'Inside the Met, it's as bad as you ———
it's the casual, ubiquitous misogyny that was witnessed by
Lloyd-Rose that really chills the blood . . . elegantly written.'
Richard Morrison, *The Times*

'A compelling snapshot of modern policing.'
Andrew Anthony, *The Observer*

'Lloyd-Rose's writing is vivid and forensic, giving a keen sense
of the characters he met on both sides of the thin blue line.'
*Financial Times*

'Extraordinary . . . The account of what he experienced
is lyrical, funny and often poignant.'
*The Daily Telegraph*

'A valuable, direct and honest account of a personal journey
to the end of the Brixton night, as witness and participant,
in the impossible complexity of urban policing.'
Iain Sinclair, author of *Lights Out for the Territory* and
*The Gold Machine*

'A textured, compassionate book about cities, loss, wounded
souls. What kinds of care has our society outsourced to the
police? What could they learn from the work of nurses or
teachers? Matt Lloyd-Rose asks so many crucial, haunting
questions . . .'
Sukhdev Sandhu, author of *Night Haunts*

# INTO THE NIGHT

Matt Lloyd Rose has worked as a carer, primary school teacher, police officer and in leadership roles across the charity and social sectors. He is the author of *The Character Conundrum: How to Develop Confidence, Independence and Resilience in the Classroom* (Routledge, 2017), and co-author, with Henry Eliot, of *Curiocity: An Alternative A-Z of London* (Particular Books, 2016). He is based in South London with his wife and two young children, and balances writing with work supporting organizations to bring about social change and increase their social impact.

# MATT LLOYD-ROSE

# INTO THE NIGHT

## A YEAR WITH THE POLICE

PICADOR

First published 2023 by Picador

This edition first published 2024 by Picador
an imprint of Pan Macmillan
The Smithson, 6 Briset Street, London ECIM 5NR
*EU representative*: Macmillan Publishers Ireland Ltd, 1st Floor,
The Liffey Trust Centre, 117–126 Sheriff Street Upper,
Dublin 1, DOI YC43
Associated companies throughout the world
www.panmacmillan.com

ISBN 978-1-0350-0428-7

A CIP catalogue record for this book is available from the British Library.

Typeset in Scala by Palimpsest Book Production Ltd, Falkirk, Stirlingshire
Printed and bound by CPI Group (UK) Ltd, Croydon, CRO 4YY

Visit **www.picador.com** to read more about all our books
and to buy them. You will also find features, author interviews and
news of any author events, and you can sign up for e-newsletters
so that you're always first to hear about our new releases.

*For Lyd, Flo & Sebby*

# AUTHOR'S NOTE

The events and dialogues in this book are real, but names, identifying features and some locations have been changed to protect the identities of those who appear in these pages.

This is not the work of a criminologist or career police officer: I am a former carer and primary school teacher and this is the lens through which I look at policing. My time with the Met was fascinating, shocking, poignant and full of surprises. Coming from a care and education background, what surprised me most was how relevant those experiences felt. This book is about policing, but it is just as much about questions of community, inclusion, care and control.

As a carer and educator, the main agenda I bring to this book is a long-held and urgent desire that we get better at supporting the most vulnerable groups and that we bring them from the margins to the heart of our society, amplifying their voices and recognising how much they have to give, as well as how much they need. Rethinking the role of the police is part of that process – but only part.

The police stir up strong feelings – and for good reason. This book is neither a defence of the police nor a polemic against them. Rather it is an attempt to direct a steady gaze at our most fraught, complex institution, at the entrenched social challenges we send police to deal with and at our current system, which fails so many.

Whatever your views, I hope this book expands empathy in all directions and provides the imaginative resources for a richer conversation about where we are now, how we got here and where we go next.

## LOOK AFTER YOURSELF

There are many moments within this book – racist and misogynist incidents, accounts of domestic abuse, a graphic sequence in a mortuary – that could upset some readers. I have tried to avoid being gratuitous, whilst never minimising or neutralising the incidents that appear. If you think this book could be triggering, please look after yourself. If you feel you need to talk to someone for whatever reason, there is a list of helpful organisations below.

### SAMARITANS

Confidential support for people experiencing feelings of distress or despair.

116 123 (24-hour helpline)
www.samaritans.org

### NSPCC

For adults concerned about a child.

0808 800 5000 (24-hour helpline)
www.nspcc.org.uk

### MIND

Mental health information and signposting service.

0300 123 3393 (9 a.m.–6 p.m., Monday to Friday)
www.mind.org.uk

Clearly it is necessary that it be known *what* needs to be done before anyone can venture to say *how* it is to be done well.

In the case of the police, this sets up the requirement of specifying the police role in society.

Simple as this demand may seem on first glance, it presents difficulties that are more commonly avoided than addressed.

— EGON BITTNER, CRIMINOLOGIST AND AUTHOR OF
*The Functions of the Police in Modern Society* (1970)

1

Nobody had reported a wallaby missing. Nevertheless, a grainy image had made it onto the evening news, confirming that a wallaby was indeed at large in London. We were patrolling Vauxhall when a report of a nearby sighting came in. Our core operation that night was to tackle robberies and drug dealing outside local clubs. Nothing was happening, so we radioed to accept the call and drove away from the lights and music.

We pulled up next to a dimly lit row of garages, squinting at the pixelated outlines of bollards and bins, alert for signs of movement. It was almost midnight and the street was completely still. Someone passed around a pack of Percy Pigs and we each took a handful without lowering our gaze, scanning left and right. After five minutes, the Sergeant decided to drive around a bit, in case the wallaby had moved since the caller spotted it. We circled the area for ten minutes but found nothing, looping round and round the same few streets. What had seemed plausible when we accepted the call began to feel improbable, and then absurd.

A call came out: a robber on a bike, IC1 male, late teens, was making a getaway not far from us. The Sergeant switched on the blue lights and siren and raced towards Stockwell, pumping the bull horn at each junction. She turned sharply into the estate the robber had cycled into. 'Hold tight!' she shouted, and we gripped the headrests in front of us, bracing as the van hit a speed bump, then another and another.

We followed the chase on the radio. We had been hoping to reach the robber first, but we could hear a response car ahead of us closing in on him. A minute later, they caught him in a car park and, by the time we pulled up, the young man was in handcuffs, blood pouring from his nose. 'Honestly, Nathan, that was the worst getaway I've ever seen,' an officer was saying, searching through his first-aid kit for a dressing. 'We're on an estate. I'm in a car, you're on a bike. There are tiny alleyways everywhere. What were you thinking, turning in here?' Nathan did not reply. He had made a sudden turn into the car park and attempted to duck below the security barrier, a daredevil limbo that resulted in him headbutting the pole and being knocked backwards off his bike. Nathan's phone rang and the officer answered it for him. 'Hi, yes, Nathan's phone . . . I'm afraid Nathan's not really free to speak at the moment . . . He's standing next to me in handcuffs . . . Yeah, he'll call you back.'

The situation was under control, so we left the officers to it. As we were driving out of the estate the Sergeant spotted a group of IC3 males from the ABM gang in the stairwell of a high-rise and suggested we do some searches. 'We'll go in there, see if it stinks of cannabis and, if it does, there's our grounds,' she said, 'which should be easy, because those hallways always stink of cannabis.' Half of us went through the front door, the Sergeant shouting 'Boo!' as she entered. Six teenage boys ran out of the back door, where our colleagues were waiting for them.

We told the boys we suspected them of possession of cannabis and were going to search them. They spread their legs and raised their arms, as though they had been tagged in a game of Stuck in the Mud. We emptied their pockets, skimmed their waistbands, slid the backs of our hands up the insides of their legs, attempting conversation all the while. How's your summer been? Have you been away at all? Why have you got five phones? 'This has been a bone summer,' one boy replied.

A friend of theirs, IC3 female, early twenties, walked over shouting at us. 'You're completely out of order! This is our lives! This is our lives!' She walked up to each of us, holding a notebook and pen, writing down our shoulder numbers. 'Why you got the right to do this?' she asked. 'What gives you the right to do this?' We did not find any drugs or weapons on the boys, so we wrote our 5090s, said goodnight and got back in the van. 'Who was she?' someone asked the Sergeant. 'Yeah, we know her,' the Sergeant replied. 'She spent five years inside for firearms. She was hiding them for ABM.'

It was nearly midnight. We were about to stop for a break when a harassment call came out. An IC2 male, mid-thirties, was harassing an IC2 teenage girl at the centre of an estate in Brixton. We sped there on blue lights, arriving within five minutes, but when we pulled up everything seemed quiet and calm. We got out of the van. It was a handsome brown-brick estate, five storeys high with a neatly trimmed lawn in the middle. 'Over here!' someone shouted. An IC2 female, early twenties, emerged from a doorway and pointed at a silver car on the other side of the lawn, two silhouettes just visible inside. 'I'm her older sister,' the woman said. 'Every night, for like, two hours, they sit in that car. He's thirty-five, she's fifteen. It's not right.' We walked across the grass, knocked on the driver's window and asked the pair to step out. 'We're just friends,' the man insisted, 'we're just friends talking . . .' He paused for a moment and looked at the girl. 'We're both lonely,' he continued. 'We understand each other.' He was interrupted by shouting across the courtyard. A tall IC2 male was walking towards the older sister – the man's cousin, who had come to stick up for him. The cousin and the sister began to argue and the girl from the car began to cry. 'I don't have any friends my age,' she said. 'Honestly, we're just talking.' We separated everyone, told them an officer would visit to investigate further, and sent them all home.

We were overdue a break and drove to the Kebab Company on Clapham High Street. It felt good to be in a warm, bright room, sinking into a black leather chair, shoulder blades hooked over the seat-back, legs stretched out below the table. We sat in silence for a moment, inhaling the roasting meats and waiting for our numbers to be called. 'Evening, officers!' an IC1 male, seventies, shouted from his table at the back of the restaurant. 'You see how I'm sitting here, officers,' he said. 'I always like to sit with my back to the wall so I can see who's coming into a place. I used to be a villain, you see.' Suddenly the Sergeant pointed at something outside. An IC1 female, sixties, not much over five foot, was walking past the window. She had hunched shoulders and moved with quick shuffling steps, her head bent so low it was hard to believe she could see where she was going. 'Watch out for that one,' the Sergeant said, 'she's horrible and I never want to stop her again. She spits and bites and is just totally hideous.'

Back in the van, we did some circuits of Clapham, sagging slightly after our pittas, entering the most soporific phase of the night and waiting for the uplift that comes at three and carries you through till dawn. We were on one of the dark roads that cuts across the Common, passing Honest Tom's snack wagon, when we heard on the radio that there were about fifteen IC1 males throwing bottles and wielding baseball bats outside Honky Tonk on the High Street. We were less than a minute away and we all sat up, suddenly alert, readying our batons and CS spray. If we were lucky, we would be the first to arrive. We dashed to Honky Tonk, lights and siren pulsing, and scrambled out of the van onto the pavement, looking around for the men, hands hovering above our holsters.

A moment passed. We looked round again, then we looked at one another. There was no sign of a disturbance. We asked the bouncers whether they had seen anything and they said no, all was calm, not a bat or a bottle in sight.

2

## YouTube: *Police vs Teenager UK London*

247,984 views

### Dr Sanguine Sunrise

I think English/British police officers need to get
'hard'. I mean, two trained and paid officers should be
able to take down some random teenage prick –
surely?

#### dounga99

They need some Brazilian jiu jitsu class.

#### G Fuentes

They're not used to arresting anyone anymore, UK
police are mainly in the business of community
outreach now.

### Paul Morris

What did the filth pull him for?

**anonymous one**

he was wanted for hand bag snatching from old ladies, but of course hes innocent and it's police brutality because some guy filmed it for you tube. . .

**George Radcliffe**

If he "didn't do nothing" why did he resist for 5 minutes?

**Joe Jones**

It escalated because the kid was too strong for them and their restraint is terrible. If someone has two hands on the back of your head pushing your face to the ground how can you not fight back.

**mike h**

"i can't breathe" errr stop resisting then dick

**Kieran Ladbury**

If u can't breathe how are u talking

**BigBleedinSteve**

Thank god he's white 😊

**Bahnstormer**

Why are all these people standing around not helping.

**blobby nobby**

nice to see nobody helps pigs

**Atreyon**

England always has such pretty ivys growing every-where. Makes it look so green and lush.

**TheK9Queen**

as a brit I haven't really noticed but when you point it out, it is really green, huh? 😄

**Fred Sausage**

Beautiful ivy. I was upset that they damaged some of the ivy by wrestling in it.

'Make yourself a tea if you want one. The milk's in the forensic fridge.'

'CRIME ACADEMY', says the polished steel sign outside. 'Please remind students not to attach the defibrillator pads to each other', says a notice on the corridor wall.

The first day of training. We are shown CCTV footage of a pair of police officers reprimanding an IC1 male for urinating in a shop doorway. While they are talking to the offender, his friends appear, argue with the officers and then attack them, beating them with their own batons. 'Why are you here?' reads the caption at the end of the video. 'Because this could be you.'

Policing is all about communication, they tell us on day one. 'Tactical Communication: the use of communication skills with the purpose of achieving control . . . You're *professional communicators* . . . Effective communication is like throwing a bucket of water on two dogs fighting . . .' Communication, we are told, is 7 per cent verbal, 38 per cent vocal and 55 per cent non-verbal. 'Beware of non-verbal leakage,' the instructors warn us, 'the things you communicate without even realizing it, through your expression or your posture' – the fear, irritation or confusion that leaks from your face, your hands, your shoulders, involuntary as sweat.

'Above all, be firm,' they conclude. 'You don't feed a dog to stop it biting you.'

Officer Safety Training in the high-ceilinged gymnasium. 'Eighty per cent of our job has no violence,' they tell us, 'but you work for the twenty per cent.' We learn to do knee, elbow and open-hand strikes, the one-handed push away, two-handed push away. 'Always maintain a reactionary gap . . . Stay out of the fighting arc . . .'

Baton training. 'It's very simple, really . . . You've got a stick and you hit people with it. It's an easy concept to get your head around.'

Handcuff training. 'Always backload your handcuffs . . . Cuff on or below the wrist . . . Check the tightness and ask how they feel before you double-lock them . . .' We cuff one another repeatedly, in various styles and positions – front stack, rear stack, back to back, lying down, standing up – so that our wrists are raw for days afterwards. When we have mastered the basics, the instructor adds some violent resistance, teaching us to control a half-cuffed prisoner by jerking their cuffed wrist backwards, sending darts of pain through the joint, and forcing them to the ground.

CS training. We are lined up on a field and sprayed in the face by an instructor in a gas mask. Coughing and howling, it feels as though chillies have been scrubbed into our eyes, mouth and nose. More commonly known as tear gas, CS is an incapacitant with a three- to ten-foot range, ten- to fifteen-minute recovery time and a one-in-ten failure rate. 'Whatever you do, don't try to CS a dog,' the instructor tells us, 'you'll just make it angrier. Leg it or use a fire extinguisher.'

CS reacts to water and it reactivates in the communal showers afterwards. We screw up our faces and howl and laugh in a naked huddle beneath the jets.

There is a lot to learn. Fortunately the police really go in for mnemonics.

SOAP, JOG, POP, PLAN, OATS, STAIRS, PAW, DIE, CHAP, PAIR, PEACE, PIPES, COW, MEAL, DOTS, PEEP, ESCAPE, BIRO, PEPSI, WIFE, SHACKS, SAMPLE, RA-RA, CHAMPS – mnemonics that explain everything from notebook protocol to reasonable force to the criteria for hate crime.

Some mnemonics are more than one word long: SAD CHALETS, GO WISELY, NO ELBOWS, TED'S PIE. Some are short absurdist phrases: A TAP ON JAW FOOD (how to give a traffic ticket), JACK FED HOT PIG RAM (how to book in lost property). Some are neologisms, barely words at all: IDCOPLAN (arrest conditions), NASCH (name, age, sex, colour, height), CHAMPSDG (traffic collisions involving animals). Some mnemonics are multiple words beginning with the same first letter: the 6Cs for firearms, the 4Rs for drunks in custody. Some of the simplest mnemonics are double or triple booked. There are three competing ABCs: Airways, Breathing, Circulation (first aid); Accuracy, Brevity, Clarity (writing statements); Assume nothing, Believe no one, Check everything (dealing with fires).

–

We are taught the definitions of common offences.

> An assault occurs when one person intentionally or
> recklessly applies force to the person of another
> without the other's consent.

There is a concision and precision to legal language – language distilled, as far as it can be, to pure meaning.

> A person is guilty of affray if he uses or threatens
> unlawful violence towards another and his conduct is
> such that it would cause a person of reasonable
> firmness present to fear for his own safety.

Legalese is the opposite of literary language. Gaps are filled, mystery removed, double meanings expelled. Each offence is carefully defined, each term within each definition defined in turn. Each definition is a Russian doll of nested definitions, an attempt at total clarity. Yet at times their precision has a poetry of its own.

> A person is guilty of theft if he dishonestly
> appropriates property belonging to another with the
> intention of permanently depriving the other of it.

In the definition of theft, there is a musicality to the phrasing, a beauty to the density. The definition expands, pivots, then folds back in on itself. Each word is essential and exactly where it needs to be; in combination, they encapsulate perfectly the factors that must be present to prove the offence. These are known as the 'five fingers of theft': (1) dishonestly (2) appropriates (3) property (4) belonging to another (5) with the intention of permanently depriving the other of it.

We are surprised to learn that two of theft's offshoots, robbery and burglary, are different things. Robbery: using force, or threat of force, to steal. Burglary: entering a building as a trespasser, with intent to steal, or forming that intent once inside. Most of us used the terms interchangeably.

Class after class, handout upon handout. Videos, role plays, props and PowerPoints. We are taught to search, taught to arrest. 'You are detained for the purpose of a search . . . You do not have to say anything but it may harm your defence . . .' We search one another in the corridor, hide flick-knives in our waistbands, fake drugs in our socks.

We sit through a long session on public order offences, the delicate business of determining the point at which unpleasantness becomes unlawfulness: what counts as threatening behaviour and what constitutes harassment or abuse. 'For Section 4, Harassment with Fear of Violence,' explains our instructor, 'the victim must fear violence against *themselves* and no one else . . . i.e. *Unless you come out with me tonight and watch* Fatal Attraction, *I'm going to kill your bunny rabbit* is not Harassment with Fear of Violence.'

We learn about racially aggravated offences: 'Criminal Damage, Harassment, Assault or Public Order offences motivated by Colour, Origin, Religion or Nationality . . . Or, to put it another way, if you've got CORN on your CHAP, it's a racially aggravated offence.'

There is a long session on handling extreme situations. We watch video after video of things we must not do: actors in police uniform chasing armed robbers down back alleys, dashing into burning buildings, leaping into canals to save someone. In times of high stress, 'red mist descends', we are told. 'You will do things you would never do if you were thinking straight.'

We are blasted with information. *Actus reus*: guilty act. *Mens rea*: guilty mind . . . PNC: Police National Computer . . . TSG: Territorial Support Group . . . Offweps: offensive weapons . . . ABH: actual bodily harm. GBH: grievous bodily harm . . . 'If you take a statement it's *their* statement, if you take someone's property it's *your* exhibit' . . . 'Some animals are property, others aren't' . . . 'The porcelain on the end of a spark plug can be used to break car windows' . . . 'Deflating someone's car tyres is criminal damage. Spray painting someone's cat is criminal damage.'

We click through dozens of online training modules: Firearms, Human Trafficking, Equality and Diversity, Dealing with Dangerous Dogs. We are shown the reporting systems – CRIS (crime), CRIMINT (criminal intelligence), MERLIN (children and missing persons) – and introduced to official documents: Form 5090 (stops), Form 9993 (harassment warning), Form 124D (domestic violence), Form 372 (near misses), Form 9002 (ordering new trousers or skirts), Paper Sack 420 (evidence bag), Form 420b (sticky label on evidence bag). Then there are the logbooks in the station front office: Book 66 (property involved in crime), Book 89 (items found in street), Book 99 (recording lost items), Book 105 (property booked in).

'I appreciate there's an orgy of information in front of you,' the instructor says. 'I like that word *orgy*. In fact, there's just the right amount of people in here.'

At the end of our training, at a ceremony attended only by ourselves, we are given warrant cards and sworn in as police officers – Special Constables, unpaid volunteers with full police powers, who work at least two shifts a month. For the volunteer, it is an opportunity to learn something new. For the Met, it is a way to boost numbers on busy weekend evenings. There are four hundred of us at the ceremony, about to be dispatched to London's thirty-two boroughs. I asked to be placed in Lambeth, the borough where I lived and where I had, until recently, worked as a primary school teacher. Among the other Lambeth Specials are a banker, a bus driver, a printer, a civil servant, a supermarket manager, a pastor, an HR director, a stay-at-home parent, a hospital receptionist, a stagehand, a custody officer, an executive PA and a criminology student.

We recite the oath: 'I do solemnly and sincerely declare and affirm that I will well and truly serve the Queen in the office of constable, with fairness, integrity, diligence and impartiality . . .' Then we form an immense snaking queue around the auditorium and troop across the stage to collect our warrant cards and shake a magistrate's hand. We are instructed to clap ourselves for the duration of the presentations – twenty minutes' solid clapping.

'As cliché as it is, you have the power to impact on lives, save lives and take people's liberty and freedom away,' says the magistrate. 'That is a massive responsibility, so when you are on duty, keep that in mind.'

'Even when you're off duty, you're never really off duty,' one of our instructors tells us. 'It can be lonely out there sometimes. God knows why when there's so many people.'

Lambeth, where I lived, taught and policed, is a long narrow borough just south of the Thames, home to a third of a million people, and one of the most densely populated places in Britain. It begins on the heights of Norwood, Streatham and Gypsy Hill, drops down to the twin poles of Brixton and Clapham, then continues to Stockwell, with its Portuguese cafes and bars, the Oval with its iconic cricket ground, and on north to Kennington, where politicians conspire in curry houses, Vauxhall, which teems with spies by day and clubbers by night, and Waterloo with its big wheel, buskers and brutalist buildings. The neighbourhoods are crammed tightly together, one flowing into another, but each has its own distinct character. Lambeth runs out when it hits the Thames, and the Houses of Parliament look back from the opposite shore.

Underneath it all runs a hidden river – the Effra, which once ran above ground, rising in Upper Norwood, then passing through central Brixton and flowing north to the Thames. The Victorians integrated it into their sewer system and now the Effra runs unseen, sweeping waste along with it, channelling its waters to the Crossness Sewage Treatment Works. In downpours, the Effra emerges from the depths, discharging its overflow into the Thames at Vauxhall.

Lambeth is a theatrical place, home of many stages – the National Theatre, the Old Vic, the Young Vic – and home to many remarkable performers. Charlie Chaplin grew up in Kennington. David Bowie was born in central Brixton. Punk legend Poly Styrene grew up down the road, near Myatt's Fields. Dub poet Linton Kwesi Johnson came to Brixton as a child and still lives on Railton Road. Music hall greats Marie Kendall and Dan Leno lived in the borough. And a few streets south of the National Theatre, behind Waterloo station, is the site of the first modern circus, Astley's Amphitheatre. Lambeth's theatrical character spills out onto its streets. It can feel larger than life. It reminds us, in Toni Morrison's words, that 'life *is* that large'.

All of the new Lambeth Special Constables were invited to a welcome briefing. We were greeted by a rosy-cheeked Sergeant we had spoken to on the phone during the recruitment process. He was responsible for settling in new Specials and it was easy to see why: he was affable, avuncular, always pleased to see you, always had time for a chat. Even when I called with a boring admin issue, he would answer with the exaggerated conviviality of an estate agent. This was the first time we had met in real life. He ushered us into a large room, smiling and patting our shoulders.

There were a dozen new Specials at the briefing. When we were seated, two senior police officers walked in and the room went quiet. 'Lambeth is London's, if not the country's, premier borough for policing,' an Inspector said. 'In terms of risk and excitement, we are right up there.' I had a sense of Lambeth's challenges from my time as a primary school teacher in Brixton. It consistently rates among the top boroughs for poverty, violent crime, gang activity and mental ill health. In a city of extremes,

Lambeth stands out. 'You'll be spending a lot of time in Vauxhall, Clapham and Brixton,' the Inspector continued. 'Three of the hottest spots in the Met.'

'Brixton is an emotive word for everyone, of course,' she said, alluding to the riots of 1981 and 1985, 'although relationships with the public are light-years ahead of where they were thirty, forty years ago. And Stockwell has a slightly sadder recent history . . .' she said, referring to the 2005 police shooting of Jean Charles de Menezes, an innocent twenty-seven-year-old mistaken for a terror suspect two weeks after the 07/07 London bombings.

The Inspector looked around and began to wrap up. 'You'll have an amazing time. You'll see more in a night than you would in a year in rural Hampshire . . . Get stuck in, get hands-on – that's the only way you'll learn – and enjoy it.'

The front office was closed when I arrived for my first shift, so I rang the doorbell. There was no answer, so I tried the bell again, then walked around the side of the police station. Every single room in the four-storey building was lit, but there were no signs of life. I returned to the main entrance, rang the bell again and banged on the door several times with my fist. Still no one came, so I phoned 101, the police non-emergency number, and asked the operator to send somebody to let me in. As I was hanging up, I spotted a tall man coming out of the station's side gate. I ran over, pulled out my warrant card and he let me past.

The yard was dark, stacked with temporary road signs and scuffed riot shields. I walked past them and pushed open the back door, entering a corridor with a dozen blue doors along it. I did not know where to go, so I knocked on one door after another, opening them to find near-identical rooms with chipped blue walls, hairy brown floors and banks of old computers. The offices were deserted, but people had been there recently. There were half-drunk Cokes on the desks. The computers were on and Microsoft logos were bouncing around the fat black screens.

The door at the end of the corridor led to the station canteen, a small room posing as a big room, packed with so many tables and chairs that there was barely space to walk between them.

The tables were littered with cups, cans, the day's free newspapers. At one end of the canteen was a kitchen, its worktops dotted with crumbs, butter, tea bags and the damp traces of tea bags. A steel sink was jammed with unwashed mugs and plates. 'AS YOU CAN SEE WE HAVE CLEANED THE STATION', read a sign above the toaster. 'PLEASE CAN WE KEEP IT CLEAN AND TIDY'. A second sign, over the sink, said, 'PLEASE CAN YOU DO YOUR OWN WASHING UP IT'S NOT THAT HARD'. On the back wall of the canteen was a large cork pinboard, black mould spreading from its edges to the centre. The only thing pinned to it was a red T-shirt with the slogan 'PEACE ON THE STREETS', its sleeves pulled taut by brass tacks.

I found the Lambeth Special Constabulary office at the top of the building. There were four desks, strewn with kebab cartons and blue latex gloves. The floor below them was covered with broken biros, metal shoulder numbers and a pair of lacquered red high heels. Along one wall was a noticeboard covered in posters. One showed a photo of the Commissioner, frowning above the slogan 'TOTAL POLICING' and announcing 'a total war on crime'. Another showed a woman with a puffy purple face. 'URGENT MEANS URGENT', it read. 'The average response time to urgent domestic violence calls is 2 min 46 slower than for other emergency calls.'

There was nobody in the Specials office either – I had arrived far too early. I sat on a swivel chair and waited. A moment later my phone rang, an unknown number. It was the police. A pair of officers were waiting outside to let me in.

'This shit has to stop, boys! No more fruit in the locker room!' Someone had left a banana in his locker and now the overheated basement was swarming with fruit flies. One officer was trying to kill the flies with a crow bar, cracking it against the lockers and the white brick walls. Others were shouting at the banana's owner. 'Boys, boys!' he protested. 'Boys, boys!'

'Fuck off you mouldy banana cunt!'

We went upstairs for the briefing, forty of us seated in five tight rows. The Inspector clicked through a PowerPoint, photos of criminal men and criminal cars, details of current operations. Above her head, a neon-blue fly-zapper crackled, flashing orange with each kill. 'Be aware that Essex Police have launched Operation Thunderbolt to tackle violence between rival motor-cycle fraternities,' she said. 'They've asked us to report sightings of biker gangs passing through Lambeth.' She paused. '*Thunderbolt* . . . We could learn from that. What was the name of that operation we ran recently? Operation Napkin? It doesn't exactly set the blood racing, does it?'

There is a briefing at the start of every shift to give us the latest intelligence on our area. No two briefings are the same, but most are fairly similar. Top Five Robbers, Top Five Burglars, anyone wanted or missing, vehicles to look out for. We jot down names, dates, number plates, and stare at the faces flashing past, trying to stamp them onto our minds. Some details stick in the memory more easily than others. 'Suspect last seen doing press-ups topless on the roof of his car' . . . 'Suspect has attached a machete to the wall by his front door' . . . 'Suspect evoked Section 61 of the Magna Carta and attempted to headbutt police.'

At the end of a briefing, we are given our duties for the evening, assigned to areas and teams. 'Did you bring your hi-vis jackets? No? You're all fucking useless!'

—

Boots, trousers, shirt, necktie, kit belt, stab vest, hat – and a face hidden somewhere in the middle of it all, lost among the black, white and blue. Putting on a police uniform for the first time is a peculiar experience. It feels like fancy dress, like a joke taken too far.

The police uniform transforms a stranger into a familiar figure, a person into a personification. As a police officer, you become someone less specific. But what you lose in individuality, you gain in access to other individuals. In uniform you can talk to anyone and anyone can talk to you.

'Nice to see you, officer. How you doing? All right? . . .
Quiet, yeah. Too quiet if you ask me.'

People approach you and, at times, you feel as if you have been mistaken for someone else. They pick up a conversation midstream, beginning where they left off last time they bumped into you, even though it was not you they bumped into.

'Don't worry officer. I've got your back. If anyone tries
to mess you around, just tell 'em Angel will sort 'em
out if they do.'

In uniform, each of you is any of you. When you interact with a member of the public, you embody the sum of their experiences and impressions of the police. You do not know whether you will be treated as the heroic officer who did X or the hated officer who did Y.

'Don't talk to me! Don't even look at me!'

Uniform flattens, makes the wearer two-dimensional. If someone dislikes the police, you can be friendly, but the outfit speaks first and speaks louder.

'Don't you have anything better to do than coming round here wasting our time?'

If fashion is a language, then uniform is its starkest expression – clothing that relays a message as directly and simply as possible. A uniform should mean the same thing to everyone, though this only happens if the public are treated uniformly.

'Will you arrest our friend when he gets here? It'll be so funny. Just pretend to arrest him. Honestly, it'll be so funny.'

Putting on the uniform for the first time, dressing in front of the mirror, you watch yourself disappear. Then, out on patrol, you look for yourself in car windows, shop windows, the mirrors in people's hallways, your head on a police officer's body.

'Excuse me, officer. What's the best way to get to Aldershot?'

Every Friday night, we would be put on patrol in either Brixton town centre, Clapham High Street or Vauxhall. For the first shifts, though, we simply circled Lambeth in a van: three new Specials in the back, two regular officers in the front, getting a flavour of what the borough has to offer. One of the regulars turned around in his seat. 'Right guys, you tell us what you want to stop. We're looking for slaggy cars, rundown cars, pimped-up cars . . . Or normal cars driven in a slaggy way or by slaggy-looking people.' Someone pointed at an old red Ford Focus as it turned sharply down a side street, as though trying to avoid us. We followed the car, pulled it over and got out to talk to the driver, an IC3 male in his late forties. We took down his details, ran a name check on the radio and learned that he lived in North London and had previous convictions for drugs. Could he account for his presence in this part of town? No, he could not. We searched the car, shining torches into the foot-wells, picking through the wrappers and Rizlas around the gear stick, then searched the man himself. Emptying the pockets of his puffer jacket, we found dozens of small paper bundles: drugs, wrapped and ready to sell.

'How do you explain these?' we asked.

'They're psalms!' the man said. 'They're prayers!'

We dug our thumbnails into the fine grey paper and unrolled a couple. There was nothing inside them and the crumpled paper was covered in fine black print. They were prayers, as he said. Tiny scrunched psalms, rolled up to hand out. We said goodnight and sent the man on his way.


When we stop a person or vehicle, we radio to check whether they are known to police and whether there is anything we ought to be aware of. The operator consults the Police National Computer and gives responses in code. Alpha – ailments, Delta – drugs, Echo – escaper, Foxtrot – firearms, Mike – mental health, Sierra – suicidal, Victor – violent, Whiskey – weapons, Whiskey Mike – Wanted/Missing.

Codes are also used to describe a person's ethnicity. IC1 – White, North European; IC2 – White, South European; IC3 – Black; IC4 – South Asian; IC5 – Chinese, Japanese or other South-East Asian; IC6 – North African or Arab; IC7 – Not Recorded or Unknown.

One evening we stopped an IC1 male on Norwood Road, radioed in his details and found out he was wanted. The man overheard the call. 'Whiskey Mike? I'll have a brandy Coke,' he said, before we arrested him.


'How do you know when to stop someone?' we asked one of the regulars. 'Who should you stop?' He thought for a moment. 'Let's say you're walking along and you see someone hanging about on a corner. What do you do? Well, first you've got to think: *Have they ever been arrested?* Then you think: *Yeah, probably, if they live round here.* So you stop them, you talk to them and you try and get grounds for a search. If you get grounds – maybe you smell drugs, or they can't explain what they're doing there, or they're acting suspiciously – you search them.'

We passed an IC1 male, mid-twenties, lingering on a dark corner. He was swaying and looked dazed. 'What are you up to, mate?' we asked as we approached. The man looked up, drew an uncapped hypodermic needle from a trouser pocket and held it out to us. We took it from him gingerly and laid it on top of a bollard, then we ran a name check on the man and told him we were going to search him. 'Do you have anything else on you that could hurt you or us?' we asked, snapping on a pair of latex gloves. He said no, but we were afraid to put our hands in his pockets and pulled them inside out instead, catching the contents as they fell from the lining. One of the regulars passed us a sharps tube and we sealed the hypodermic inside. The man was known for drugs but he was not carrying any, so we left him on the corner stuffing his possessions into his pockets and climbed back into the van. As we did, our driver jumped out, picked something up, and handed it to the man. 'Dropped your bank card, mate,' he said. 'Don't lose that.' Back in the van, he slammed his door and turned around to look at us. 'Now, I know you're new,' he said. 'But he's standing there waving a needle and you walk right up to him? What were you thinking? He sticks that in you and bang, you've got AIDS. I mean, guys – this is a fucking reality check.'

Policing is a contact profession. We frequently touch and are touched by people we know nothing about, whether searching them, bandaging them, restraining them, or simply shaking their hand. This contact carries risks, for us and for the people with whom we interact: physical risks like violence and disease, and psychological risks like trauma and humiliation. Where possible, before touching someone, we put on a pair of blue latex gloves to make contact safer and more clinical. The gloves put a barrier between one body and another, turn a stranger's hands into the familiar blue hands of a technician. The needle in the pocket is our greatest fear, the point that pierces the protective layer.

We drove down Tulse Hill and spotted an IC3 female, mid-twenties, sitting in a parked car at the edge of the estate. We walked over and she wound down her window.

'Are you aware you're in a robbery hotspot?'

'Have you come to rescue me?'

'We're just checking you're all right.'

'Well that's very nice of you.'

We talked to her through the open window. She had lost the key for her building and was waiting for a neighbour to get back and let her in. One of the regulars walked over. 'Get her out of the car,' he whispered.

We asked the woman to step out and we took down her details in a red pocket notebook. While our driver ran a name check she told us about her kids, leaning into the car's footwell and pulling out a pair of Peppa Pig lunchboxes, which she placed on the car roof to take into the house later on. Our driver signalled that the checks were OK so we said goodnight and that we hoped somebody would arrive soon with a key.

Back in the van our driver turned around in his seat. 'Officer safety: you get her out of the car, you treat everyone the same. You don't know that woman, but we do. She's known to police. We checked her name and it flashed Whiskey and Victor. Her brother's high up in TN1 and has a major firearms record. She's got a history of violence against police and carrying weapons. You're treating her as though she's harmless and she's acting up to it. Why do you think she got the lunchboxes out of the car? She's playing you. She's seeing what she can get away with. How do you even know what's in those lunchboxes? It's not necessarily a fromage frais and a packet of Quavers, let's just say that.'

We were warned about this kind of thing in training – that in policing there are only two types of risk: high and unknown. 'Anybody with a sufficient level of crisis in their life can be a threat to you,' we were told. 'There is no such thing as a low-risk situation.'

Policing requires you to be open to others while being open to the possibility that they may not be what they seem. You are expected to approach the apparently harmless with the same blend of caution and friendly professionalism with which you approach the apparently volatile. In a role in which people frequently attempt to deceive you, you must not compound the issue by deceiving yourself.

'What's TN1?' someone asked.

'TN1? It's one of the most violent teen gangs round here – based in Tulse Hill. There are lots, but TN1, GAS in Angell Town, ABM in Stockwell . . . Those are the big ones.'

'What does it mean?'

'What, TN1? Tell No One . . . Trust No One . . . Depends who you ask. All 'Bout Money, ABM. Guns and Shanks is GAS . . . Gangsters Always Shoot, I've heard too.'

—

We drove towards Clapham. On the way, we spotted a white van being driven erratically, drifting between lanes, then blocking the path of an ambulance. We chased the van on blue lights, but it did not stop, so we drove along next to it, gesturing through the window and letting off yelps from the siren. The van ignored us and kept going. 'This is the slaggiest driving I've seen for a while,' said the Sergeant. When we hit a patch of dense traffic an officer jumped out to bang on the driver's window. The van still did not stop. The officer in the road opened the driver's door, reached over him and pulled on the handbrake. We parked in front of the van and instructed the driver, IC1, thirties, wearing a grey woollen coat and a trilby, to step onto the pavement.

'I would have stopped. I was planning to,' he said. 'It's just that this is a rental van and the handbrake is in a different place from my car.' The man appeared distracted, struggling to maintain eye contact and unsteady on his feet. We ordered a breathalyser and I wrote out a Fixed Penalty Notice for Driving Without Due Care and Attention. He would get a £100 fine and three points on his licence. 'A hundred pounds?' he said. 'That's all right. You're not going to believe this, but I've just inherited fifteen million.'

A response car arrived with a breathalyser. The man blew into it and we were surprised when it came back clear. We gave him his ticket, told him to take more care, and sent him on his way.


We did a sweep along Clapham High Street, looking for an unlicensed hot-dog vendor who was notorious in the area, an IC2 male in his sixties who always worked Friday and Saturday nights, frying sausages and onions on a crudely welded sheet-metal cart.

'There he is, the fucker!' our driver shouted. We scanned the pavement and spotted him: a short man with craggy features, tending a steaming silver hotplate. He was wearing black jeans, a black anorak and a black beanie pulled down low so it covered his eyebrows. His eyes were on the hotplate, his face set in a stern, appraising expression. As we were parking, the hot-dog vendor spotted us, dropped his tongs and ducked down a side street, his cart bouncing along the tarmac in front of him. We followed, brought the van alongside and rolled down a window, driving at his pace. The hot-dog vendor kept jogging, looking straight ahead, as though he had not noticed us. We drove quietly next to him, waiting for his patience or puff to run out. After twenty metres he stopped. 'I'm working. Leave me alone!'

'Go home,' we said, 'or we'll confiscate your cart.'

We looped back to the High Street and drove slowly up and down it, 'talent spotting'.

'That one?'

'Fuck off, mate.'

'How about that one?'

'Not bad. That is not half bad.'

White high heels, tight leather skirt. 'She'd get fucked.'

Sequined top, high-waisted jeans. 'I'd do her.'

There were debates about the quality of this arse or that arse, whether a face lived up to an arse, an arse to a face. 'If you see a woman from behind,' someone asked, 'can you tell how fit her face will be, just by looking at her arse?'

During the shift I had been discreetly making notes on my lap in the dark. As my colleagues talked and laughed, I continued to write – then felt a flush of fear. What if someone noticed?

How would they react if they saw their banter recorded verbatim on an index card? I tucked the cards under my thigh, like a child hiding a note from a teacher.

It was getting late and we were circling backstreets when we spotted an IC3 teen peering through the rear window of a white estate car.

'It's hard,' a Special said. 'You see a Black guy alone at this time of night and you can't help thinking certain things.'

'What kind of things?' replied one of the regulars, 'because that sounds a bit racist.'

As our van turned into a neighbouring street a car alarm went off. We jumped out and ran back around the corner to find the boy in the driver's seat of the white car, jabbing the dashboard and talking breathlessly into his phone. He leapt from the car as we approached and the nearest Special, a mental health professional by day, flicked open his baton and raised it above his head.

'Get onto the pavement! Get onto the pavement!'

The boy complied, eyes wide, his attention caught between us and his phone.

'Hang up the phone!'

'No, man, it's the owner! I'm speaking to the owner! It's the police,' he said into the phone, 'they think I'm stealing your car!' He looked up at us. 'I'm just moving the car for my uncle. He sells cars and he's put me on the company insurance so I can move vehicles for him.'

'At 2 a.m.?'

'I know how this looks.'

We took details from the man on the phone and ran checks

on the car. The boy produced the keys and we confirmed that he was on the insurance. He really was moving cars for his uncle. We all laughed and said goodnight.

Back in the van, our driver turned around to look at us. 'What was all that about? I come round the corner and it's all gone fucking mental. Why did you pull out your baton? Can you justify that? I mean, fucking hell – I'm police, but that was pretty aggressive.'


Skirting the edge of the Angell Town Estate, we spotted an IC3 teen walking alone and pulled up next to him. He was wearing a black tracksuit and had two teardrops tattooed below his right eye. We told him that he was walking in a robbery hotspot and we were going to search him. He said nothing, stuck his chin out and looked at the rooftops behind us. He put up no resistance to the search and acted, instead, as though he was scarcely aware it was happening. He did not look at us or acknowledge us in any way. The boy was sixteen. A name check revealed that he had previous convictions for knifepoint robbery, but there was nothing suspicious on him so we said goodnight and got back into the van.

'Which Spice Girl has aged best?' our driver asked as he pulled away.

The shift finished at four. Buzzing and beyond tired, I caught a bus home outside the police station, travelling through the very streets we had been circling in a van. My wife and I were living in a flat at the top of Brixton Hill. I got off the bus at New Park Road and felt my energy give way to exhaustion. Arriving home, I pulled off my clothes in the dark and climbed into bed.

When I woke later that morning, I decided to go out for breakfast and type up my notes from the night before. I stepped outside and looked down the road. From our doorstep, we could see the roof of HMP Brixton, its chimneys glowing in the morning light. Living at the top of the hill, we were constantly aware of the prison. We were the perfect distance from it: not so close that our light was blocked by its walls, but near enough to appreciate its austere Victorian grandeur. It appeared serene and silent from the outside. I found it hard to believe it contained hundreds of people. Now, as a police officer, I viewed it with renewed interest. I was part of its supply chain.

I walked along New Park Road, past the grocery and the hardware store, past Angela's Cafe, Chicken Treat, and Airy Food & Wine. In an area as busy as Brixton, New Park Road is a reassuringly manageable place – a primary school, a brown-brick estate and a single row of shops, surrounded by tightly packed terraces. My wife and I had found a little flat there and liked how quiet and local it felt. We liked knowing the family we bought our fruit and veg from and chatting to the owner of the off-licence while he stood outside for a smoke. Overseeing the bustle of New Park Road was the unsleeping eye of 7000 Cars, as friendly at 4 a.m. as they are at 4 p.m. My wife and I booked them whenever we needed a ride to or from the airport, and time after time they had proved themselves reliable and kind. When we retreated inside at night, it was reassuring to know that they were there, watching over the neighbourhood.

It was only a ten-minute walk from New Park Road to the centre of Brixton, but as my warrant card gave me free transport I caught a bus. I flashed the card at the driver and went to sit on the upper deck. At the top of the stairs there was a screen live-streaming the footage from seven CCTV cameras. Without meaning to, I found myself staring at it, watching my journey in real time, the passengers getting on and off, close-ups of people's faces, the back of my head. A camera downstairs was trained onto a passenger's newspaper and I could just make out the headlines.

I got off outside Morleys department store and walked to the Phoenix cafe on Coldharbour Lane, a small, friendly greasy spoon I had frequented once or twice a week since moving to Brixton several years earlier. The manager waved and I found a seat at the back.

The Phoenix was always bustling, although it was a tiny place and only contained seven tables. The interior was many shades of brown: dark brown chairs strung with light brown wicker, black-brown panels on the lower half of the walls, tea-brown above. The floor was a checkerboard of brown and beige tiles. Each Formica table was supplied with brown sauce, ketchup, malt vinegar and salt and pepper in royal blue shakers.

Across the entrance was a plywood privacy screen, shielding clients from the curiosity of passers-by. There was a fan on the ceiling that was never switched on. Ventilation came from slatted panels above the shop window, filtering the sounds of the street into the cafe's calm interior. Mirrors on opposite walls expanded the space, bouncing endless images off one another so that the cafe seemed to stretch beyond its walls, right along Coldharbour Lane.

The centrepiece of the Phoenix was a monumental stainless-steel tea urn on the counter, two hot-water tanks with a tall central flue – a baroque contraption resembling a steampunk jetpack. The manager and a waitress laboured on a narrow patch of floor behind it. The kitchen was out the back and a bell rang whenever an order was ready.

The Phoenix must have been there for thirty or forty years. Unremarkable in its day, it had become remarkable as times and tastes had changed around it. Black and white photos taped to the wall showed what the cafe used to look like, which was what it still looked like. Same space, different faces.

A mug of black coffee appeared while I was spreading crumpled yellow index cards across the table, the notes I had made during the previous night's shift. They were barely legible, written on my knee in the dark. I found a card covered in sexist banter and felt confused. The same officer who challenged a Special's racist language had taken us 'talent spotting'. Why had he upheld one set of standards and not another?

Reading the comments, I was shocked but not surprised. I recognized them from the corridors and changing rooms of adolescence. The tone was identical, as was the giddy mutual encouragement, one lewd remark giving permission for the next. I had said nothing. I told myself this was because I wanted to see and hear what police did, without intervening. But it was also because I was new, and anxious, and caught off guard.

The waitress brought my breakfast, a plate of toast, beans and bubble and squeak: leftover potato and cabbage fried into a charred grey patty. I have always loved the way it looks awful but tastes tremendous. Not many places serve it. I pushed aside the index cards. I was struggling to write anyway, tired and distracted, my head swimming with memories that felt like dreams.

I barely knew London before I moved there in 2008, and I did not know Brixton at all. I had heard the name, I had heard 'The Guns of Brixton', I knew there had been some riots. I had seen other young white professionals raise an eyebrow when I said I was moving there.

I first visited Brixton in the height of summer and I loved it the moment I emerged from the tube: the steel pans outside Iceland, the bustle of the market along Electric Avenue, the reggae booths in the railway arches, the smells of incense and fish and dust and weed and blood and disinfectant. I felt I had rarely been anywhere as teeming and pulsing with life. Within minutes, it was one of my favourite places and I could not wait to live there.

I went house-hunting with two friends and we visited an ex-council property a five-minute walk from the school where I was about to start teaching. Afterwards we went to the Dogstar pub to discuss whether to rent it. We liked it, but the house was small and two of the three bedrooms were tiny, made by bisecting one already-small bedroom with a plywood wall.

We looked out at the junction of Coldharbour Lane and Atlantic Road, night falling and trains passing. The location and price were good, so we decided to take the house, clinking pints of Hoegaarden to celebrate. When we moved in, the two of us with the tiny rooms removed the beds and slept on the floor to make space for our things. At night, we could talk to each other through the wafer-thin wall.

Our new home was at the junction of Leeson Road and Mayall Road. I did not know until much later that this had been the front line of the 1981 Brixton uprising, or that our house was on the site of the Windsor Castle, a pub destroyed by rioters, or that our entire council block had been built on the wreckage of forty-eight hours of violence between police and public three decades earlier.

Our house backed onto Bob Marley Way. A man called Bob lived there; he became a friend and would occasionally come over with his guitar to play Bob Marley covers. Bob's son went to the school where I taught and most of the other pupils lived close by.

Bob Marley Way was generally peaceful at night, so we were surprised one evening to hear a thunderous banging, as though people outside were hitting oil drums. I looked out of my bedroom window and saw a dozen teenage boys running over the tops of the cars parked in the cul-de-sac, jumping from the boot of one onto the bonnet of the next, racing round and round, denting the metal as they went. I had no idea what they were doing or why. It looked like some kind of ritual, as if the boys were summoning something in the centre of the circle of cars. The noise roused the street, doors began to open – but before anybody could confront the boys, they jumped down from the cars and ran away.

Walking through Brixton late at night I often saw the shapes of teenagers, or heard the sound of running feet, and I wondered who they were and what they were up to. In the *Evening Standard* there were frequently stories about gang stabbings and shootings. One night, a boy ran into our front garden and crouched behind the wall, panting. We were shocked and, without thinking, banged on the kitchen window. He leapt to his feet and ran on.

I was the Year 3 teacher in the local primary school, teaching thirty seven-year-olds, and I wondered about the connections between those small children and the boys and girls I saw on the streets at night. A couple of my pupils had older siblings in gangs, several had absent fathers, two had young fathers in prison. One of the boys, when he was six, had been caught rolling make-believe spliffs from scrap paper, copying the gestures he saw his brothers making at home. Looking around my classroom, I could not help spooling forwards and wondering whether some of the children would find themselves caught up in the violence that played out in the surrounding streets.

My class was considered the most challenging in the school. I had never taught before and was not sure why I had been given them. In our first lesson, a boy stood on his desk, shouted, 'I'm King Kong!' and karate-chopped another boy in the windpipe. While I tended to the injured boy, noise and movement erupted around me. I attempted to carry on with the lesson. 'Shut up, you wasteman!' someone yelled. That lunchtime, a group of my pupils surrounded a new teaching assistant in the playground, took off their shoes, and pelted them at him, chanting 'Dickhead! Dickhead!'

My class had a reputation, but the extreme behaviour was as much a product of my inexperience, my inherent looseness and gentleness. A more capable teacher would have been sufficiently firm at the outset to avoid the loss of credibility and slide into chaos. As it was, I lost control and shambled through one lesson after another, attempting to reverse the vicious cycle, trying to establish enough calm to teach fractions, fairy tales or dental hygiene. Each morning I woke to feelings of doom and guilt, walked along Railton Road to school and resumed my uphill struggle from bad to mediocre. By the end of the first term, I had managed to stabilize the situation: outright defiance gave way to reluctant compliance. The children learned and made progress, but time had been lost that could not be regained.

I was better prepared for my second term and, to begin with, posed as a rock-like authoritarian. In the first lesson, I kept a pupil in at lunchtime for writing in pen instead of pencil. If pupils came into the classroom chatting, we would go straight back outside and practise coming in silently. If they put their books away messily, we would get them out again and put them away tidily. I once made a child write me an apology letter for sighing loudly in a lesson. On another occasion I spotted a child passing a note and pounced to intercept it. 'I feel happy!' it said when I unfolded it. I expected total obedience, overlooked nothing and fixated on the most minor details. And I was surprised to see how much the children not only respected but liked the structure and discipline. They knew where they stood, so they relaxed and acted like small children. Then I relaxed, and acted more like myself, and we had a good year.

As I got further from those turbulent first weeks, I shifted out of survival mode and my thoughts turned to how to support every child to succeed. It was bewildering: some children were struggling with the basics of reading while others were reading Harry Potter; some children were doing multiplication while others struggled to tell the difference between addition and subtraction. I could not fathom how teachers met all these needs simultaneously, and most nights I was up late, hammering together lesson plans.

Often the plans backfired. There was the time they dismissed my fumbling explanations and decided that magnets were powered by magic. Or the unit we did on healthy eating, which culminated in them designing the ham-jam-and-crisp sandwich as their example of a well-balanced meal. Or the day we put dirty coppers in Coca-Cola and the children concluded, when the coins came out shiny, that drinking Coke would be a fantastic way to keep their teeth clean.

In the gaps between lessons, we passed out percussion instruments and made music. I brought my guitar to the classroom and we learned sea shanties and Bob Marley songs, the children dancing among the low tables. Working as a primary school teacher is the most challenging thing I have ever done, but the most joyful and rewarding too.

As much as the teaching, I enjoyed feeling part of the community: knowing people when I walked down the street, chatting to children's parents and grandparents in the shops, being given a surprise hug by a parent while eating with friends in Brixton Market. I liked supporting families through challenges too: sitting in meetings with social workers, making sure children were safe, making sure the classroom was a haven, even if life outside was unstable.

I stopped teaching after two years and became an educational researcher. In my new role, I travelled to schools in low-income communities, filming lessons, interviewing teachers and pupils, and investigating how great teachers change lives. I loved watching other people teach, but I missed working directly with young people, so I decided I would do some volunteering, maybe mentoring. Then I spotted an advert on the tube for the Met Special Constabulary.

Everyone I knew was surprised when I said I was going to join the police. I was surprised too. I had never given a thought to policing and could not imagine myself doing it. Nevertheless the decision was less haphazard than it appeared. For as long as I can remember, I have been fascinated by care, education, community and inclusion. This generated an appetite for working with vulnerable or marginalized groups that began in my teens and has never left me. I have done stints at an elderly care home, a toddler group, a homeless shelter, a refugee mentoring programme and a mental health helpline. Before moving to London, I spent a year as a live-in carer for adults with learning difficulties.

I did it because I enjoyed it. But, looking back, I can see that I was exploring the same set of questions from multiple angles: How do we live well together? What are our responsibilities to one another? How do we value and empower every individual, at every stage of life?

Becoming a primary school teacher was part of that process. So was joining the police. When I became a Special Constable – a volunteer with full police powers – I was attracted not so much by the role as by what police see and experience, their proximity to vulnerable groups at their most vulnerable moments.

I thought policing might help me to think about how, and how well, our society was set up to tackle entrenched social issues. Social workers felt overloaded. My colleagues in education were divided over whether teachers should play a wider role in children's lives. Local services had been cut in a huge government austerity drive, from mental health provision, to youth clubs, to libraries, to the bowling green where my grandma used to meet her friends to play bowls. In such circumstances, I wondered whose job it was to grapple with our most complex social challenges – homelessness, loneliness, gang violence, poverty, mental illness, domestic violence – and I suspected that the police were the people who confronted these issues at their most raw. I was intrigued to see how they responded to them. Thinking about it, I realized I was not even sure what the role of the police was in relation to these problems. I knew that the police tackled crime and kept order. I was not sure what they did with the rest of their time.

Even as it became clear that policing would help me explore these deeply held interests, I still felt reluctant. Policing seemed like something I would not do – perhaps should not do – and I wondered why that was. What was it about this job that was simultaneously so compelling and so unappealing? The more resistance I felt, the more determined I was to try it.

The rosy-cheeked Sergeant was there to greet me when I arrived for my second shift. He helped me find a kit belt and stab vest that fitted better than the sagging items I had been issued, then picked through boxes of pins to find my shoulder numbers. As we searched, he chatted about the job and how good it was that we Specials volunteered to do this. I told him I still needed a can of CS. 'No problem,' he said. He disappeared for a minute, then came back waving a shiny grey cylinder. 'Just give it a spray to check it works,' he said with a wink.

We were back in the van for this shift. Cold late autumn, night long fallen when we set out at 7.30. We drifted north from Clapham to Stockwell to Vauxhall, requests for help coming out of the radio, hanging in the air, then being picked off by response teams.

Thousands of emergency calls are made in London every day. Processed centrally, they are transmitted to the relevant borough. 'There's a tall man screaming outside Clapham Common tube' . . . 'A woman's called from St George's Wharf, she says she's been punched by her husband' . . . 'A unit's required at Max Roach Park: a group of males is fighting with sticks.' Messy situations are stripped to essentials: people, problem, place. Narrative fragments mingle with jargon and code. 'A mother's phoned up and said her daughter should have been home four hours ago' – 'Send it to Five Eight One Nights' – 'Show Lima X-Ray Five One Zero Five over.' When we accept a call, we go to the address, meet the people, and hear the whole story. If another unit responds, that five-second fragment is all we get.

'A figure's been sighted climbing across a pre-school roof,' we heard, 'just off Kennington Park Road.' We were less than five minutes away, so we called to accept the job.

We turned on our siren and lights and swung back south, Lambeth Walk to Black Prince Road, Kennington Road to Cleaver Square. Shops, pubs and houses blurred. The terraces seemed more tightly packed than normal. I knew these streets, but not at this speed.

'Next left,' someone said.

'No, wait, no. It's wrong on the map.'

'Get your phone out,' the driver shouted. 'Get your phone out and check.'

'Left here . . . straight on . . . straight.'

Within five minutes, we reached the pre-school and radioed our time of arrival. We stepped out of the van and squinted at the roof. It was too dark to see if anyone was up there, so two of us shinned up the perimeter wall while the others surrounded the premises.

We lowered ourselves into the playground. We were surrounded by bulky shapes and, at first, I was not sure what I was looking at. The plastic see-saws and Little Tikes cars, gaudy by day, were squat, colourless outlines. The silhouettes of the climbing frame and Wendy houses looked like an encampment. We muted our radios and crept towards the main building, alert for signs of life. In the low light, the air was full of grey static, so that everything around us seemed to be moving. We did not think we could see or hear anyone, nor could we imagine why someone would scale a pre-school roof, but it was difficult to be sure that there was nobody there. We passed a line of sand and water tables. We stepped over a knee-high fence and reached the pre-school itself. I boosted my partner so that she could see onto the flat felt roof. There was nobody up there, so we did a circuit of the school and checked the doors and windows for a break-in. Returning to the playground, we opened the doors of the Wendy houses and checked behind the climbing frame. There was no sign of an intruder, so we radioed to say that all was well, squeezing our update between the latest requests for help. It was a dull autumn evening, but there was plenty going on: a shoplifter, a stabbing, a few domestics, a couple of robberies, a disturbance in a bar.

Driving towards Brixton, we flashed our lights and stopped a moped with only one mirror. 'Is everything all right?' asked the driver, an IC4 teenager. We told him why we had stopped him and asked to see his licence. 'The other one got knocked off,' he said. 'I thought it was legal to drive with one mirror.' It is legal, but it was also a good reason for a chat. We took the boy's licence and ran a name and vehicle check.

There are different radio channels for different patches of Lambeth and invisible lines where the channels change. Each patch has a main channel and a support channel for checking people's details. Compared to the main channel, with its urgent calls and unfolding situations, the support channel makes for tedious listening: one officer after another spelling out names and addresses, endless Alphas, Bravos, Kilos and Victors, mind-numbing strings of numbers and code.

I reached the front of the queue and read out the boy's details, struggling with the phonetic alphabet, feeling foolish when P and U would not come and I swapped in Pancake and Unicorn.

The phonetic alphabet is a peculiar mishmash of names, places and objects. I did not know it before policing and at first I thought of Lima and Quebec when I said their names, of friends called Charlie and Mike, of people playing Golf and dancing the Tango. As I began to use the phonetic alphabet regularly, I noticed the meanings fade. Within a matter of weeks, only the sounds remained – although I still imagined a polished marble floor each time I heard Hotel, thought Romeo when I heard Juliet, and saw a flash of amber whenever I said Whiskey.

When the checks came back clear, we thanked the boy on the moped and said goodnight. 'I'm driving home from work,' he said. 'McDonald's.' He unzipped his puffer jacket and showed us the yellow uniform, his name badge pinned to the breast pocket.


More calls. 'A male's threatening a female outside the Dogstar' . . . 'There's been a stabbing on the Stockwell Gardens Estate' . . . 'A handbag has been snatched outside Gypsy Hill train station' . . . 'A unit's required to deal with a group of individuals who are picnicking in the middle of Streatham High Road.'

The police radio is a reminder that we are a tiny node in a vast network of activity, a structure we can sense but cannot see. Even with the volume low, we can hear the unfolding drama of crime and response. During my first shifts I was fascinated by the radio, by the operators cataloguing the city's suffering. At times it seemed like a random-event generator, not just relaying situations but inventing them. It took me a couple of shifts to realize that the stories we hear on the radio are reports, not certainties. When a call comes, we take it at face value, but it is not uncommon to rush to a giant street fight, only to find an empty road. When we arrive at a location and there is nobody there, no indication as to whether what was reported took place, it can be hard to know the truth.

There had been an abandoned call from the New Park Road Estate, next to my flat. Someone had dialled 999 and hung up. The operator had called back twice with no reply, so we radioed to say we would go and investigate.

We drove up Brixton Hill and turned onto New Park Road, passing Chicken Treat, the 2012 Quantum Shop, Mareeg Coffee, Angela's Cafe. It was strange to be a hundred metres from my bed, and my wife asleep in it. I often wondered whether I had done the right thing by asking to police in the borough where I lived. Regulars told cautionary tales of colleagues being hassled off duty by people they had stopped on shifts, or by local teenagers who followed them home.

We drove to the centre of the estate and got out. I felt uncomfortable: these were my neighbours. I might see them in the shop. We found the right building, rode a cramped lift to the top floor and walked along the balcony to the caller's address. There was no answer when we knocked. We knocked again loudly. 'It's the police, open the door!' The door inched open. Five thigh-high IC3 children were giggling behind it. A moment later two women, a mother and a grandmother, appeared behind them. 'Is everything OK, officers?' We explained what had happened. 'Now! Which one of you kids called the police?' the grandmother asked. There was a subdued silence. 'Come on now!' The silence was broken by a five-year-old boy who whispered, 'Well . . . I dialled 9, 9, 9, then 1, then 2.' There was a pause, then the women burst out laughing. 'Well, at least he's honest, hey officers? Now you see what happens, don't you, Charles?'

It was midnight and we were driving down a wide residential road connecting Brixton to Clapham. Red houses with small front gardens, pavements dotted with young trees. We spotted a tired-looking Corsa with patchy brown paintwork and a broken headlight. We flashed it and pulled it over beside a squat breeze-block church with a sign on its lawn. 'Let's meet at My House. Sunday before lunch. GOD.'

We mimed to the driver, an IC6 male in his forties, to roll down the window. 'Turn off the engine, put the keys on the dash and step onto the pavement.' The driver did what we asked, but shiftily, his shoulders tense, his eyes darting between our faces. 'Take your hands out of your pockets so we can see them,' we said. His eyes widened and he jerked his hands from his coat pockets and thrust them above his head. 'No, no, bring them down, mate. Just relax.'

The man's name was Hassan. He was stout and balding, wearing a brown jacket and trousers that were too big for him. We explained that we had stopped him because of a broken headlight and were going to run some routine checks. Hassan nodded but did not say anything. He shifted his weight from one foot to the other and looked back along the road in the direction he had come from.

Our checks showed that the Corsa was uninsured – something Hassan already knew. In stumbling English, he explained that he had just bought the car from a friend and had tried to buy insurance, but the payment had bounced. His girlfriend had advised him not to drive, but there were things he needed to do tonight so he had decided to take the risk.

We radioed for a tow truck and explained to Hassan that we were going to confiscate the Corsa. There would be a considerable fee, several hundred pounds, to reclaim it. We stressed how serious it is to drive without insurance, how unfair it is on other road users. Hassan listened in silence and put his hands back into his pockets.

We worked through the car seizure form, filling in Hassan's details, then the car's, then reeling off a long list of Yes/No questions. 'Do you want the car to be scrapped?' we asked as we neared the end.

'Yes,' he replied.

'You want the car scrapped?'

'Yes.'

'Are you sure you don't want to pick up the car?'

'Yes,' said Hassan. 'I want to pick up the car.'

We tore off a carbon copy of the form, handed it to Hassan and told him he could collect his belongings and go. He unscrunched a black bin liner and walked around the car, emptying the glovebox, boot and footwells into it, and then he looked at us and gave a half nod. We said goodnight and wished him well. Hassan nodded again and set off in the direction he had been driving. We sat on a garden wall to wait for the tow truck and watched him walk away, bin bag swinging from his fist.

We heard laughter behind us. There were three twelve- or thirteen-year-olds on the fire escape of the evangelical church, an IC1 male, an IC1 female and an IC3 female. We walked towards them and, as we did, they clattered down the steps and walked away with the exaggerated strides of children who want to run but have been instructed not to. They turned a corner. By the time we reached it they had vanished.

I woke thinking about Hassan and how random it was that we stopped him. I wondered where he was now, whether he was home, whether he had crossed London on foot, how he would even have done that. I had seen him take his phone from his pocket as he was preparing to leave, glance at it, then put it back. It was an old Nokia with a tiny black and white display. No WhatsApp, no internet, no maps. It made me think of the time, as a student, I came to visit a friend in London and tried to navigate from King's Cross to her house in West London using a tube map, presuming that the lines were as straight as they looked, the gaps between stations a true gauge of distance. I had walked for two hours, then gave up as night fell, many stops from my destination.

I left the house, caught a bus down Brixton Hill and went to the Phoenix. I ordered a plate of bubble and squeak and sat in the back corner, closest to the heat and smell of frying from the kitchen.

We could so easily not have stopped Hassan. What did it mean that we had? We were not systematically checking that cars were insured – we had stopped him because of a broken light. I was not convinced that the risk we had exposed him to, leaving him miles from home in the middle of a cold winter's night, pushing him further into financial precarity, was greater than the risk to which he was exposing others.

I had made an effort to explain the seriousness of driving uninsured. In a roundabout way, I think I was trying to make Hassan feel better, as though understanding the gravity of his offence might make our response seem less harsh.

The confiscation seemed both minor and massive. What could be more routine than impounding an uninsured car? Yet I could imagine how difficult and disruptive the experience might be for Hassan. I was also struck by the casual power I now held as a police officer. I was the one who had spotted his car. I pointed at it, suggested we pull it over, and the next thing I knew, a man was on the street holding his belongings in a bin bag. I was troubled that I had noticed his car simply because it was rundown. Already, on my second shift, I could see that our attention was drawn to people who could not disguise their precarity. We applied pressure to the people already under significant pressure – because they were easy to spot and we were looking for something to do.

The fact that bothered me most was that Hassan was not a calculating criminal. He was a man whose insecure circumstances had led him to take risks that he might not otherwise have considered. And because of those circumstances, the consequences of his risk-taking would be particularly severe. It is an ancient dilemma, perfectly expressed by the writer Anatole France: 'In its majestic equality,' he wrote, 'the law forbids rich and poor alike to sleep under bridges, beg in the streets and steal loaves of bread.' Something about the drab banality of the confiscation made me feel this afresh.

Being stranded miles from home in the middle of the night is a problem. Having your car confiscated with big fines to reclaim it is a problem. For Hassan those problems had rolled off the back of other problems and would surely generate fresh problems of their own. There was a compounding effect, problems multiplying uncontrollably, the field of available options narrowing.

I knew next to nothing about Hassan. I did not know whether the confiscation of his Corsa was an inconvenience or a final straw. But it dawned on me that the most mundane-seeming stop could be a moment of life-altering proportions. This realization gave an unanticipated gravity to community policing. We stopped people, we dealt with minor incidents, we logged them on the computer, but we had no way to take the measure of that moment for the people involved.

I paid the bill and left the Phoenix. It was lunchtime. Brixton was getting busy. On the bus ride home, I thought about the adolescents we had spotted and lost the night before. Perched on the railings of the fire escape, they had looked like children on a climbing frame.

On our next shift, we were sent to Clapham High Street on foot patrol, monitoring the Friday-night crowds in the pubs and clubs. The rosy-cheeked Sergeant gave me a wave as I arrived at the office and asked how things were going. I was still missing all sorts of gear, I admitted – evidence bags and traffic tickets, a clip for my radio and a holster for my baton, both of which I was storing in a pocket of my stab vest. He rootled around in an over-stuffed cupboard which had long ceased to have any system or order. Five minutes later, to my amazement, he had found all the items and handed them to me with a smile.

I was still getting used to the uniform. The beat helmet in particular – an elongated plastic cone that felt like it might topple off at any moment. It was neither comfortable nor functional and I could not understand why we wore it – especially as it made us look faintly ridiculous. The public took us less seriously when we were wearing the helmet. Tourists asked to try it on, drunks tried to knock it off. The female officer's bowler hat, although less of a direct target, scarcely commanded more authority.

Over time, though, I realized that this was the point. Wearing funny hats, we are more approachable. My preference for the sleek military cap I wore on vehicle shifts was also a preference for the extra degree of authority it gave me – the additional degree of respect the public displayed when I was wearing it. Although the beat helmet makes us physically bigger, in a more important way it makes us smaller. The bowler and the beat helmet signal that we are good-natured community servants, not an occupying force. They are a detail, their impact subliminal, but they reduce the distance between the police and the public.

At the end of each working week, thousands of people flock to the half-mile strip of Clapham High Street to drink and dance. They emerge from Clapham North and Clapham Common tube stations with a look not just of relief, but of determination, as though they have come to settle a score. Then they drink in Honky Tonk, dance in Infernos, and end the night at KFC, the Kebab Company or in the queue for an unlicensed hot dog. At eight o'clock the High Street was already heaving. Our task was to walk back and forth until everyone went home again, to deal with any issues and remind the excited crowds that the eyes of the law were on them.

Alcohol is a superb producer of crime. On Clapham High Street on a Friday night, it provokes a degree of high spirits, violence and confusion not ordinarily found outside a school playground. Alcohol distorts personalities and perspectives. The people who step off the tubes and buses are not the people who will leave seven hours later.

An IC1 male, early twenties, rushed up to us, wide-eyed and out of breath. 'My friend's just dropped his Oyster card! And some guy – some guy's just picked it up and walked off with it!' He pointed down an alley, where two groups of intoxicated men were shouting at each other in an unlit car park. We walked towards them. 'All right guys! That's enough! Calm it down!' We separated the groups, identified the man who had taken the Oyster card and insisted he return it. When he refused, we threatened to arrest him for theft. Weighing his options, he tossed the Oyster card onto the tarmac in front of him. Then he began to run around shouting, 'I just got arrested! I just got arrested for an Oyster card!' He ran over to us: 'I can't believe I just got arrested for an Oyster card!'

'You haven't been arrested,' we said. 'The best thing you can do is go home.'

Getting drunk in public has a ritualistic quality. People take a mind-altering substance and make themselves vulnerable en masse, trusting that sober non-participants – bouncers, bar staff, police and paramedics – will keep them safe.

There was an argument on a traffic island between two IC1 males, early twenties, one with a bloody mouth.

'He's my boyfriend,' the other said. 'He's just been punched in Vodka Revs. He wants to report it, but I think we should just go home.'

'Give us a description and we'll go over and sort it out.'

'No, no, come on, let's just go home and watch *South Park*.' The man with the bloody mouth nodded and began to cry. His boyfriend put his arm around him and they walked towards the tube.

Gone midnight, passing Infernos, we were approached by an IC1 female in a short black tasselled dress. 'What's the easiest way to get to Hammersmith from here?' she asked. 'Sorry, no idea,' we replied. The tube had stopped for the night and we did not know the bus routes. She lifted her left foot and placed it on a garden wall. 'Do you want to see my tattoo?' she said. Before we could reply, she had hitched her dress up to reveal a vibrant image covering her left thigh: the head of a sausage dog, wreathed by fruit and flowers. We stared in silence. It looked like a memorial to a much-loved pet.

'It's my sister's dog,' the woman said.

'Is it dead?' we asked.

'No,' she said, 'but I feel guilty . . . I was meant to be looking after it tonight. Now I'm worried about it and I don't know how to get home.'

We looked again at the dog on the woman's thigh: its chin was raised, its eyes were wide and it had a manic smile on its face. An IC1 male walked towards us and paused as he passed. 'That looks well dodgy!' he shouted.

We left the woman and walked away from the High Street. Turning a corner, we saw an IC1 male in suit trousers and a white shirt asleep against a garden wall, elbows hooked over bent knees, his chin touching his chest. 'Mate. Mate, wake up. This is a bad place to sleep.'

Patrolling the High Street, watching people laughing, playing, crying, it seemed that the transformation alcohol offered was a return to the carefree, impulsive, present-tense experience of childhood. I thought of the paediatrician and psychoanalyst Donald Winnicott. 'No adults are all the time adult,' he wrote. That seemed true here. When drunk, adults do childish things. And the more they drink, the more they regress, until they can barely look after themselves, sinking deeper and deeper into a state of delicious dependence.

—

There was a long queue at the illegal hot-dog vendor's trolley. 'You'd have to be pissed out of your head to eat that shit,' my partner said. 'God knows what's in those sausages.' We looked on for a moment and then cut to the front of the line. 'Mate, you need to pack up and leave.' The hot-dog vendor looked straight past us and continued to take orders. We stepped between the man and his customers and he flapped his arms in exasperation, smacking his spatula onto the grill. 'I'm working, I'm working!' he said.

'Go home,' my partner replied. 'I swear, if we see you around again tonight, we'll take your cart and throw it in a skip.' The hot-dog vendor scowled, scraped the sausages into a cardboard box and wheeled his trolley down a side street.

The queue remained in place for a few moments after he had left, hanging there until the news spread along it and people drifted away.

3

## YouTube: *Crazy London Gang Fight*

198,831 views

### Jahangir Hussain
who is fighting who????

#### Sabotaz80
No matter how many times I watch this I still can't entirely tell, looks like one of them switches sides half way through lol

#### tadeasle
I seen three guns and u tellin me ain't nobody get shot

##### hot video
Did the gun have blanks or does someone need to go specsavers this is just too much i saw a sword a chopper a batton but no one was killed and everyone walked away

**Sabotaz8o**

After reading the police and court reports on this I've finally cracked what the fuck is actually happening in the video lol. There's 5 guys fighting in this video, not 4 as originally seems. The two guys we first see outside the shop are together with the guy inside wearing the fur hooded jacket. These 3 (who are of Jamaican/black British origin) are fighting against 2 other guys (who appear to be of Somali origin). The Somali gunman chases the 2 hooded guys into the shop, one of whom fires a shot back himself, where they join their mate in the fur hood. All 3 of them awkwardly get chased around the tiny shop, trying to avoid getting shot. The Somali guys gun fortunately seems to jam as he is trying to shoot them in the shop, at which point one of the hooded guys meat cleavers him in the face, and then starts grappling with him for dear life, while the other hooded guy from outside runs off, not to be seen again (smart choice).

**gtmoney007**

Seen a lot of fights online before, that was a mad one

> **SOFIA labrune**
> So good! trop bien!

**biogroveblade**

Literally no loss to society if any of these die.

**Liam Eaton**

let them kill eachother, they dont contribute
nothing good to this planet

**SOUPRUN01**

this planet is being destroyed by human beings
anyway. Plastic takes 450 years to break down.
Most people consume alot of plastic. Causing
flooding in bangladesh.

**Aaron Chisholm**

Wtf dat was my local shop

**Chubby Greyhound**

Christ, I was in there just the other day happily
buying some Wotsits and a croissant (a huge let
down sadly). Funny world.

We were patrolling South Lambeth in a van, looking for people and vehicles to stop. As we were driving up Tulse Hill, a ball of white light skimmed across our windscreen, the magnesium flare of a firework. We looked in the direction it had come from and saw an IC3 male in his early teens sprinting towards the estate. We swerved to the kerb, threw open the van door and gave chase, catching the boy just before he reached the entrance.

'I didn't do it!' he shouted.

'Why did you run if you didn't do it?'

'I thought you was going to beat me up. Isn't that what you do, beat people up? I seen it on *Road Wars*.'

One Special rolled on a pair of blue latex gloves and began to search the boy while a regular asked him questions.

'We've got better things to do than deal with little shits setting off fireworks. Where do you live?'

'On the estate, with my aunty and baby cousin.'

'We could take you back to your aunt now and give her a fine for eighty pounds. Does she have eighty pounds to give us? I doubt it.'

The boy shrugged. After the initial shock of being caught, he now looked bored.

We heard shouts from the estate and then, a moment later,

half a dozen hooded figures appeared at the entrance – teenage boys, bigger and older than the boy we were searching. 'Let him go!' they shouted. 'He ain't done nothing!' Then they began to drift towards us, as though they might be coming to rescue their friend. I felt my knees give slightly, sweat seeping through the armpits of my shirt. I felt completely out of place, a teacher in a police uniform, unsure what I would do if the situation escalated. The boys hovered ten metres away from us, shouting and gesturing, watching our every move.

The search did not uncover any more fireworks so we took the boy's details and let him go. Once he had joined them, the teenagers withdrew into the estate and we got back in the van. 'You want to be careful in there,' said our driver. 'They're not fans of Old Bill. One patrol car that went in there had its windscreen smashed by a brick dropped off a balcony.'

We drove back down Tulse Hill, past the Hootananny, a club in an old hotel, and onto Effra Road, which roughly tracks the route of Brixton's buried river. We followed Morval Road, Dulwich Road, and on past the dark and silent playground of the school where I used to teach. Through the railings, I could see my classroom door. We turned onto Railton Road and drove the route I had walked to and from school every day. We went past my old house, past shops where I knew the shopkeepers, past the drawn curtains of friends and of children I had taught.

I had walked lines of children through these streets to museum trips and swimming lessons, holding the hand of the child at the front, turning my head to check we were all together, clapping rhythms to get their attention, which the whole class would clap back, getting the attention of everyone passing by.

It was curious. I knew this area, I was part of the life of this place, and yet, at night in a police van, it felt remote, like a known place in a dream. I had hoped that policing would bring me closer to my community, but here I felt I was seeing it at one remove, as though I were floating above or outside of it.

We drove along Coldharbour Lane, passing the Ritzy Cinema and Windrush Square in front of it. It had not been called that when I moved to Brixton, although I could not remember its old name. When the square was redeveloped, the name was put to a public vote and Windrush was the winner, commemorating the ship that brought the first Caribbean immigrants to the UK after the Second World War. Looming over Windrush Square is a giant faded advertisement for Bovril, painted on the end of a Victorian terrace – one of London's ghost signs, a reminder of how haphazardly certain slivers of the past persist in the present.

We continued along the High Street, past KFC, Morleys, Iceland, the tube, and on towards Angell Town.

Police and teens have a distinctive relationship. The street is where teenagers meet and where police hunt for crime. When most people are indoors, police and teens are outside hoping something will happen, police in their fleeces, teens in their puffers. We share the night-time streets and, on uneventful nights, we become events for one another.

We stopped for a break in the Kebab Company and I asked a regular officer how much time they spent dealing with teenagers. 'Too much,' he said. 'It stops us doing the job we're paid to do. I joined the job to arrest criminals, not to be a social worker. There's all these effed-up families expecting us to be social workers, but we're not.'

We drove along Clapham High Street and saw a pair of officers dealing with the hot-dog vendor outside the Clapham Picturehouse. 'You've got to admire his work ethic,' our driver said. 'Rain or shine, he's always out. He's crafty, mind. If you tell him to go home, he just wheels the cart around a bit then sets up somewhere else. I've thrown his sausages in the bin before, but as soon as you leave he fishes them out and puts them back on the grill. Now when I see him I take the valve off his gas canister – that way I know he'll have to stop.'

We were waiting at a traffic light next to Clapham Common tube and a curly-haired IC1 female tapped at the front passenger window. One of the regulars opened it and asked what she wanted.

'Someone took my purse and I really need it. I really need to get it back. It has my residency card. I was on a bus and a Black man grabbed it and ran away.'

'He's long gone now,' the officer replied. 'The best thing you can do is report it at a police station in the morning.'

He wished her goodnight and wound up the window. 'She'd get fucked,' he said as it slid shut.

My face felt hot and I felt my shoulders tense. I looked around the van, trying to gauge my colleagues' reaction. If they were shocked, they did not show it. The moment passed without comment. What did it mean that words like these were permitted in a police van?

We circled around Clapham, deflated and bored, looking for someone to stop and waiting for interesting calls. A Special was talking about the bus route he drove for his day job. 'Fuck that route,' said the regular. A domestic violence call came out of the radio, a woman being threatened by her partner. 'Fuck that call.'

We saw a car full of IC3 teens, two in the front, three in the back. We flashed our lights and pulled them over. The driver stepped out with a smile. 'Today's my birthday, you know!'

It was almost 1 a.m. Someone passed around a packet of Percy Pigs and I took a couple, rolling the gummy pig heads between my fingers before putting them in my mouth. I chewed them slowly, savouring the sweetness and the rubbery texture. I never normally ate sweets. They reminded me of my childhood.

We spotted two bikes propped against a fence outside a car park – left there perhaps by a pair of teen robbers. We stopped the van and tiptoed inside, alert to any movement, hoping to disturb a drug deal or the exchange of stolen goods.

Near the road it was easy to see what was what, but visibility deteriorated the further we walked into the car park. The scene shifted before our eyes, as though by moving through the darkness we were disturbing it, like swimmers stirring up silt. Objects became outlines, then blurs, then faded altogether, until, instead of tidy rows of cars, all we could see was an agitated grey fuzz.

We could not see or hear anybody. Perhaps no one was there. We turned on our torches and searched between and below the cars. On the way out, examining the bikes, we realized they were chained and had been left for the night.

I boarded a bus home at the end of the shift. There were no double seats free on the top deck, so I walked to the back and sat next to an IC3 teen in a baseball cap. His head was leaning on the window and I thought he might be asleep. I straightened my trousers and tucked my rucksack between my feet.

'Move,' the boy said. I was surprised, unsure whether I had heard correctly. 'Move,' he said again, louder and slower. I turned to look at him. His head was still leaning on the window. 'Move!' the boy said, raising his voice. I stood up, picked up my bag and said something about manners, respect, public transport. Then I took a seat further forward, next to an older man in a camel-hair coat.

I arrived home at six o'clock and got up four hours later with the jet-lagged glow that sometimes accompanies a long night and a short sleep: a feeling of weightlessness, a sense of not quite belonging to the waking world. I went for breakfast in the Phoenix and thought about the boy who fired the firework.

As a former teacher, I did not feel comfortable chasing, grabbing and searching children. Stop and search seemed very adult to me, crossing boundaries that should be crossed only in extremis and then only with the utmost care. A crowd of uniformed officers surrounding a thirteen-year-old – I could understand why the other boys had come out of the estate. The imbalance was striking, the jeopardy real. I was surprised he had not appeared more afraid.

I thought about teaching and policing. The roles seemed incomparable; I had turned from an educator into an enforcer. But as I drank my coffee, I reflected that they were more similar than they appeared. The things children do in schools are criminal offences in the world of adults. Pushing someone over is assault, taking their football stickers is theft, scratching a swear word onto a radiator is criminal damage. Aspects of teaching are like policing in miniature. But when under-eighteens transgress, it is generally thought of as misbehaviour. Up to the age of ten, this attitude is enshrined in law. The very young are considered *doli incapax* – 'incapable of ill doing'. 'We can't arrest them,' we were told in training, 'but if we see a little one up to no good, we don't just walk away from our responsibility because of this kryptonite ten thing.'

In my second year of teaching, I took my Year 3 class swimming every Thursday morning. Year 4, my old class, had the slot before us and would leave the water on our arrival, changing while my class was in the pool. On one of those Thursday mornings, a Year 4 boy urinated in the shoes of a Year 3 boy called Danny. Getting changed half an hour later, Danny, the best in the class at football but very shy otherwise, was so distraught at his discovery, he could not even tell me what had happened and another boy had to come over and explain. I looked for alternative footwear, but the only spare shoes we could lay our hands on were a pair of girls' trainers a classmate had brought in her swimming bag. Danny would have to walk a mile through Brixton in pink girls' trainers, carrying his ruined shoes in a Tesco bag. When I told him about this second humiliation, the desolation on his face deepened. Seeing this, Elijah, another boy in my class, offered to wear the girls' trainers on the long walk back and lent Danny his dry black Kickers.

Thinking about Danny's shoes, 'incapable of ill doing' did not seem quite right. James Baldwin described the innocence of children as 'both real and monstrous'. Without an adult's capacity for empathy and imagining consequences, he wrote, children 'intimidate, harass, blackmail, terrify, and sometimes kill one another'. Urinating in another child's shoes. It was grotesque. Then I thought about Elijah's gesture, an outsized act of generosity and loyalty. Childhood is an extreme time.

My bubble and squeak arrived. Steam was spurting from the top of the tea urn.

I was accustomed to interacting with young people in schools. It had been disconcerting to find myself in a stand-off with them on the street, acting like the boys' adversary, not a caring, authoritative adult.

Facing the boys, I had felt an almost overwhelming urge to hold up my hands, to shout, to bring us all to our senses. I thought we might actually end up fighting them. Then I had realized how rehearsed the situation was. My colleagues seemed unconcerned; they had been there before. There would be some noise, some drama, and then it would sub-side. I wondered how the boys had seen the situation and what it meant to them.

One of the reasons policing appealed to me was the oppor-tunity to see sides of my area that I would otherwise struggle to access. Living in Brixton, I was always conscious of how much I was not seeing, and particularly of the hidden lives of the teenagers in gangs. They seemed to occupy a parallel universe. They were right there, I saw them all the time, but the city they lived in was far more dangerous than mine.

It made me think of China Miéville's novel, *The City and the City*, which tells the story of two rival nations whose capital cities share the same location. It is a bit like East and West Berlin, except no wall carves the city in two. Instead, the cap-itals are intermeshed, with certain zones allocated to one city or another, and others that belong to both. These 'crosshatched' areas are used by residents of both cities simultaneously, but they are not shared spaces. The occupants of the two states not only ignore one another, but are actively trained to 'unsee' one another. '[Here] it was a quiet area,' writes the protagonist, 'but the streets were crowded with those elsewhere. I unsaw them, but it took time to pick past them all.'

Brixton felt like a crosshatched area, with some of its teenagers caught between the city of order, routine and school rules, and the city of conflict, risk and rule-breaking. London may not be 'a dangerous city by global standards', writes the rapper and writer Akala, but 'it is hard to overstate just what a scary place London is to a working-class black male teenager.'

I went to pay. The Phoenix's manager was training to be a black-cab driver, preparing for the Knowledge, the gruelling assessment cabbies must pass to get their licence. He was reading the London *A–Z* and put it face down by the till when he saw me approach. Outside, small children were bouncing along Coldharbour Lane in front of parents with heavy bags of fish and vegetables from the market. On the corner of the High Street, outside KFC, I could see a group of teenagers with a sound system. A girl was singing Gospel music and some boys were handing out flyers about Jesus.

For our next shift, we were assigned to Clapham High Street. I arrived late and ran in sweating, out of breath, still in my daytime clothes while the other Specials were kitted up and ready to go. The rosy-cheeked Sergeant waved hello, batted away my apologies and sent me to change.

In the van on the way to the High Street we paused next to Clapham South tube station. On the Common opposite is a large brown-brick cylinder covered in graffiti – the entrance to a Second World War bomb shelter. This was the place where arrivals on the HMT *Empire Windrush* were given temporary accommodation in 1948, sleeping in bunks deep below the city while, in the daytime, they looked for work and a home. The immigrants, from across the Caribbean, were instructed to register at a Labour Exchange. The nearest was at 372 Coldharbour Lane, next to the entrance to Brixton Village Market. They went there to find jobs, and many took lodgings nearby, beginning the process that would see Brixton become the symbolic heart of the Afro-Caribbean community in Britain. We drove on and the van dropped us off outside Londis.

On the High Street in hi-vis, we walked back and forth between Clapham Common and Clapham North tube stations, passing Honky Tonk, Infernos, the Kebab Company, Vodka Revs, Roosters Spot and KFC, passing them again on the way back, then passing them over and over and over. An IC1 female, mid-twenties, pink hair, walked towards us, making eye contact and smiling. 'Knobheads,' she coughed as she passed.

'You get used to that,' my partner said. 'A lot of people hate the police. Until they get their bag stolen.'

It had been dark for several hours, but it was still early and the Friday-night crowds were just ordering their first drinks. There was not much to do, so we did a sweep for people begging at the cashpoints.

The first was an IC1 male, fifties, sitting on a piece of cardboard outside Barclays. He was perfectly still, his chin on his chest, not even looking up to ask for money. He did not seem to mind when we asked him to move, chatting as he gathered his possessions. 'I've got a room in a hostel,' he said. 'I know I'm luckier than some, but I hate it. There's some tough characters living in there, I'll tell you.'

Although begging is illegal, we rarely arrest people for it. Instead, we move people on, a phrase that sounds euphemistic but is entirely literal. When we ask someone to move on, that is all we expect them to do. We nudge the problem down the road. My partner told me that arresting a beggar can be a good technique for finishing a shift on time. 'At a certain point in the evening,' he said, 'it's good to get off the streets, so that you don't get drawn into something serious just before you're due to finish. There's this one chap, a prolific aggressive beggar, he's got an ASBO that means he's not allowed to beg, but he still does it all the time. He can be a really easy body. You spot him and nick him and you know that's you tucked up for the rest of the shift.' I knew who he meant: a man in Brixton who approached me several times a week. He was remarkably active, working the bus stops, the markets, stopping hundreds of people an hour, moving briskly from one to the next. His energy was astounding.

The second person begging was an IC3 male, forties, his dreads tucked into a woolly hat, sitting by a NatWest cashpoint with a Staffie next to him. 'I'm just trying to get some money for food,' he said. 'I'm just begging, aren't I? It's not exactly the biggest crime in the world.'

'I'm afraid we need you to move,' we said.

He stood up and clipped a lead onto the dog's collar. 'Come on Ruby, let's go.'

It is not uncommon for people begging to get frustrated when we move them on. They accuse us of picking on them, tell us there are more important things we could be doing than making their lives more difficult. As with teenagers, so with beggars. Those who spend the most time on the streets are the most susceptible to policing.

I was struck by the futility of our actions. Several of us were walking around Clapham, looking for people begging. We had an opportunity to engage with people in need of support. What were we doing with it?

Former Met Commissioner Robert Mark described the distinctive power of the police as the 'power to inconvenience'. The inconvenience is meant to serve a greater purpose. Here it seemed an end in itself.

In my education research job I worked in a privately owned office complex by the Thames in London Bridge. Instead of police, security guards patrolled the grounds, chasing away beggars, skateboarders and anyone who disrupted the sleek corporate tranquillity. Patrolling Clapham High Street, we were not working for a private client – yet it looked as though we might be. Our approach was identical.

Homelessness is rarely just about lack of a home. Addiction, mental illness, poverty, and trauma are often in the mix. I thought about the language we use to describe the most vulnerable. They are 'outsiders'. They are 'in the margins', they have 'gone off track' or 'slipped through the net'. Our language suggests they have gone somewhere else. Or we say that they have been 'left behind', as though the rest of us have moved on without them. The irony is that often no one goes anywhere. The most vulnerable continue to share the same spaces as everyone else and life goes on around them, their part in it no longer secure.

We watched Ruby and her owner disappear into the darkness of the Common, then we set off in the opposite direction, back past Infernos, Vodka Revs, KFC. We found a pair of IC1 eighteen-year-olds, wearing tartan and leather, sitting on cardboard beneath the railway bridge. The young woman had a ring in her nose and the man had a blue line tattooed across his face from ear to ear. They were squatters down on their luck, buskers turned beggars after selling their instruments. 'I play accordion, he plays guitar. We play tunes by Cher and Lady Gaga mainly.'

Before entering the Phoenix I looked along Acre Lane, stretching away to Clapham. Although I knew Brixton before joining the Met, I had never even visited Clapham. Now I knew it only at night, through the eyes of a police officer.

I pushed open the door of the Phoenix, greeted the manager and sat down to type up my notes – to get my memories on paper before they began to blur. This was something I did outside policing too. Since childhood I have been an obsessive note-taker. I began keeping a diary when I was eight. To the perpetual amusement of friends and family, I have been writing life down ever since.

I am not sure what urge lies behind my note-taking, but it is driven by compulsion, not duty. When I have a moment alone, it is my first and strongest instinct. As a Special Constable the habit intensified. On shifts I would scribble rough notes on index cards stored in the pockets of my stab vest. The next morning I would type it all up – and, in the process, think it all through.

I spread out the previous night's index cards and stretched my legs below the table. They were stiff from walking up and down Clapham High Street for eight hours. I thought about the beggars we had moved on and wondered how they had spent the night.

When I was a student I volunteered on Fridays at a much-loved local night shelter. For the first hour, I caught up with the residents, then when everyone had gone to bed I cleaned the kitchen, the bathrooms and the lounge, before grabbing a blanket and sleeping on one of the sofas. The night shelter was in the basement of a church, with high windows looking out at the pavement and the feet of passers-by. The lounge was never really dark because of the glow from the street lights. It was never really quiet either, because one of the residents snored in an armchair in one corner. He had spent so many years sleeping upright that he could no longer sleep in a bed.

I saw some guests each week for months, others only once. Over mugs of tea, I heard stories of people breaking down, running away, dropping out, being dropped: a man who lost his job, house and wife in the same week; a woman fleeing domestic abuse; an out-of-work sailor trying to get to an Italian port; a Cambridge physics prodigy thwarted by alcohol; a cheerful man who described himself as 'a professional touring tramp'. Some of the older men had been on and off the streets for much of their adult lives.

I became particularly close to a man called Tom, who had become suddenly homeless in his sixties. He moved into the hostel while I was volunteering there and began selling the *Big Issue* outside Sainsbury's. Tom had a mischievous smile and I was impressed by his positive attitude. He was sure he was going to turn his life around – and he embraced this new chapter with enthusiasm, unideal as it was. We would talk through his options on my night shifts, his progress through various waiting lists, and we would chat and laugh outside Sainsbury's when I passed. But then I watched with distress as Tom's optimism gradually drained away and it became clear that there was no fast track back to normality and a flat of his own. We continued to chat in the hostel and on the street, and Tom continued to smile, but his pace slowed, his condition declined and every time I saw him he seemed to have lost another tooth.

During my night shifts in the hostel, we only had to call the police once: the evening a guest started arguing with the manager and tried to stab him with a fork he had pocketed during dinner. The manager and I backed the guest into the entrance hall and locked him in. He raged behind the reinforced glass, brandishing his fork and demanding that we let him out. When the police arrived, they surrounded the front door and waited for him with batons drawn.

On Saturday mornings, getting back to my student room before most people were awake, I always felt as if I had returned from somewhere remote, even though the shelter was only a ten-minute walk away. I had a similar feeling in the Phoenix, finishing my bubble and squeak. Clapham was just along Acre Lane, past the big Tesco.

I knew that, but the place I had spent the night felt far off and inaccessible.

After spending our first shifts patrolling, we were due to spend a night dashing to emergency calls in response cars. I was excited by the prospect of drama and speed, and by the thought of a night in a warm car, rather than pacing backwards and forwards for miles.

The station was quiet when we arrived. The only person in the briefing room was the rosy-cheeked Sergeant, who told us there had been a serious gang fight, with multiple stabbings, and that everyone had rushed to the scene. I noticed my reaction and felt a flush of guilt: rather than feeling concerned, I felt disappointed to have missed it.

Half an hour later the regulars returned and we were each sent out in a car, racing on blues and twos from one call to the next.

Blues and twos is police slang for emergency response driving: blues for the lights, twos for the siren with its two-tone nee-nah wail. There is nothing in a city more attention-seeking than an emergency response vehicle. Our cars had luminous Battenberg paintwork, multiple lights with multiple settings, and a whole suite of noises, including a chirp, a wail, a yelp and a bull horn. Response cars are designed to be unignorable on streets where shopfronts, hawkers, buskers and billboards compete for attention with headphones and handheld devices. The siren's shriek and the spinning lights override everything for the seconds required to carve a way through.

Our first call was a domestic violence incident: a man had phoned to say his brother had assaulted him. We knocked on the door of a council flat on the ground floor of a high brick stack. The regulars had been there before. After a moment, the door opened an inch onto an unlit corridor. 'I'm naked but just come in anyway,' said a man's voice. 'No, Jamie. We'd prefer it if you put some clothes on first.' We waited a minute, then Jamie, IC1, late twenties, opened the door wearing shorts and a jumper. We gestured towards his fly. He looked down, grinned, and tucked his penis inside.

'What happened, Jamie?'

'It's my brother – you've got to do something about him.'

We walked in and Jamie shut the door behind us. We were in a hallway, but it felt more like a tunnel, lit only by the dull orange glow of the frosted glass above the front door. I felt a prickle of claustrophobia and we asked Jamie to turn on the light.

'Right, start at the beginning.'

'You've got to do something about my brother.'

'What do you mean, Jamie?'

'It's not on, the way he's treating me.'

'What's he been doing?'

'He's been really violent.'

'In what way? Tell us what happened today.'

'What do I need to tell you? He's been violent. You've got to do something.'

'Jamie, we need you to be more specific. What happened today?'

'You know. *Violent*. Kicking me, punching me, stuff like that.'

As we pressed Jamie for specifics he began to get agitated, the tendons tightening on his neck, his voice getting higher and faster, his fists clenching and unclenching. Jamie's brother sat quietly in a room across the hall, one leg crossed over the other, his hands folded in his lap.

'What am I supposed to tell you?' Jamie shouted. 'I nearly killed myself earlier!'

'But you're still here, aren't you, Jamie?'

'Don't take the piss! This is serious. I almost killed myself.'

'Jamie, we can't arrest your brother without a specific allegation. What happened?'

'I'm gonna kill myself! What don't you understand?'

'We can call an ambulance for you, Jamie, so that you can get the help you need.'

'Arrest *me*, then! You'll just have to arrest *me*!'

'We're not going to arrest you, Jamie. You haven't done anything wrong. Now, do you want to make an allegation against your brother?'

'A – Rest – Me!'

'Jamie, we're not going to arrest you. Why don't we call you an ambulance?'

'Oh, just fuck off then! Fuck off out my house!'

As is common with domestic incidents, we left Jamie's flat unclear what had taken place and uncertain how to proceed. Walking outside, I wondered again what we were for. We had been deployed, servants of the state, to visit Jamie in a moment of crisis. There was an opportunity there for something – but what? Support? Connection? To leave him in a better state than the state in which we found him? We had not even managed that.

As we returned to the car, I thought about the different emotional realities of teaching and policing. Teachers foster learning and growth. The possibility of change is something they witness daily. The police, by contrast, turn up when something has gone wrong, and they interact endlessly with people who seem locked in damaging cycles.

The regulars seemed irritated, as though they were unsure whether we had done too much or too little. 'Until next time,' one of them said.

Back in the car, we listened to the requests coming out. 'There's a woman outside her house using suicidal body language' . . . 'There's an aggressive family at Lambeth Town Hall. Staff are trapped in a room with only one entrance and exit' . . . 'A woman's called to say her brother has stolen her iPad.'

We raced from call to call on blue lights, moving through the congested city with unnatural ease, dense traffic parting, pausing, moulding itself around us. We accelerated towards lamp posts and traffic islands and swerved back into lane just in time, weaving through the streets in a high-paced slalom, free from limits and laws. Brixton, Clapham, Stockwell flashed past, our lights reflected in shopfronts and car windows. It was unexpectedly peaceful. The city beyond the windscreen appeared frozen, as though time had stopped for everyone but us.

'A couple have called to say that a neighbour is harassing them.' We accepted the call and drove to their address, an upstairs flat in a yellow-brick apartment block. We knocked on the door and an IC1 female, early thirties, opened it, whispering a greeting and explaining that their young son was asleep. She ushered us to the living room, past the boy's bedroom, and past the kitchen, where a blue bedsheet was tacked up over the window.

The couple explained that an IC1 male in a wheelchair was harassing them. Some months earlier, without apparent cause, he had begun heckling them and following them and would not desist. They had reported his behaviour multiple times and applied for a court order. Nevertheless, that evening, the man had sat below their kitchen window, shouting up at them for two hours while they put their son to bed and tried to ignore him.

They described the situation for the umpteenth time, anger, distress and exhaustion coming and going on their faces. We took a report, said that we understood how upsetting it must be and told them to call straight away if it started again.

In training we got a sense of what a slippery, subjective concept harassment can be. There is no neat yardstick. To prove it in court, you must demonstrate that a 'Reasonable Person' would think that the conduct in question amounts to harassment. The Reasonable Person is what is known as a 'legal fiction', a kind of psychological mannequin on which thoughts and behaviours can be displayed and examined. When debating messy individual situations, this helps to quantify the harm being done as precisely as possible.

There is a whole host of legal fictions, including the 'Reasonable Parent', the 'Reasonable Landlord', the 'Officious Bystander' and the 'Fair-minded and Informed Observer'. There is a 'Person of Reasonable Firmness', who allows the likely distress caused by an action to be evaluated, and a 'Person of Average Appetites', who helps determine what is obscene. The 'Reasonable Person' appears most frequently. Neither heroic nor endowed with special intelligence, they are a benchmark of ordinary, acceptable thought and behaviour.

There had been complaints about a noisy house party on a nearby estate. We drove over and knocked on the door of the flat. It was answered by an IC1 female, twenties, wearing zombie make-up. The regulars smiled at her and said nothing for an uncomfortably long time. The young woman stared back, then said, 'I'm sorry, I'm really sorry. We'll turn it down.'


A call came out. An IC3 male on a bike had snatched an IC1 female's handbag. We were near her flat and went round to take a statement and circulate a description of the robber. The young woman was badly shaken and could not give us much of a description. IC3 male, late teens, about six foot, in blue jeans and a grey hoodie. He had yanked her bag off her shoulder as she was walking home and ridden away before she could get a proper look at him. She stood in her kitchen crying, the heel of one hand pressed over her eyes, one foot crossed over another. She looked defeated. Along with her bag she had lost, at least for now, her sense of life being safe and predictable. We filled out a Victim Care Card and said someone would be in touch. 'See this number?' my partner said. 'Eight seven three five? That's your unique number: it means that you were the eight-thousand-seven-hundred-and-thirty-fifth person to call the police today. That's in the whole of London. Eight million people.'

Hearing that number, I had a moment of vertigo imagining the vast quantity of incidents the Met dealt with every week. I found it even stranger to think how similar many of them were to one another, the same few scenarios being played out over and over by different casts of characters. The patterns were so dependable, it was as though the incidents we attended were pre-programmed. Another robbery, another domestic, another drug deal.

Working alongside regulars, it was clear that what seems dramatic at first does not remain so. The repetition was numbing. We had to remind ourselves that each incident was unique and significant, even as our experience suggested otherwise. We had to identify patterns, but without mistaking those patterns for reality. It required a kind of deliberate mental longhand, a rejection of the mind's attempts to auto-fill details.

Nothing we dealt with was ever quite a one-off, yet no two things were ever quite identical. It reminded me of something the writer and philosopher Walter Benjamin wrote: 'The illusion of novelty is reflected, like one mirror in another, in the illusion of perpetual sameness.' Police officers are confronted endlessly with novelty that is not novel and sameness that is not the same.

The night passed quickly, one situation rolling into the next. The regulars were constantly writing things down – I could see why. After weeks of response shifts, dealing with dozens of similar situations in dozens of similar homes, you would struggle to pick them apart.

A particular challenge of policing is the need to remember an incident while experiencing it, to retain snippets of speech, the movements of a body, the shape of a scar, the precise order of a sequence of events. As an incident unfolds, we hoard important details in our short-term memory, anxious to offload them.

The writing in our pocket notebooks is often scrawled in a hurry. Even so, it is an official document, often referred to in court, and we are expected to follow strict rules to ensure we cannot go back and alter what we have written. Blank spaces must be ruled off so that nothing can be added. Mistakes remain legible behind a straight ruled line. Sevens are written with a bar to differentiate them from ones, zeros are crossed with a bar to differentiate them from Os. We even have a 'pocketbook signature': our name written as plainly and legibly as possible. Just as the mess of a crime scene must be preserved, so must the mess of our thinking, noting and noticing. 'If it's not written down, it didn't happen,' we were told in training.

We accepted a call to a children's home, a four-bed terraced house with white walls, coarse brown carpet and a television playing to an empty lounge. A fifteen-year-old boy had just assaulted the home's manager. While he was being given his weekly allowance, the boy had demanded the rest of the cash in the safe. The manager refused and the boy shoved him and pinned him against the wall.

The boy was gone. The moment we were called, he had run out of the back door and jumped over the garden wall. We went upstairs to the office and took a statement from the manager, an IC3 male in his forties. He shrugged and shook his head. 'We do what we can, officers,' he said. 'We do so much for that boy.' We checked he was all right and asked him to call when the boy came back; we would return and arrest him then. As we were leaving, another resident was arriving, an IC3 teen in jeans and a cap. We held open the front door and said good evening. 'Don't even talk to me!' he replied as he passed.

There was a lull and we circled the north of the borough. We were driving towards Vauxhall when we passed a series of long black skid marks scorched onto the asphalt. A few days earlier a helicopter had crashed into a crane on top of the St George Wharf Tower, a fifty-storey skyscraper being built beside the Thames. 'Anything can happen in Lambeth,' our driver said.

It was gone 2 a.m. A call came out: a woman's sixteen-year-old daughter was still not back from school. We drove to their house in Oval, disturbing a stand-off between a fox and a long-haired white cat as we parked outside. A woman, IC3, forties, buzzed us in and we found her in an upstairs living room, empty except for a black leather sofa and a white plastic table and lit only by the street lamp outside the window.

'She's probably at a friend's,' the woman said, 'but I don't know and she's not answering her phone.' We checked that her daughter was not hiding anywhere, searching the wardrobes and the bathroom until we were confident that there was nobody else in the flat, where only the woman and her daughter lived. We told the mother to call us straight away if she heard anything, then went back to the station to put a MERLIN on the system.

Sitting at a bank of computers, we completed our paperwork. There were dozens of boxes to fill in, the computers were slow, and it was gone 4 a.m. by the time we finished.

My radio started chirping. It was the rosy-cheeked Sergeant: my wife had made an emergency call to report the fact that I was not yet home. She was worried something had happened. I said I was fine and would send her a message. Ten minutes later, another Sergeant called with the same information. Again, I said that I was fine.

I went to the Special Constabulary office to sign off and return my radio. When I arrived, the rosy-cheeked Sergeant was waiting with a printout of my wife's emergency call, which he presented to me like a certificate, the other Specials laughing. 'You're lucky you've got someone who cares,' he said.

When I woke, I could still feel the motion of the police car, the thrill of the speed. It felt as if the bed was moving beneath me. I liked the fast driving more than I had expected and felt a rush of excitement each time we put on the lights and siren. On blue lights, we got to drive the way joy riders drive. Out on shifts, I found myself craving emergencies.

For as long as I can remember, I have had dreams about running but not moving. I run to something I am late for, but I cannot reach it. In these dreams, there is always, somehow, more time before the exam or encounter I am running towards. More time, that is, for me not to be able to get there, for despair to mount, and frustration to shade into panic.

Racing around London on blue lights provided an unexpected antidote. Dream-like itself, it offered an experience of unobstructed speed and fluidity, of a world that, far from trying to thwart you, is responsive to your every move, opens wherever you turn and parts to let you pass.

I went into Brixton to have breakfast and type up my notes, grabbing a book about the police as I left the flat. On the way to the Phoenix, I thought about the night before: the visit to Jamie, the family being harassed, the noisy party, the lost daughter, the children's home. Most of the calls had less to do with crime than with mental health and other people's relationships. What did we have to do with all that? Were we the most appropriate people to deal with the issues we faced, or were we just the closest to hand?

I had begun reading about policing and crime to try and make sense of my new role, amassing an intimidating stack of books with names like *Law and Order*, *The Great British Bobby*, *In the Office of Constable*, *Introduction to Policing*, *Aspects of Police Work*, *The Politics of the Police*, *Observations on the Making of Policemen*, *The Functions of the Police in Modern Society*. I ordered them from second-hand bookshops and every few days another arrived, with a similar title, and a similar blue cover to all the others.

I had cleared a shelf and begun dipping in. At first it all felt new, but the more I read the more I noticed the same ideas and examples cropping up and I started to feel as if I was reading the same book over and over.

There was one voice, however, that immediately stood out.

Egon Bittner was a sociologist who, in the 1960s, studied the police in Denver's skid row neighbourhoods, accompanying them on shifts and watching their work. Bittner observed what officers spent their time doing and compared it with the crime fighting they were 'supposed' to be doing. Constables were pulled into all sorts of situations: law enforcement, social regulation, dispute mediation, community support, care giving, providing help and advice . . . The institution's tough talk might suggest otherwise, but police did much more than just chase criminals, even if the public, and even many police officers, saw that as their primary function. Bittner concluded that 'no human problem exists, or is imaginable, about which it could be said with finality that this certainly could not become the proper business of the police'. Police are available at all times and in all places. A suitable police task is simply 'something-that-ought-not-to-be-happening-and-about-which-someone-had-better-do-something-now!'

The phrase made me laugh when I first read it. But then I realized it was spot on. The urgency of the 'now!', the vagueness of 'someone' doing 'something', capture the paradoxes of policing perfectly. There are problems that cannot be ignored – and the police deal with them because they are the around-the-clock stop-gap service. They turn up and do what they can, regardless of what is actually needed.

Drawing on his observations of policing, Bittner published a series of books and articles that outlined his ideas of what the police are for, what makes them distinctive and why their role can feel so blurry and problematic. Underpinning his investigations was a desire to determine 'what police work could be at its very best'. Browsing my new books, I found Egon Bittner's writing the most faithful mirror for my experiences, and a brilliant description of why policing is such a strange job – why it feels as if it is multiple jobs rolled into one.

What grabbed me first was his voice – it was wise, lyrical, impassioned, not at all what I expected. It was as though a poet or prophet had stumbled into a criminology department. No description of the police I had read compared with sentences like these:

> [The police officer] is ambivalently feared and admired, and no amount of public relations work can entirely abolish the sense that there is something of the dragon in the dragon-slayer. Because they are posted on the perimeters of order and justice in the hope that their

presence will deter the forces of darkness and chaos, because they are meant to spare the rest of the people direct confrontations with the dreadful, perverse, lurid, and dangerous, police officers are perceived to have powers and secrets no one else shares. Their interest in and competence to deal with the untoward surrounds their activities with mystery and distrust.

Bittner wrote about policing in mythic terms, highlighting the role's inherent ethical murkiness. He looked directly at the crudeness and imperfections of police work, examining the way that they arise from the role itself, as much as from the people who perform it. And he confronted the irony that representatives of a tainted institution go out every day and tell other people they are doing something wrong. Few people, Bittner wrote, 'are constantly mindful of the saying, "He that is without sin among you, let him cast the first stone . . .", but only the police are explicitly required to forget it'.

Bittner became an important thought partner. Policing was not what I had expected and it was not what it seemed. Much of it appeared to be care work and youth work conducted bluntly, reluctantly, even punitively. A lot of the officers I met wanted to catch bad guys, not support vulnerable people. It was not that they thought that was unimportant – they simply did not think it was their job.

The more Bittner I read, the more intrigued I became. I wanted to know more about him, and how he had seen so deeply and differently into the world of policing. There was surprisingly little online, only references to his publications, a death note on a university website, and a ten-line Wikipedia entry that said he had been born in Czechoslovakia in 1921, emigrated to the States after the Second World War, and died in 2011. I found a single photograph: a headshot of an old white man in a houndstooth blazer, checked shirt and striped tie. He has a wry expression, soft dark eyes and a dense silver moustache. He retired before the arrival of the internet. Apart from his work, he seemed to have left little trace.

I ate my bubble and squeak one-handed while reading *The Functions of the Police in Modern Society*. I noticed another customer looking at me and felt self-conscious. Just as I did not flash my warrant card off duty, I felt I was exposing too much by reading Bittner in the centre of Brixton. I pressed the book's cover to the Formica table.

We were being briefed before a shift patrolling Brixton. Our Sergeant for the night was urging us to be proactive: to stop people, talk to them, and get grounds for a search where possible. 'I've done more shit stops than you've had hot dinners,' he said. 'If you look at someone twice, that's enough to stop them to at least have a chat. What you'll find is that you get a feeling, then you talk yourself out of it – but that's your sixth sense and, more often than not, you'll find something.'

There are different kinds of stops, according to the level of suspicion: 'stop and talk', 'stop and account', 'stop and search' and 'stop and arrest'. 'Stop and search is the most powerful tool in our armoury,' the Sergeant told us. 'Your job is to go digging. Do people hide things in the groin area? Of course they do. If you're not making them uncomfortable, you're not doing it right.'

We looked at the Top Five Robbers: all young IC3 males.

'Isn't there a risk of stereotyping people?' someone asked.

'It's not stereotyping, it's based on intelligence,' a regular replied. 'They know why you're there. They are the problem or they know the problem. My own experience as a young Black man? I've been searched many times, many times. I still get searched. I used to get out my warrant card at the start, but now I just let them find it.'

It was another cold evening. Most people were rushing between places, rather than loitering on the street, and there were not many obvious targets to stop for a chat. At the end of Coldharbour Lane, outside the Dogstar, we saw a group of IC1 males smoking. One of them tucked something out of sight as we approached. 'What have you just hidden in your pocket?' we asked. The man was in his late twenties, with blond stubble and an electric-blue spike through one eyebrow. He pulled a joint from the front right pocket of his tight white jeans. A puff of smoke came out with it. 'Anything else we should know about?' He pulled a transparent tube containing an unsmoked joint from the front left pocket. 'This is a bit awkward – I'm a civil servant,' he said as we wrote out a Cannabis Warning.

I was patrolling with a regular. We walked down to Railton Road and wove around its backstreets.

'Where are we?' the regular said suddenly. 'What's the street name?'

'Leeson Road,' I replied.

'How did you know that? Did you read the street sign?'

'No. I used to live here actually. There's my old house.' There was a light on behind the mesh curtains on the kitchen window.

'Doesn't count, then,' she said. 'I was trying to catch you out. One of the things you learn as a copper is you've got to know where you are. All the time. Every street you walk down, you've got to clock the sign and remember it.'

'In case you see a crime and need to report it?'

'In case you get into bother. Imagine something happens to you. Imagine you're in trouble and you've got a couple of seconds to call for help, what are you going to say? *Urgent assistance, I'm somewhere in Brixton?*'

We continued along Railton Road, towards the school where I had taught. I felt awkward being so near it on foot. My pupils lived on these streets. We passed Chaucer Road, Spenser Road. I spotted a woman, IC3, late thirties, walking towards us: the mother of one of the boys I had taught. I braced myself for the moment of recognition. But then she walked straight past, barely glancing at us.

I felt mixed emotions. I did not really want to be spotted in my uniform, but nor did I like this sense of distance from a place I knew well. As a police officer, I had greater access to people, but less of a connection to them. The way we approached people, it often felt as if we were an external agency supervising the community, rather than an active part of it.

We passed my old school, walking straight past its play-ground. As we did, my mind flooded with memories of playtimes and PE lessons, children running and dancing, falling out and making up. Thinking about standing there on lunch duty, mediating disputes while identically dressed children raced past, it occurred to me that I had rarely sat down as a teacher. Policing seems like the more physical job, but over the course of a day, I must have walked similar distances to a beat officer, just in tighter circuits: loops of the playground, figures of eight around the low red tables in my classroom.

I felt a pang of nostalgia for the children I had taught and the hours we spent in that room. Then I suddenly remembered Mr Foodface: a giant cardboard head, collaged with photos of different foods, which hung from the back wall, manically grinning. Mr Foodface loomed above my lessons in my second year as a teacher, a kind of unsettling Big Brother figure. Visitors tended to react with alarm, but the children, who had made him, loved him.

Every afternoon I said goodbye to my class and they chanted goodbye in unison. One day, as well as saying goodbye to me and the teaching assistants, they began adding: 'Good afternooon Mr Fooood-faaace.' And from then on, they wished Mr Foodface a good afternoon every single day, until we held a raffle at the end of the year to decide who would take the giant head home.

It had been a while since I had thought of Mr Foodface or the day-to-day life of my classroom. Out policing, I missed the sense that I was building something with a specific group of people – habits, routines, a shared culture. I thought about some of the teachers I knew and what good police officers they would make. They brought the best out of people. I was not sure why, as police officers, we did not see our role in the same way.

We left the school behind, emerging onto Dulwich Road and passing a tall green pole that looked like a lamp post without a lamp. 'It's a stink pipe,' I said to my partner. 'There's a sewer down there.' I had learned about stink pipes in my final term as a teacher, when I took my class on a local history walk. Stink pipes let noxious fumes escape and reduce the risk of explosions. The sewer below us was the River Effra.

Turning onto Shakespeare Road, we spotted an IC3 teen approaching. When he saw us, he stiffened and seemed to conceal something in his palm. We stopped him and searched him for drugs. 'Where are you going tonight?' we asked. 'It's my eighteenth birthday,' he said, 'I'm going to meet some friends.' We found nothing so we thanked him and said goodnight.

We walked along Railton Road towards central Brixton. A white Ford Astra with flames stencilled along both sides streaked towards us, did a sharp turn, and pulled up in Marcus Garvey Way. We walked over and knocked on the driver's window. He rolled it down, an IC3 male, late teens, and looked up at us with a blank expression.

'You need to pay attention to your speed round here,' said my partner.

'How fast was I going?'

'That's not what I'm saying,' she replied. 'I'm saying you were going very quickly and there are a lot of drunk people wandering around this area who could walk into the road.'

'How fast was I going, then?'

'You know that we haven't recorded your speed, we're just having a word.'

'So why are you stopping me if you don't know how fast I was going?'

'All right then, if you want to do this properly: you're not wearing your seatbelt so that's a ticket right there. Turn off the engine and get out of the car.'

'Nah, listen to me. Listen. I just get annoyed because police see my car and they assume I'm a boy racer. That's why I'm asking how fast am I going, because police always stop me because of this car.'

'Did you do all of this yourself? The stencils?'

'Yeah – all of it!'

He got out of the car and started to show us around, pointing out the sound system, the under-car lighting, a skull stencilled on the roof, and the flashing LEDs on the gearstick. My partner was into cars and followed the young man, asking questions.

'Really nice work,' she said as the tour ended. 'Now you look after yourself.' She waved and we walked away.

'Take care, yeah,' he shouted after us.

I was bemused. At the start of the interaction, I had felt certain it would result in a fine, or at least a search. The young man's sudden warmth had saved him. The turnaround reminded me of something Egon Bittner wrote, about how a person's attitude often determines the outcome of an encounter with the police. If we feel respected and can walk away without losing face, we are more likely to be lenient. If someone causes us grief, we are more likely to do something. The officers Bittner observed tended to detain people they perceived as 'inappropriate in their manner, vaguely dangerous, dissolute, disruptive, or in various other ways a bane'. And in this way, he wrote, laws become 'all-purpose control devices' and arrests are 'not preliminary to punishment' but 'punishment in themselves'.

We walked to Brixton High Street and bumped into the illegal hot-dog vendor outside the tube. He had probably already been dismissed from Clapham High Street. We told him to go home and watched as he scraped the sausages and onions into a cardboard box, placed it on a shelf under the hotplate and wheeled his trolley past Iceland and down Electric Avenue.

We looped round to Atlantic Road and walked past the shutters of the butchers and fishmongers. There were pools of blood and disinfectant in the gutter, red mixing with blue, the smell of both mixing in the air. An IC1 male walked past us, FUCKING CRIMINAL stamped onto his belt in steel letters.

We heard angry shouts from Electric Lane and ran around the corner to find two large groups of IC3 teens facing off.

'We're friends, we're friends!' they said when they saw us, and started laughing. 'Calm it down, guys,' we said. 'Go home.'

We walked away, but as soon as we turned the corner the shouting resumed and we ran back again. 'We've told you once,' my partner said. 'Go home or get nicked.' The boys dispersed and we kept walking.

On the street behind the police station, we spotted a van with a broken rear light and knocked on the window. A six-foot IC3 male, early thirties, stepped out. He grinned and spread his arms wide, as though about to embrace us. 'If you work round here, you've got to smile, you know. Look at your face! It's like you've already decided I've done something wrong!'

In the Phoenix the next morning, I thought about the Sergeant encouraging us to stop people, to go digging. I could see the logic – the more we look, the more we find – but it made me uncomfortable. We were only looking in certain places. We were 'distributing surveillance and intervention selectively', as Bittner put it, and in the process making certain groups of people feel like a target for our attention – which they were.

A search is a throwaway moment for a police officer, especially if it yields no result, yet it can have an indelible impact on the person searched. Rebekah Delsol, a specialist in the effects of stop and search, interviewed Black men about their experiences being searched by the police and found that men in their late fifties and early sixties could remember everything about their first search: 'They could describe in detail the first time they'd been stopped by an officer [. . .], exactly what the officer said to them, what the officer had done to them, how it felt to be a teenager stopped by the police.' For the officer, the moment is so run-of-the-mill it can slip from our mind immediately, for the person we stop, the moment can become frozen in time, never to be forgotten.

Abuse of stop and search sparked the 1981 Brixton uprising and the practice still generated tension and mistrust. In uniform in Brixton, as a white officer often stopping young Black men, I was conscious of being part of a painful and unresolved history.

Neither my initial police training nor my induction to Lambeth focused on the decades of police racism that followed the arrival of the *Windrush*. We did not hear the name Cherry Groce or learn about the Brixton riots of 1981, 1985 or 1995. My awareness of the Met's litany of failures emerged haphazardly, gleaned from conversations, blogs and books.

Brixton was cold and calm outside the window. A butcher walked past, pushing a frozen pig in a shopping trolley. Just down the road I could see a refrigerated truck, its doors open, revealing many more pigs hanging from meat rails. Looking out at central Brixton, at the trickle of pedestrians passing the window, I found it strange to think that battles had been fought on these streets, and that they were still vivid in the minds of many in the community – maybe even some of the customers around me, reading the papers and drinking their morning coffee.

When I lived on Leeson Road, I soon learned about the 1981 riots – or 'uprising', as locals called them – which erupted on the streets around my house. The headteacher at the school where I taught told us how it had got caught up in the action. 'This school was surrounded and cordoned off,' she said. 'People couldn't get in, people couldn't get out.' Many of the parents and grandparents who came into the playground each day, she reminded us, had lived through that moment and were, in different ways, still living with it. 'Our parents remember the riots,' she continued, 'they're still a subtext for how they see police, how they see officialdom, how they see our role. You've got to be aware of that when you see resistance and fear and lack of trust.'

Several years passed before I heard the whole story and

learned that the uprising had its origins in a fire on New Cross Road. I was listening to a radio show featuring the poet Jay Bernard, who had decided to write a book about the fire after realizing they had 'grown up as a black British Londoner with a piecemeal understanding of the event and the consequences'. *Surge* reconstructs the horror, rage and repercussions of that moment, weaving together voices and artefacts from the archives, and demanding that we never forget.

It was Saturday, 17 January 1981. Yvonne Ruddock and Angela Jackson were celebrating a joint birthday party at 439 New Cross Road. Yvonne was turning sixteen, Angela eighteen. There were sixty guests and the party lasted all night. Early on Sunday morning a fire broke out and spread rapidly. The stairs collapsed. The house was full of smoke. Many of the guests were trapped. Some jumped out of second-floor windows to escape.

Thirteen young Black people, aged between fourteen and twenty-two, died in the blaze, including Yvonne Ruddock and her older brother Paul. Many more were injured. One of the survivors took his own life two years later. Initial signs suggested that the party had been firebombed – a racist attack – but the cause was never officially established.

There was a muted response from Margaret Thatcher's government. This prompted the Black Parents Movement, the Race Today Collective and others to form the New Cross Massacre Action Committee and organize a Black People's Day of Action. Writer and activist Darcus Howe travelled around England spreading the word, attracting attendees from across the country. On 2 March 1981, twenty thousand people marched through central London chanting, 'Thirteen dead, nothing said'.

A month after the Day of Action, with South London still reeling from the fire, police in Brixton launched an operation called Swamp 81, viewed by many as a response to the Black community's show of strength. Constables stopped and searched hundreds of locals – mainly Black men – using the so-called 'Sus Laws', historical powers that enabled police to stop, search or arrest anyone they considered suspicious.

Even before Swamp 81, resentment against the Sus Laws was high. They were routinely used as a justification for stopping and arresting Black men. In his memoir, *A Search for Belonging*, Michael Fuller describes the hysterical reaction from his colleagues when, as a young Black officer in the 1970s, he used the Sus Laws to arrest a white man trying to break into a car.

'Mate, what colour is he?'
I said: 'White. Why?'
    They stared at me and all burst out laughing. At
every desk a man in wide lapels and a broad, striped
tie was clutching his sides or falling off his chair. I
watched them with total incomprehension.
    Finally, one of them explained to me that the sus
laws were a device for white officers to arrest black
people who had pissed them off. Word got around the
station that I had arrested a white man for sus and
that seemed to tickle pretty much everyone.

The name 'Swamp 81' may have been chosen to reflect the way officers saw Brixton, or to echo Margaret Thatcher's comment that 'people are really rather afraid that this country might be rather swamped by people with a different culture'. A perfect name for a punk band or rap crew, it was a provocative choice for a police operation.

One hundred and fifty plain clothes officers conducted over a thousand searches in Brixton in six days. 'I was stopped and searched every single day of that week,' wrote Darcus Howe, who was living and working in the area. 'If you were black and male, you were under the power of the police. Young white boys in plain clothes, they literally swamped the area and stopped anything black that moved.'

Swamp 81 enraged the community, as officers must have known it would. Then, in a moment of confusion, while officers were giving first aid to a Black man who had been stabbed, it exploded into two days of violent clashes, with Railton Road at its centre.

Police were ill prepared for a full-scale onslaught with bottles, bricks and petrol bombs. Michael Fuller was one of the officers policing the uprising, the only Black officer in the ranks. 'We were the police,' he writes, 'but they were staring us out as if we were an occupying army. "Babylon! Get out of Brixton!"' There were about three hundred and fifty casualties. Over a hundred vehicles and more than thirty buildings were set alight.

The Race Today Collective published their monthly journal out of offices on Railton Road, edited by Darcus Howe with deputy editor Leila Hassan, poet Linton Kwesi Johnson, writer Farrukh Dhondy and others. They had window seats at the uprising. The collective interviewed participants and documented the violence unfolding on their doorstep.

Darcus Howe had come to national attention a decade earlier as one of the Mangrove Nine, a group put on trial for incitement to riot after leading a protest against repeated police raids on the Mangrove restaurant, a vibrant community hub in Notting Hill. The group were cleared of the charges and at the end of the fifty-five-day trial the judge stated that there was 'evidence of racial hatred on both sides' – the first ever official acknowledgement of racism within the police.

The events of April 1981, and their significance, remain contested – a dynamic visible in the tug of war over how to refer to them. The word 'riot' suggests hooliganism. It lays the blame for violence and damage at the feet of the rioters. But when a community erupts in rage after protracted humiliation and abuse by those paid to protect them, the label feels problematic. '"Riots" is not really the right word,' wrote Darcus Howe, looking back twenty years later, 'this was an insurrection against the British police [. . .] Anger that had been stored up in the black community over the years suddenly exploded.'

I had only a vague sense of all this while I was stopping and searching people in Brixton. It was a resounding absence in my police training – yet, as a police force, it was our recent history, it was the backdrop for the way the community interacted with us. I found it bizarre that we could be sent onto the streets without knowing it.

There is now a plaque on 439 New Cross Road, installed in 2011 by the Nubian Jak Community Trust: 'New Cross Fire took place at this site on January 18, 1981, claiming the lives of 14 young people'. The pristine brown-brick terrace is opposite another of London's 'Ghost Signs'. 'BRITISH MATCHES FOR BRITISH HOMES, BRYMAY SAFETY MATCHES', it reads, compressing the fear of both foreignness and fire into just eight words.

There is nothing in Brixton marking the site of the uprising, no plaque on the estate where I lived describing when and why it was built. Online, I found a black and white photo of the charred shell of the Windsor Castle pub, the site of my house on Leeson Road.

I tried to superimpose the street as I knew it onto the scene of devastation, but try as I might, the images would not join up. I could not see them as the same place.

We were patrolling Clapham in the van. It was perishingly cold, snowing heavily, and there were few people or cars on the streets. There was a gusty wind and the snowflakes were small and sharp on the face. It was going to be a slow night. There were domestic violence calls coming out, but it was too cold for street crime.

On Clapham Park Road, we spotted a white car driving without headlights, difficult to see amid the snowfall. We pulled it over and two IC1 males got out, brothers in their mid-twenties, on their way to collect their sister from Heathrow. 'Oh god, I'm so sorry. I didn't even realize,' one said. We began to fill out a £30 Fixed Penalty Notice for driving without headlights. 'Come on, it's quiet on the roads, it was a mistake.' We worked our way through the long form, writing a whole statement at the roadside, while the white car buried itself. The brothers were not wearing coats and they shivered, stamped and sighed, the snow turning to slush at their feet.

We looped around the residential streets behind the High Street, finding them deserted. It had only been snowing since the afternoon, but a couple of centimetres had already settled. As we drove through the fresh snow, I wished I could watch our circuits from above and see the patterns we were etching onto the city: tight circles, giving way to loose spirals, then seemingly random meanders.

Lambeth looked pristine. The whiteness made the streets look simpler and less overloaded. Details disappeared, outlines softened. The only signs of life were the footprints on the pavements and the temporary graffiti on some of the cars: TWAT, CUNT, giant cartoon cocks.

'What are your favourite swear words?' our driver asked.

'You know what? I really don't like all the swearing in the police,' a female Special replied. 'I can't stand it when people use the word cunt.'

'But swearing's an important part of the job. Actually, my current favourite is shit-cunt.'

We stopped a black car on the street behind Infernos. An IC3 male in his mid-twenties jumped out, short, with a puffy gilet and a patchy beard. He smiled as we approached. 'Wow, you guys are tall! I want some of what you've been eating!' We told him that he was driving without lights. 'Man! I'm an idiot. I had no idea. I'm such an idiot!' We ran name and car checks and learned he had previous convictions for GBH and Offweps. 'I'm a family man,' he said. 'Totally reformed!' We pointed out the dangers of driving without lights. 'You're right. You're so right. It's totally up to you, officers. If you want to give me a ticket, I'll understand.' We warned him and said goodnight. He got back in his car, flicked on the lights and drove away.


I had the realization when I began policing that, although we have less status and influence than those further along in the legal process, we determine who enters in the first place. By arresting one person and not another, giving a verbal warning for one offence and a ticket for another, we decide what becomes a criminal matter and what does not. Faced with two identical situations, we can turn one into a matter of permanent record and make the other disappear. We set, in Egon Bittner's words, the 'outer perimeter of law enforcement'.

Sometimes, instead of arresting someone, we broker an informal solution. Sometimes we cannot bring ourselves to give a person a ticket because they are young or old or charming or vulnerable. Sometimes we let a person off because it is late and cold. On other occasions, when we are feeling fastidious or we do not like the attitude of the person in front of us, we stick to the letter of the law, regardless of how minor the offence. We 'have, in effect,' wrote Bittner, 'a greater degree of discretionary freedom in proceeding against offenders than any other public official'.

Before becoming a Special, I had not realized how idiosyncratic police work is. The neat regularity of the uniforms, the thoroughness of the law books, belie the fact that we will never act as consistently as a state might like. Who we are affects how lenient we are and who we are lenient towards. Police uniform is less an expression of homogeneity than a cloak for its opposite.

Bittner's point did not seem to be that the discretion and flexibility of police officers is avoidable, or even undesirable, when applied wisely and decently, but that it is not sufficiently acknowledged. As such, constables exercise 'a power that is certainly not officially assigned to them'.


We circled South Lambeth in the van. 'Percy Pigs?' someone said, passing the bag. Apart from DV calls, nothing was coming out of the radio.

'All this waiting around annoys me,' one officer said.

'All right,' said our driver, 'you've got to summarize your sex life with a film title. And don't say *Free Willy*.'

On slow nights, time feels alternately stretched and squashed. The spaces between incidents expand, while the incidents themselves compress and are over too quickly. Time passes on half-speed or fast-forward.

The snow began to fall more heavily and the wind intensified, sweeping the snowflakes in all directions, fuzzing the windscreen and confusing vision. Millions of tiny white dots swarmed through the air, like pixels pulling away from an image, as though the night were coming apart.

I was in the back row of the van and, while the others were talking, I fell asleep, then woke up and tried to stay awake, my cap on my knees, my forehead resting on the cold glass. It is hard not to fall asleep when it is late and you are inside a moving vehicle, all warm in the back row where nobody can see you, with nothing to distract you but identically lit streets of identical brown houses.

Just after 2 a.m., the wind and snow stopped and we drove along Clapham High Street. It should have been the busiest time of the night, but nobody was out and everywhere was shut. For once, there were no drunks cradling chips, no smokers outside Infernos, no illegal hot-dog vendor, just pristine pavements and a line of dark windows. We reached Clapham North and looped around behind the station, past the mural to Billy Cox, a teenager who had been stabbed a few years earlier.

We drove along the High Street again, slowly, and looked more closely at the shut shops and bars. The windows were dark, but we could just make out seated silhouettes in Roosters Spot, the outlines of bodies in KFC, and we could see figures standing inside Vodka Revs, packed tightly together like an opera chorus waiting behind the curtain. The High Street was not shut – there must have been a power cut. The only light came from a pair of candles on the counter of the Kebab Company.

The next morning, New Park Road was dusted with snow. I decided to walk down the hill to the Phoenix instead of taking the bus, then regretted it as my gripless Converse skidded across the pavement.

I thought about the previous night's shift, drifting around Lambeth in a blizzard. I thought about the swearing in the van. It had been funny. Everyone had laughed. But the female Special had stated a boundary and our driver had immediately crossed it. There was an aggression to his response that I had overlooked the night before.

I liked him. He was considerate towards new Specials, he was caring and thorough in his interactions with the public, he was friendly and easy-going, even when tired or bored. When he said, 'but swearing's part of the job', and shared his new favourite swear word, his tone was affable, almost apologetic, as though he empathized with the Special's perspective but it was simply not tenable.

Moments like these gnawed at me throughout my time as a Special – it seemed that to join the Met was to consent to a certain kind of sexualized, macho culture. It was in the air and there was no escaping it: the 'talent spotting', the chat about one another's sex lives, the sexual jokes and banter. Watching a new Special trying to object, I saw that this culture was particularly keenly enforced for female officers, whose participation was clearly both necessary and exciting for some male officers. And, just as some female officers made a show of their ability to handle physical confrontations, some of them also made a show of being as willing and able to be laddish as the lads. The alternative, which I had just witnessed, was to shut down. Either way, female officers were expected to fit themselves to a culture in which casual misogyny was the currency of workplace connection.

Filtering, holding, dealing with all of that, on top of an emotionally and physically draining role – it sounded exhausting, just as being a Black or Asian officer at any time in the last sixty years sounded exhausting: going to work every day and deciding whether to prioritize pragmatism, protest, or self-protection.

The feminist scholar Sara Ahmed talks about 'the work some of us have to do *just to be* in institutions': to enter them, to stay in them, and to stay well within them. Make a reasonable request, state a plain fact, and 'you'll be heard as complaining'. Object to the existing culture and you risk 'heightening your visibility and vulnerability' and 'being pathologised by your peers'.

I could not believe that this culture – hidden from no one inside the Met – had not been stamped out. Relative to how precisely officers watched their words when it came to race, there was something wild and unstable about the use of sexual and sexist language. It was so blatant, as though officers felt irreproachable. *Shit-cunt. She'd get fucked.* Even used playfully, there was a violence to this language – and violence has no more place in policing than it does in teaching. Yet, for the police, permitted to use force, it is always tantalizingly close. It is not a big step from force to violence, and I sensed, in this language, a conscious flirtation with the darker possibilities of the role.

Challenging racist language and attitudes within the Met was not sufficient to stamp out institutional racism, but it did make a difference. It sent a message. It curtailed the flow of toxins. In their attempts to quash racism, the Met's leadership seemed aware of the way organizational culture can normalize behaviour that should not become normal. Somehow this logic did not carry over to misogyny. There was clearly no belief that behind-the-scenes banter existed on a spectrum with real-world violence and abuse.

The Special who objected to the swearing had said nothing in reply to the driver. Nor did I. Nobody backed her up and the conversation moved on.

The road outside the Phoenix had been dug up. The Victorian water works were being replaced, teams of workmen criss-crossing Lambeth, pulling out rusted pipes and dropping in blue plastic tubes.

I sat near the window, keen to see what lay beneath the streets I walked down every day. Looking into the hole, a cross-section of asphalt, mud, metal and rock, I found myself wishing the city's history was preserved in such neat strata so that I could stand in a place, drill backwards from the present, and see everything that had come before. I thought of the lost River Effra and wondered how deep I would have to dig before I reached it.

Since moving to London, I had become slightly obsessed by its hidden histories, particularly the stories of little-known or overlooked lives. I had even started a magazine with a friend, mapping different aspects of the city. While I was teaching, I had learned that the mother of a child in another class was researching a local woman who had died in 1979, aged twenty-seven. The mother was the Uruguayan artist Ana Laura Lopez de la Torre and the project was called 'Do You Remember Olive Morris?'

In 2006, living in Brixton, De la Torre had come across a

photo from the 1970s of a young, barefoot Black woman with a wry expression, holding a sign reading: 'BLACK SUFFERER FIGHT POLICE PIG BRUTALITY'. Captivated by the woman's fearless appearance, she had decided to find out who she was.

The basic details came quickly. The woman was Olive Morris, an influential squatter, activist and community organizer. Morris was a member of the British Black Panther Movement, the founder of the Brixton Black Women's Group and a founding member of the Organisation of Women of African and Asian Descent. She had died tragically young from Hodgkin lymphoma at St Thomas's Hospital in Waterloo. There was a council building named after her on Brixton Hill. 'A council building named after a female Black Panther,' wrote De la Torre. 'It seemed to defy belief [. . .] A council building named after a female Black Panther and squatter. A building dedicated to Housing Services'.

As De la Torre sketched the outline of Olive Morris's existence, she sensed that she had stumbled on a life that was historically important. But then the information dried up. Olive Morris had made a big impact in a short time, but there was almost no record of it.

The breakthrough came when De la Torre was introduced to Liz Obi, an old friend of Olive Morris, who had squatted with her on Railton Road. Obi was passionate about preserving her friend's legacy. In 2000, she had curated 'Remembering Olive, Remembering the Times', at Brixton Library, displaying all the artefacts that she and Morris's boyfriend had held onto. De la Torre and Obi met for coffee in Brixton Market. 'That morning I learnt more about Olive Morris than in a whole year of searching in archives and the web,' wrote De la Torre. Obi was initially sceptical: 'My reaction was, why was this white woman interested in our history? What did she plan to get out of it?' But the pair clicked and bonded over a shared belief that 'a project exploring the life of Olive Morris' might provide 'a platform for young women to explore their own political identities'.

Together they established the Remembering Olive Collective, a group of women who met monthly and undertook the painstaking work of tracking down the information locked in the minds, drawers and photo albums of those who had known Olive Morris. They would create a 'collective portrait' before it was too late.

While I was teaching, I followed the collective's efforts on their blog. I had a long shelf of books about London; it was invigorating to encounter a story that did not appear in any of them – a life that opened onto other stories of abuse and resistance that needed to be captured and shared. I was impressed by the intensity of the collective's efforts: putting out calls to the public, gathering information, building a case for Olive's significance. Later, as a Special, I noticed how much the campaign had in common with a police investigation: tracking down evidence before it decays or disappears.

My bubble and squeak arrived and I ordered a second mug of coffee. The Phoenix was quiet for a Saturday. There was a man reading the papers, a woman doing a word search, a couple complaining that their landlord had still not fixed their broken shower. I looked out at the hole in the road and the blue plastic tubes.

Next to them, the old iron piping looked like something rotten that had been eaten away by maggots. It was difficult to distinguish from the surrounding mud.

On our next shift, we were sent out in plain clothes to patrol a robbery hotspot. At the evening's briefing, the Sergeant showed us a map of recent attacks, each marked with a red star. 'That's our hotspot,' he said, drawing a triangle around them. Most of the robbery victims were IC1 females walking alone. He passed round a printout of the likely suspects, a dozen IC3 gang members aged between twelve and eighteen.

We set out from Brixton Police Station, passing one of the hot-dog vendor's confiscated trolleys in the yard, and walked towards the recreation centre. I scanned the streets and spotted a blue plaque on the front of a red-brick mansion block. 'HENRY HAVELOCK ELLIS: Pioneer in the scientific study of sex lived here', it said. My partner saw me looking. 'Sounds like a randy bugger,' he said. 'I can think of a few officers who'd sign up for his experiments, mind.'

In uniform, we signal our presence, and people's behaviour changes accordingly. Patrolling in plain clothes was an exhilarating contrast. On our way to the hotspot, winding through backstreets, we passed three IC3 teenagers sitting in deck chairs in a small front garden, relaxing in a cloud of cannabis. We took out our warrant cards and they jumped to their feet. 'Where did you lot come from?' one of them shouted. We put gloves on and searched the boys and the garden. 'This is my second search today, you know!' another boy said. The cannabis was hidden in a plant pot. We seized it but chose not to take further action.

Taking their stash, I felt more like a teacher confiscating sweets than a police officer tackling crime. We had to take the drugs, yet it felt somewhat petty and pointless to do so. 'Look, lads, if you're going to smoke weed, do it indoors,' said the Sergeant. 'If you do it outside, this is what happens.'

The hotspot was a subdued, dimly lit cluster of streets with high hedges, dark corners and little foot or vehicle traffic – a perfect place for robberies. We patrolled the area in pairs, walking slowly and keeping our distance from one another, restarting our circuit every ten minutes or so.

A few cars drove past, a couple walked home hand in hand. We walked past another stink pipe releasing gases from the River Effra. We followed the route in our pairs, making small talk, persuading ourselves that it was still early and we just needed to wait a while longer before a robber appeared. My guts churned, imagining the encounter. After an hour, though, when we had seen nothing suspicious, we were so eager for something to happen that all caution and tension evaporated – we desperately wanted a knife-wielding teen to jump from a hedge, a shadow to chase down an alley.

We spotted an intoxicated IC1 female on tall white heels, talking into her mobile phone and decided that we should advise her to take extra care. She lowered her phone and listened with a cocked head. 'Right, thanks,' she said and walked away. 'Yeah, it was the police,' we heard her say. '*Apparently* I'm in a robbery hotspot.'

Walking in circles quickly becomes boring. Once it becomes

clear that there are no immediate threats, there is little to recommend it. Nevertheless, the monotony of policing is permanently tinged with hope. Even at the most intensely tedious moments, there is always the possibility that something dramatic will happen. We walk for hours, it gets late, we grow despondent, and then, out of nowhere, we stumble on a drug deal, or we hear that we are just around the corner from something that should not be happening. When we least expect it, drama bursts through the boredom.

Looping around the hotspot, we wondered whether we had scared the robbers away. Perhaps we were acting as a deterrent, preventing robberies, deterring the very things that would make our night interesting. 'We're not even preventing crime,' my partner said, 'we're just pushing it off our ground onto someone else's,' as though crime were a lump in the carpet we could move but never flatten.

By midnight, dozens of circuits later, we were worn out, sitting in a line along a garden wall. 'Let's go to McDonald's,' said the Sergeant. 'If we sit on this corner much longer, we'll get a call asking us to investigate a group of suspicious characters.'

Open twenty-four hours a day, seven days a week, and a participant in the Community Toilet Scheme, Brixton McDonald's performs an important social function, offering a warm, supervised, brightly lit space to anyone, anytime. We walked in and joined the queue, indistinguishable in our jackets and jeans from the other customers. Our orders arrived quickly, except for my veggie wrap, and we waited at the counter in silence. Across from us, an intoxicated IC1 male took huge bites from a multistorey burger, chewing slowly, eyes fixed on a point in the distance.

'Hi, we're waiting for a veggie wrap. We've been waiting for about ten minutes.'

'Yeah, it's coming. We couldn't find one, but we have now and we're just heating it up.'

Leaving McDonald's, we decided not to go back to the hotspot and instead walked to Coldharbour Lane. As we passed the Prince Albert pub, we saw a topless IC1 male lying on the floor, kicking his legs in the air. 'This is an advantage of plain clothes,' said my partner. 'If we were in uniform we'd need to do something about him and it would be time-consuming and slightly pointless, but in plain clothes, we can just keep going.'

The man on the floor was about thirty, alarmingly thin, with wild bulging eyes. As we passed him, he leapt up and made a dash for the door of the Prince Albert. The bouncer blocked his entry and the man stumbled backwards down the steps and into the road. The oncoming cars braked sharply and the man slapped their bonnets as he staggered between them and onto the opposite pavement, where he hissed at some passers-by, unzipped his fly and urinated into a bin. 'Having said that,' my partner continued, 'this isn't really something we can ignore any more.'

By the time we reached him, the man had collapsed in the doorway of an off-licence. We sat him up, then lifted him to his feet. As soon as he was upright, he started to dance, grinning and twirling his wrists, wobbling his head and shooting seductive glances at us. Then he collapsed again. We sat the man up and put a jacket around him. His pupils were dilated and his skin was clammy and mottled like uncooked chicken. He told us his name was Mike and that he had been kicked out of his flat. We searched him for drugs, but all we found in his pockets were warning letters and bills.

An intoxicated IC3 female spotted Mike and walked over to us.

'Let me help him!'

'That's kind, but we're fine, thank you.'

'No, no, you've got to let me help him!'

We thanked her again more firmly and she began to cry.

'You've got to let me help him. I just have such strong feelings for him!'

While we waited for an ambulance, we asked the bouncer at the Prince Albert whether he had seen Mike before. 'He's been coming around here for a few nights now. He was here earlier today and police called an ambulance for him then too. He was gone for a few hours but he's come straight back.'

The ambulance arrived and we left Mike with the paramedics. Then we followed a group of IC3 teenagers in hoodies, keeping our distance to watch what they were doing. They looped from Coldharbour Lane to Rushcroft Road, through Windrush Square, along Effra Road, Kellett Road, past the Effra Hall Tavern, then onto Atlantic Road and back up to Coldharbour Lane. They just seemed to be wandering around, much as we had been a couple of hours earlier. They stood in a huddle talking and we watched them from the bus stop opposite the Phoenix. While we were standing there, a pair of IC1 males, one late teens, one late twenties, ducked down Electric Lane, right next to us. We were less than five metres away, looking straight at them, but we were in plain clothes so there was no reason for them to notice. The younger man palmed some cash to the older one, bent down, fiddled with his shoe, then emerged from the alley to slip back into the stream of late-night revellers. We let him walk a few metres and then apprehended him, pulling our warrant cards from the pockets of our casual clothes.

'What were you doing with that man in the alley?'

'We were just talking.'

'What about?'

'Nothing really.'

'It looked like you bought something and put it in your shoe.'

The young man's name was Alexander. He was nineteen and had finished school a few months earlier. We searched him and found a heart-shaped pill in his left sock.

'What's this?'

'I don't know.'

'You bought it and you don't know what it is?'

'It's probably MDMA, I guess. But I wasn't going to take it.' He paused. 'I didn't even buy it, actually. That guy just gave it to me. I was talking to him and he gave it to me for free.' He paused again. 'Actually he threatened me. He forced me to accept it, so I did, but I wasn't going to take it.'

The grimace on Alexander's face implied that even he was not convinced by his story. We arrested him and called for a van, then radioed our colleagues and asked them to go after the dealer.

'Man, my dad is not going to like this,' Alexander said. 'He's going to be furious. You know, I'm supposed to be starting uni this autumn. History.'

'Were you going to take that pill?'

'Probably, yeah.'

Standing next to Alexander, I thought about how arbitrary it was that I had seen his drug deal. A ten-second delay, a single divergent choice, and I would have missed it. I had versions of these thoughts on every shift – stopping people, searching cars, coming across fights, smelling drugs – and knowing a different route would have yielded a completely different set of situations.

Beat policing is dictated by chance. Who we encounter depends on a random mixture of decisions and deflections. Few institutional roles leave such a large space for the accidental, the aimless, the arbitrary. In my books about policing, I had read that only 10 per cent of crimes are reported. There were more illegal acts occurring on our patch than we could possibly detect. Dealing with whatever lay in our path, we were sampling crime, not stamping it out.

The noticeboards in Brixton Police Station were covered with TOTAL POLICING posters, announcing the Met's 'total war on crime'. On the poster, the Commissioner is wearing a peaked cap with a black and white chequered hat band. The pattern is not difficult to interpret. It suggests the orderliness, inflexibility and black-and-whiteness of the law. Encircling the head, it implies that the mind within is objective and unbiased. The check on the cap is a neat grid with no centre and no gaps, a fantasy of the city as a chessboard where the pieces are visible and victory is possible. Out on the beat, I saw how far from 'total' our policing was.

The more I thought about it, the more problematic the slogan seemed. A 'total war on crime' sounds impressive – until you consider its implications. It would require total surveillance and repression, and still would not succeed. For the Met, it was just a catchphrase. But reading Egon Bittner had alerted me to the risks of hyperbole. Bittner warned that officers develop 'maxims of judgment and conduct from figures of speech'. Slogans can change the way people think and act, regardless of how superficial the words seem. Bittner was particularly critical of military metaphors in policing. A 'community can no more wage war on its internal ills,' he wrote, 'than an organism can "wage war" against its own constitutional weaknesses'. Crime is not an outside force to be repelled, it is a product of the circumstances we create and occupy together.

In Brixton at night, encountering individuals who needed support not suppression, the idea of a 'total war on crime' felt bizarre and wrong-headed. Perhaps it helped to explain why so many of the regulars I worked alongside were frustrated by domestic violence, mental health crises, homelessness and community disputes. In this framing, the police are like soldiers, not social workers. There is little time for the patient work of care when there is a war to fight.

It took half an hour for a custody van to arrive, a slow half-hour outside Club 414, watching the night life. Looking left, I could see people queuing to get into the Dogstar; looking right, people were streaming in and out of McDonald's. Our colleagues had managed to apprehend Alexander's dealer just around the corner, outside KFC. When they reappeared without him a few minutes later we asked what had happened.

'We didn't find any drugs on him, so we let him go.'

'What?' said Alexander. 'So *I'm* the one who's been arrested!'

The Brixton Custody Suite was closed so we had to go to Peckham. We joined the queue, waiting in a big metal cage in the yard. Since learning that his dealer had been let off, Alexander was refusing to talk to us, so we sat on a metal bench and wrote our notes. When our turn finally came, we presented Alexander to the Custody Sergeant, who booked him in for the night, only a few hours of which remained. Across the custody suite, we could hear an officer saying that a missing fifteen-year-old had been found. She was in the front office, throwing anything she could pick up and trying to pull the radiators off the walls. The Sergeant suggested they move her to the custody cage. 'You can't break anything in there but yourself,' he said. We took Alexander to a small windowless room for his mugshot and fingerprints and left him there.

ANTHRAX IS KILLING HEROIN USERS, read an old poster on the wall.

When I woke the next morning, I went back into Brixton. I walked along Coldharbour Lane, intrigued by the sense that, although this was precisely the place I had arrested Alexander ten hours earlier, it was also, somehow, not the same place at all. Walking through central Brixton, I felt as if I had not been there for a long time, and that I had just returned from somewhere else entirely.

I went into the Phoenix. After long shifts and little sleep, the cafe had become a kind of decompression chamber. I could not face typing my notes at home – it felt claustrophobic. I needed to be among people, somewhere warm and neutral, a third space that was neither personal nor professional. The manager smiled, waved me to a table, then went back to staring at his London A–Z. Nobody came over. They knew my order and no longer asked. I took out my laptop and began writing down the night before, spreading my index cards across the small square table.

A black coffee appeared. The events of the shift were playing behind my eyes. I thought of Alexander, Mike and the boring hotspot. Then I found myself thinking about the teenagers we caught smoking cannabis in the front garden: the shock on their faces when we pulled out our warrant cards; the boy who said it was his second search that day. I have never been stopped and searched in my life. I wondered how it must feel to be searched twice in twelve hours.

My bubble and squeak appeared. I thought about Swamp 81 and the ongoing community anger about stop and search. Then my mind turned to Olive Morris.

I had been reading more of the 'Do You Remember Olive Morris?' project online. Her political awakening came as a teenager, when she witnessed police stopping and arresting a Black man not far from where I was sitting, at 55 Atlantic Road, a railway arch now shared by a minicab office and the New Look Hair Salon. This was the site of Desmond's Hip City, an iconic Brixton record store mentioned by Linton Kwesi Johnson in his poem 'Yout Scene':

> di bredrin dem stan-up
> outside a Hip City,
> as usual, a look pretty;
> dem a lawf big lawf
> dem a talk dread talk
> dem a shuv an shuffle dem feet,
> soakin in di sweet musical beat.

It was here, in November 1969, that police stopped and arrested a Nigerian diplomat, Clement Gomwalk, on suspicion of being in possession of a stolen vehicle. Gomwalk protested, the crowd of outraged young music fans began shouting and tussling with police. The seventeen-year-old Olive Morris was among them, about to experience activism and police abuse for the first time.

There are multiple accounts of what happened and in what order. At some point Olive Morris was handcuffed, beaten up and arrested, along with five others. The 'three cops who threw me into the van then climbed on top of me,' she said. 'Then I was turned round on my back and one cop mashed my chest with his boots and bruised my breast. Each time I tried to talk or raise my head I was slapped in the face'.

The suspicious vehicle was Gomwalk's diplomatic Mercedes. Olive Morris was charged with 'assault on police, threatening behaviour, and possessing offensive weapons'.

Gomwalk's arrest caused a minor diplomatic incident. In the House of Commons, the Home Secretary, James Callaghan, gave an account:

> Police inquiries took place on the morning of 15th November about a car which was causing a serious obstruction in a no waiting area in Brixton. The licence plate bore a different number from the Road Fund licence disc and there was a possibility that the vehicle might have been stolen.
>
> Mr. Gomwalk, who was not at this stage known to be a diplomat, returned to the car, and refused to give any explanation of the ownership. During questioning by the police, a hostile crowd gathered, a struggle took place, and in order to prevent a breach of the peace Mr. Gomwalk was arrested and taken to Brixton police station. His identity and entitlement to diplomatic immunity were established while he was there and he was released.
>
> In the meantime, a disturbance developed as a result of which six other persons were arrested, against whom proceedings are now pending. In the circumstances, it would not be proper for me to make any further comment.

'Can my right honourable friend confirm that the police in Lambeth will continue to work with all sections of the community and do what they have done hitherto – try to maintain the best possible race relations within the borough?' was the response of John Fraser, Labour MP for Norwood.

A decade later, the year Olive Morris died, John Fraser attempted to introduce a Bill to abolish the Sus Laws. 'The enmity that is felt by many young black people towards the police ought to and does cause us a great deal of concern,' he remarked. His attempt was defeated. It was not until 1981 that the Sus Laws were finally abolished, four months after they had sparked the Brixton uprising.

Back in 1969, Olive Morris was taken from Brixton Police Station for treatment at King's College Hospital. Emerging bruised and enraged, she embarked on the career of protest, activism and community organizing that defined the final decade of her life. The police, she came to believe, were the 'principal, "legal" and most brutal agents of racism'.

Olive threw herself into all of 'the campaigns and issues facing black people in 1970s Britain,' writes Liz Obi, 'e.g. police harassment, deaths in police custody, the campaign against the Sus law, bad housing conditions and homelessness, issues of injustice in the courts and the prison system and issues around education and the practice of assessing black school children as educationally sub-normal.'

In 'Yout Scene', Linton Kwesi Johnson's poem, the laughter outside the record shop also ends in violence:

> but when nite come,
> policeman run dem dung;
> beat dem dung a grung,

kick dem ass,
sen dem paas justice
to prison walls of gloom.

I finished my breakfast and walked along Coldharbour Lane. Standing outside the New Look Hair Salon on Atlantic Road, I scanned the brickwork around the railway arches. There was nothing there about Desmond's Hip City, Linton Kwesi Johnson's poem, Clement Gomwalk or Olive Morris.

Perhaps this is to be expected in a city as layered with stories as London, but still it struck me how few of the dramatic turning points in South London's recent history were inscribed on its surfaces. For a newcomer, it was easy to live in the area without any sense of what had happened here, or how the conversations we are having today were shaped by events that occurred on these streets.

I rushed to the station straight from work, arriving late and stressed. I waved to the rosy-cheeked Sergeant and dashed to the basement to change. There were seven of us going out on patrol in the van. We gathered for the briefing, jotting down number plates and staring at the faces on the screen.

We circled Stockwell in a van. It was a wet night, not many people out. The rain had been falling heavily since the early afternoon and the roads had become mirrors for the shopfronts and street lights, projecting a distorted London downwards through the asphalt.

Stockwell is the crossroads of South Lambeth, the confluence of roads to Clapham, Brixton, Vauxhall and Kennington. On any vehicle shift, we drove through it a couple of dozen times, passing the war memorial and bomb shelter on the roundabout, now vibrantly painted with soldiers, poppies and the faces of famous people who lived locally: Vincent van Gogh, Roger Moore and Violette Szabo. The mural's creator, Brian Barnes, added the face of Jean Charles de Menezes in 2005, after he was shot by police in Stockwell tube station, but the council removed it soon afterwards.

Driving slowly around Stockwell's backstreets, my eyes flicked idly across the facades of the houses, scanning for life in the lit windows, watching bodies move in and out of the frames, spotting a woman reaching for a saucepan, a man laughing at something I could not see.

The rain was keeping people at home and a steady stream of domestic violence calls was coming out of the radio. We radioed to accept the latest, a woman who had been assaulted by her boyfriend a few streets away.

We arrived at a low red-brick council block and found an IC2 female, mid-twenties, sheltering in the doorway. Her boyfriend and his family were clustered in the lobby of the building behind her. We split up to take reports from both parties. 'Yes, he hit me,' the woman told us, 'but I hit him first. He call my mother a bitch, so I push him. He push me back and I say *Why you got to push me? You don't have to push me no more.* Then he say: *Are you going to call the police? I call them myself.*' The man had called the police and his extended family had gathered to wait for us.

Domestic abuse happens on a scale far greater than I would have believed possible before becoming a police officer. DV calls seemed to be the pulse behind everything we did. According to a paper I read, a domestic abuse call is made to the police in the UK every minute – and it is known to be significantly under-reported. Every time a report came in, we had to investigate and complete a Form 124D.

Form 124D is twenty-five pages long, full of checklists, risk assessments and witness statements, and it is exceedingly time-consuming to fill out. Its length reflects the complexity of domestic abuse incidents and also, I sensed, the Met's anxiety about our ability to deal with them. 'Historically, police officers have tended to respond poorly to victims of DV,' say the form's explanatory notes, 'tending to overlook incidents as criminal offences, failing to retrieve all available evidence to prove offences, not identifying future risk to victims and leaving them in vulnerable positions.' The extensive paperwork is designed to ensure we take domestics seriously.

We stood on the pavement with the woman and worked through the form, our voices competing with the hammering rain. We explained that we were obliged to ask a lot of questions, some quite intimate.

'Do they follow or harass you in any way?'

'No.'

'Do they abuse your children or pets?'

'No.'

'Do they have use of or access to any weapons?'

'No.'

'Are they acutely jealous or controlling?'

'No.'

'Have they made threats to kill you or your family?'

'No.'

'Are you currently or have you recently been pregnant?'

'Yes, I'm pregnant.'

Pregnancy and parenthood do not inoculate a couple against domestic abuse. If anything, the reverse is true: in 90 per cent of cases reported to the police, there are children in the house.

I thought about a day when I had walked along Railton Road to school and found the mother of a girl I taught waiting outside in the dark, an hour and a half before the children were due to arrive. She told me she needed to talk to me confidentially, so I unlocked the gate and invited her to my classroom.

We sat opposite each other on miniature green plastic chairs, and she told me that she had been beaten up by her partner the evening before, and that her daughter had seen everything. She spoke quietly, looking at the floor all the while. 'I wanted you to know so you can keep an eye on her today,' she said. 'So you know why she's acting strange if she acts strange.'

Ninety minutes later, her seven-year-old daughter bounced into the classroom, smiling and chatting to her friends. I kept a close eye on her. She seemed fine. The school's learning mentor took her aside for a chat. She looked cheerful and unperturbed when she came back to class. I did not notice anything out of the ordinary that day or in the days that followed, yet the image of what had happened must have been in her mind, its effects unknown and invisible.

We completed the forms for the girlfriend and boyfriend, totting up the risk factors, and asked whether either party wanted to press charges. They did not, and as we did not perceive an immediate risk of further violence, we left.

Back in the van, rain drumming on the roof, we could hear something on the radio about the children's home we had visited a few weeks earlier, where the boy had assaulted the manager and run away, and something about reports of gunshots in Tulse Hill, response cars scouring the area.

We stopped off at the Kebab Company, jogging inside, heads bowed. Driving along Clapham High Street, we spotted the hot-dog vendor sheltering with his cart beneath a bus stop. We decided to leave him to it and drove back to the station, hot Styrofoam boxes on our laps, the van filling with the aroma of garlic, onions and kebab meat. While we ate our pittas, one of the regulars got her phone out to show us some taser videos on YouTube: taser ball (like football, only each player is armed with a taser), followed by taser bull (a game in which people taser bulls then watch them try to get up again).

–

Sitting in the station, I typed an account of the domestic. I stared at the screen, struggling to focus. With every minute that passed, I became less capable of filling in the boxes and knew that it would take even longer to get back out on the street.

For a police officer, a two-minute incident can generate an hour of paperwork. For every satisfying arrest there is a corresponding stack of dissatisfying form filling. For a domestic violence incident, which many officers would rather not attend in the first place, the process is even longer. The fluency of a lived moment is succeeded by the labour of writing. The thrill of discovery becomes the chore of documentary. There is a constant doubling back.

While writing, officers just want to get back on the streets. It is a frustration I recognize as a diarist: while you are writing life down, you are not out doing things; but the more you go out doing things, the more there is to write.


It was still raining, so we decided to drive to a road in Clapham where people sometimes have sex in their cars, a barely lit backstreet lined with trees and industrial units. There was no one to surprise, so we drove to the High Street, sharing a packet of Percy Pigs and scouring the pavements for trouble.

We listened to the radio, waiting for a call with maximum action and minimum paperwork. 'There's a child alone in an apartment' . . . 'A woman's called, saying her boyfriend's threatening to kill her' . . . 'There's a fight outside a pub, someone's using a broken bottle as a weapon' . . . That would do. We were nowhere near, but we radioed to accept the call anyway. Our driver switched on the siren and lights and we raced towards it.

When I woke up, the sun was out and the air felt fresh. I walked down Brixton Hill and reflected on the domestic the previous night, and the reluctance of many officers to attend domestic calls. It made me think of an article by Egon Bittner, 'Florence Nightingale in Pursuit of Willie Sutton', about the conflicting demands of the police role.

Florence Nightingale was 'the heroic protagonist of modern nursing' and Willie Sutton was 'a notorious thief'. For Bittner this image – a nurse chasing a bank robber – encapsulated the contradictions of policing. To do the job well, police need to exercise both care and force, often simultaneously. They need to tackle the most serious crime, confronting violence and danger, but with the skilful care and robust compassion of a nurse.

This was not how most officers thought of themselves. 'Fearing the role of the nurse or, worse yet, the role of the social worker,' Bittner writes, 'the policeman combines resentment of what he has to do day-in-day-out with the necessity of doing it. And in the course of it he misses his true vocation.'

I was intrigued to learn that half a century earlier Bittner had identified that policing is a caring role akin to nursing and social work, but that its true nature was starkly rejected by the police themselves. His insight did not seem to have been digested by the Met. Most of the regulars I met thought it was not our job to deal with messy social issues and tried to dispatch them as quickly as possible so we could get back to the real business of battling crime. They felt a mixture of pity and scorn for the Neighbourhood Policing Teams, who deal with community issues full time.

No one 'likes being obliged to do things day-in and day-out that are disparaged by his colleagues,' Bittner wrote. 'Moreover, the low evaluation of these duties leads to neglecting the development of skill and knowledge that are required to discharge them properly and efficiently.' Until we believed these complex social challenges were our business, Bittner suggested, and until we respected the officers who worked on them, we were unlikely to do this work well, or to want to do it at all.

In the Met, far from addressing those tensions, we did not even seem capable of naming them. We continued to advertise a job that bore little resemblance to the job police officers actually do.

I thought about the regular on one of my first shifts, insisting that he was not a social worker. I had encountered similar sentiments in schools: teachers who thought the extent of their role was to impart knowledge, regardless of whether the children in front of them had eaten or slept or were traumatized or stressed or were caring for someone at home. There is often a reluctance to acknowledge the thread of care that runs through these interconnected professions.

But in teaching, social work and nursing the core of the job is what new starters expect. In policing, the gap between the imagined and actual role is stark. Many officers spend their days and nights trying to bridge it, telling themselves that the bulk of what they deal with is the fluff between the brief moments when they do what they are paid for.

Five decades on, Bittner's paper felt as relevant as ever. Patrolling South London, we competed to deal with bar fights and robberies and hoped that someone else would answer the DV and mental health calls. Faced with complex social problems, we felt more like medieval doctors than pioneer nurses, applying lances and leeches to afflictions we could not hope to cure. Attending DV calls could come to seem pointless. Cynicism set in. The call came out and we would leave it hanging. We were not properly equipped, and we craved one-off situations with clear-cut outcomes. A fight was a relief, a crude act that invited a crude response.

Nurses chasing bank robbers. The fact was, in front-line policing, very few bank robbers needed chasing. And if there were a major heist, we would not be the ones sent to deal with it. Our local robbers were mainly vulnerable young people ensnared in toxic power structures. There was a mismatch between the work we wanted to do and what really needed doing, between the mentality and skills we brought to the work, and the mentality and skills required. Far from treating notorious bank robbers with compassionate care, we treated people in need of empathy and support as though they were notorious bank robbers.

4

**YouTube:** *Racist police attack black man London UK*

67,074 views

### Ramla
This isnt racism. The police asked the man to get out of the car many times and that guy keeps refusing.

#### Club Tropícana
If the police didn't enforce people having valid driving licenses then what would the reprocussions be for speeding or driving dangerously? I didn't see any evidence for racism either.

#### trump Supporter
I dont see any racism. the officer did his job well! You are no allowed to drive!

### ricccccardo
This is clearly racism to the highest levels. His only crime driving while black. The pc mite as well have said 'sorry for the mix up you all look the same'

**Veera Raj**

I know a police officer and he told me police officers only pick on ethic minority's, especially when they drive posh cars.

**Esther Daitey**

MY BLACK BROTHER, WE ARE SOOOOO PROUD OF YOU.YOU STOOD YOUR GROUND AND YOU MAKE HIM LOOK THE RUBBISH PALE WEAK PPLE THAT THEY ARE.I HAVE SHARED YOUR VIDEO ACROSS THE WORLD.WELL DONE!!!!

**percy jones**

jesus. I've never seen so much minority victimhood in one comments section. The kid should have just complied with the police officer. Dont provoke the police then cry as soon as they respond lol. I'm glad the officer smashed the window in. Maybe it'll teach the kid some respect.

**d4hda**

What the hell why did he smash the mans window

**simon B the welshman**

because he wouldn't get out and locked himself in I'm sure his insurance will cover it if he has any

**Kier Mapp**

i feel so sorry for the cop . . . what we have here is an over worked cop suffering with mild to moderate PTSD

**YB-young blood**

i feel sorry for your mom

**mimi b**

What ???!!!! Its the officer who pulled out a knife and used it on the car !! You feel sorry for the officer? would you have got out the car with a copper going that mental? Would you be understanding had he cut up your windscreen with a knife?

**gazza3166**

That pig needs to loose his job

**Jack Black**

lose

**Jack Black**

lose. Loose is something wobbly.

**axe ishmael**

He refused to get out so the police had every rite to smash his face in.

**Rafal Anonim**

Good job! Keep it this way mr police officer!

On the beat in a high helmet and a hi-vis jacket. Seven hours walking the same few streets.

'I found this wallet. It was on the floor over there.'

Walking fourteen miles within a half-mile radius. Beating the bounds of an arbitrary patch of South London.

'He manhandled me. That bouncer should be arrested!'

Two of us – but constantly appearing, reappearing, seen on this corner, that corner, from a distance, close up. Creating multiples of ourselves, the effect of a crowd.

'Can you believe the mouth on her? She's way out of order. If she was your girlfriend, you'd pepper spray her, wouldn't you?'

Next to our patch, another patch, another pair of neon walkers, ploughing their patch just as we are ploughing ours.

'What's a good place for a curry round here?'

We adopt a light rolling stride. Slow, non-urgent. It is the opposite of the commuter's busy clip. The point is to move, not to travel; to be a presence, like a teacher in a playground.

'These two guys, they came up and hugged me. It
seemed kind of funny, but then I realized they'd taken
my iPhone 5.'

Beat walking is a distinctive form of walking. Each step is light
but deliberate. The legs move with an effortless pendular
motion, the forward swing propelling the back swing, the back
swing propelling the forward.

'I've seen you three times now. You got nothing better
to do than walk round in circles?'

Back straight, chin up, minimum stress on the knees, minimum
wear to the pavement.

'I was desperate. I just had to go. I'm sorry. You know
– it happens.'

Seven hours. Fourteen miles. Dozens of casual interactions.

'Follow me, lads, I'm fucking bullet-proof!'

We were assigned to a new operation in Vauxhall called Op Shadow, addressing a spate of robberies outside the nightclubs. At the briefing we were shown the faces of half a dozen IC6 males who had begun coming to Vauxhall on weekend evenings, befriending drunk males, enticing them into the Pleasure Gardens with the promise of drugs or sex, and then robbing them. To liven up the briefing deck, the Sergeant had included some slides of cartoon cats holding guns.

Vauxhall, the north-western corner of Lambeth, was once a stretch of industrial riverside and is now a transport hub packed with sleek residential skyscrapers which loom over the MI6 building and the vibrant LGBTQ+ club scene below.

Most of Vauxhall's nightclubs operate in the arches below the railway line. Chariots Roman Spa, Union, No.65, Barcode, The Hoist, Lightbox, Fire. Behind the clubs is Goding Street, a robbery and drug hotspot lined with wheelie bins and parked cars and bordered by the darkness of the Pleasure Gardens. We were tasked to keep a close eye on Goding Street, and the tunnels leading to it, and to pay close attention to anybody lingering there. We set out wearing jeans and T-shirts below our stab vests and kit belts to make us look more approachable, and to make our presence inside the clubs less disruptive.

We began the operation with a circuit of the clubs, greeting the door staff and seeking their views on the night ahead. They were not anticipating any issues, although our Sergeant was anxious about an IC3 lesbian club night called Bad Bitches, the first of its kind to be held in the area for several months. 'They're the roughest nights to police,' the Sergeant said. 'They turn on each other, and then when you arrive they all turn on you. I'll fight anyone before I'd fight a Black lesbian – and I say that as a lesbian myself.'

I was surprised to see the shutters down on Club No.65. The Sergeant explained that the previous weekend the club's bouncers had restrained a man on the pavement for several minutes, causing him to asphyxiate, and the club had been closed while his death was investigated. I spotted the story in the *Metro* afterwards. According to the article, the man 'had battled with depression for some time and, on the night he died, he had been at a social event for fellow sufferers'.

We walked to New Spring Gardens Walk, the brightly lit tunnel connecting Goding Street and the Albert Embankment, and spotted a pair of men, IC6, late teens. They were leaning against the wall, talking. We stood watching until they noticed and turned to face us.

'We know who you are and we know what you're up to,' shouted the Sergeant.

'What? What are you talking about?' the taller of the men replied. We entered the tunnel and walked up to them.

'We know what you're up to,' the Sergeant said again.

'We live in this country too, you know,' the tall man said. 'Do you want to see my passport? Here, take it, take it.'

'What are you doing standing in this tunnel? We know what

you're up to. The best thing you can do is leave the area peace-fully now.'

'We live in this country too. We have a right to be here.'

'You know what we're talking about,' the Sergeant insisted. 'We suggest you leave.'

'Why would we leave? You've got no right to tell us to do that.'

'Yeah, you've got no right to do that!' the shorter man said, jabbing the Sergeant in the shoulder.

'Stop touching me,' she said. 'Keep your hands to yourself.'

'Come on, arrest me then. Arrest me!'

'We don't want to arrest you, we want you to leave the area peacefully.'

The shorter man stepped back and paused, looking up at the tunnel's brick ceiling.

'You know, you can lie to other people,' he said, 'but you can never lie to yourself.'

'I'm not sure what you mean,' replied the Sergeant.

'You can lie to other people, but you can never lie to yourself.'

'You've said that. I'm not sure what you're talking about.'

'You've got your mind and your heart, your heart and your mind, and that's all you've got. You can never lie to yourself.'

'I'm not sure that's entirely relevant.'

We searched the men and ran name checks. They were known for drugs, but were not currently wanted. We found nothing suspicious on them, so we left, advising them again to leave the area.

A call came for backup from a pair of plain clothes officers on Goding Street. We ran to the end of the tunnel and, as soon as the officers saw us, they knocked on the window of a black BMW known for drugs and held up their warrant cards. We joined them so that there were suddenly seven police officers surrounding the vehicle. 'Where did you lot even come from?' said the driver, an IC3 teen. 'Oh man, you guys are fast, you know that? You could ruin someone's night sneaking up on them like that!' We searched the car and its passengers, an IC3 male and two IC3 females, and took some cannabis and a grinder off them. They were friendly and relaxed, so we let them off without a Cannabis Warning and sent them on their way.

We turned around. An IC1 male was urinating against the wall. 'Do you realize you've got your dick out in a public place and that's indecent exposure?' the Sergeant shouted. 'Are you aware you could go on the sex offenders register for that?' The man fumbled with his trousers and spun around to face us. When he had apologized several times, she let him leave.

From Goding Street, we could hear shouts in the tunnel where we had searched the two IC6 males. We ran back around the corner to find that five officers were restraining the taller man against the wall and pinning the shorter man on the floor. Both men were shouting and resisting forcefully. We ran over, grabbed a limb each, and helped get handcuffs on them. 'Is this right?' the shorter man was shouting, his head squashed sideways on the tarmac. 'Tell me, is this right? Ten of you. Ten of you and two of us! What have we done?' A group of people who had been smoking outside a Portuguese restaurant drifted down the tunnel to see what was happening, as did a police Inspector, who was overseeing that night's operations.

'Is everything all right?' he asked. 'What have they done?'

'Yes, tell me!' the shorter man shouted, from the floor. 'Come on, tell me, what have we done?'

A couple of the people from the restaurant took out their phones and began filming. 'We want all of your ID numbers,' the taller man shouted. 'We're going to complain!'

Our Sergeant quietly asked an officer from the other group what had happened. 'They resisted a search,' the officer replied. The Inspector was satisfied with this response, until he heard that the men had been searched only ten minutes earlier by us.

We helped the shorter man up, uncuffed them both, explained what had happened and apologized. Back on the Albert Embankment the Inspector addressed us. 'You've all got a lot of writing down to do,' he said. 'Do you realize how bad that looked? There could easily be a complaint there. Sort your shit out.'

We did not write anything down there and then. Instead the Sergeant suggested we get away from the clubs, drive around some backstreets and see what we found. We climbed into an unmarked car, drove away from the lights and music, and wound along narrow residential roads, the Sergeant accelerating towards oncoming vehicles, laughing and shouting, 'Die you cunts!' then slamming on the brakes at the very last moment. We did circuits of the same few streets, covering and recovering our tracks, doubling back on ourselves in a way that would have looked senseless to anyone watching. We spotted an IC3 teen in a hoodie riding a bike with no lights. 'Robber!' the Sergeant shouted, prowling behind him. He cycled into a dead space by a locked gate, waiting for us to pass. We stopped alongside him and rolled down a window. He looked over at us while turning his bike on the spot, then lost his balance and fell sideways onto the tarmac. 'Mate, you're a hazard to society!' the Sergeant shouted. He stood up, shrugged and smiled.

We decided to stop for refs in the Central Communications Command Centre by Lambeth Palace. The top-floor canteen has spectacular views over Westminster and Waterloo, and while we drank tea on the balcony, the Sergeant showed us videos of her cats racing around the kitchen, singing for their cat food, trapped beneath a washing basket.

We spent the rest of the night patrolling on foot. My partner and I walked across the Pleasure Gardens, encountering two men from a homeless shelter drinking on a log, four young Frenchmen smoking on a bench, and a couple trying to have sex against the tennis court fence. There were other figures we could not make out, who moved away from us as we passed.

A call came out: an IC1 male, twenties, had run out of Chariots Roman Spa wearing nothing but a white towel. He had been sighted outside Vauxhall train station and my partner and I said we would take a look. There was no sign of him there, so we walked under the rail bridge away from the crowds.

Several other units were searching for the runaway, in vehicles and on foot, so we did not expect to find him. Then, on Vauxhall Grove, we saw a flash of white in a garden. We stood on either side of the garden gate. Something was moving by the front door. 'It's all right, mate, come out,' my partner said, and after a few moments, a man padded out of the shadows with a white towel knotted at his neck, hanging down his back like a cape. With trembling hands he was fashioning a loin cloth from a transparent orange bin bag. He had made leg holes and was now trying to tie the torn plastic beneath his belly button. We suggested he put the towel around his waist instead and asked if he was all right.

'I'm locked out of my house,' he said. 'It's just down there. I went out in a towel and now I'm locked out. Just had a shower, then popped out . . . I've never been in trouble with the law. You're not going to arrest me, are you?'

'What's your name?'

'Smith . . . Matthew . . . Oh five . . . oh five . . . nineteen eighty . . . five . . . Chariots? Yes, I did go, but I've never been before. I'm staying with my friend, she lives just down there . . . I just panicked, you see . . . Are you going to arrest me? I've never been in trouble with the law.'

'It's all right, mate. Just tell us what happened.'

'It's just that I'm an accountant. I'm not trying to brag, but I've got a good job, and I'm not really out, you see? I've got a girlfriend . . . Am I in trouble?'

'Have you taken anything this evening? Any drugs?'

'I had some vodka and Coke . . . Coca-Cola! I don't normally drink or anything. No, I haven't taken anything else. I am on anti-depressants. I'm supposed to take them every day . . . Last Tuesday, but I can really take them when I want. I'm not really depressed or anything.'

'Where do you live?'

'I'm staying with my friend up in Tottenham. He's sort of a semi-boyfriend. Are you going to arrest me? Please don't arrest me, I've never been in trouble with the law.'

'Don't worry, mate. Just tell us what happened tonight.'

'I'm not trying to brag, but a few guys were paying me attention and then I just had to get out. I just panicked and ran for it. I'd never been there before and it was just too much.'

'And what have you taken this evening?'

'Just some vodka and Coke. And some poppers . . . He's sort of my semi-boyfriend. I'm not really out, and I'm an accountant . . .'

We put a fleece round the man's shoulders, called for a car, and returned to Chariots to get his clothes.


At 3 a.m., we passed the tunnel where we had searched the two IC6 males several hours earlier. They were still loitering there, deep in conversation. 'David Cameron needs to get in for another three years to sort this country out!' the shorter man was saying.

'All right guys, you still here?' said the Sergeant.

'You know,' said the shorter man, 'let me tell you something.' He gestured for us to come closer. 'I respect you all, from the bottom of my heart,' he said.

'That's nice of you,' the Sergeant replied.

'I respect you – from the bottom of my heart. And let me tell you something else: You can lie to your colleagues . . . You can lie to your colleagues, but you can never lie to yourself.'

The shorter man tried to give the Sergeant a hug. She patted him on the arm and we wished them both a good night.

Standing at the New Park Road bus stop, I thought about the tunnel the night before, the IC6 males resisting their second search in ten minutes. The point of Op Shadow was to target young IC6 males loitering near Goding Street. The young men in the tunnel ticked every box. But it still felt absurd that they had ended up in handcuffs, pinned to the floor and wall.

Maybe those young men were robbers. Maybe if we had not been there they would have pressed on with their plan. Maybe they waited until our shift ended, then went on a spree. Whatever the truth, we had lost any moral high ground.

I thought about the Inspector saying there could be a complaint, the onlookers filming on their phones. I played the situation back in my mind: the shouts, the sight of the officers grappling with the young men, the rest of us piling on. I was not sure what else we could have done. As I ran along the tunnel, I had presumed the men had assaulted our colleagues. In the midst of the action, the only thing to do was grab a limb and speed things to a conclusion.

Egon Bittner wrote about situations where police need to act decisively with only partial information. It is impossible to reconcile this kind of action with 'error-free performance', he wrote, so 'police work is, by its very nature, doomed to be often unjust and offensive to someone'. *Doomed to be unjust.*

For Bittner the crudeness of police conduct is a feature of the job. The 'need to disregard complexity is structurally built into the occupation'. But the public expect more than that. They expect the police not just to do *something*, but to do the *right* thing. Under this 'dual pressure to "be right" and to "do something,"' Bittner wrote, the police are 'often in a position that is compromised even before they act'.

Unlike teaching, I found policing a difficult role in which to live my values. There were so many moments when the outcome of a situation was the opposite of what we intended, or when we followed our hunches, unsure whether data or prejudice was guiding our behaviour, or when it was simply unclear what our good options were. My principles and my actions often felt out of kilter.

Bittner believed that police officers could be much better than they often were. But he also challenged people to look the facts in the face. Constables simply did not have the time to give 'the subtleties and profundities' of the situations they encountered 'anywhere near the consideration they deserve', he wrote. 'Accordingly, the constant reminder that officers should be wise, considerate, and just, without providing them with opportunities to exercise these virtues is little more than vacuous sermonizing.'

I agreed with Bittner that policing could not be error-free. But I was uncomfortable with the idea that 'the need to disregard complexity' was an inevitable feature of the job. As far as I could see, community policing was a near-constant confrontation with complexity and we would be better to acknowledge that and design our approach accordingly. Then, instead of each domestic violence call or mental health crisis provoking apathy and bewilderment, we could react with clarity and purpose. We would still need to act on limited information, we would still make mistakes, but we would at least know what we were trying to achieve.

In a place like South London, responding appropriately to complex social issues is not just an important aspect of the job; it is a description of the job in its entirety. What else was there?

I thought about the Sergeant speeding our unmarked car along backstreets, shouting, swearing, suddenly braking. Her frustration with the job was palpable.

When we met the two IC6 males at the end of the night, I was surprised by how affectionately she greeted them. It was like seeing friends make up after an argument.

Six of us were out patrolling in Brixton. It was a beautiful spring evening, one of the first warm evenings of the year, children racing along the pavements, families laughing outside barber shops. The streets were full of conversation, reggae, the smell of smoke and meat.

On Coldharbour Lane, we stopped off at the Neighbourhood Policing Office, a dingy space containing a few lockers, bikes and computers. One wall was covered with black and white headshots of IC3 teenagers from the GAS and TN1 gangs. Prison bars had been drawn onto the photos of those currently serving time. Without intending to, I scanned the photos for the faces of former pupils, relieved not to find any, although the more faces I looked at, the more difficult I found it to focus on any one face in particular.

Just as saying a word repeatedly makes it sound unfamiliar, looking at the same thing repeatedly can make it seem alien. Did this apply to police officers and IC3 males? Seeing them on PowerPoint slides, Blu-Tacked in rows on office walls, in groups on street corners, we were constantly scrutinizing their faces. For Met police officers, the face of a Black teenage boy attains a kind of heightened reality, becomes both more and less than a face.

We were walking past Morleys department store when a call came out about a stabbing inside the Tesco Express in the Esso garage on Brixton Road. There was an angry crowd at the scene, including members of the victim's family, and the officers needed backup. We boarded the first bus going that way, jumped off three minutes later, and ran from the bus stop to the garage. By the time we arrived, though, the crowd had gone quiet. The victim had been carried into the ambulance and its light was spinning silently, bathing the forecourt in its antiseptic blue.

We walked past the petrol pumps to the scene of the stabbing, leaning through the sliding doors to look at the spatters along the confectionery aisle. 'Good bit of claret,' said an officer guarding the entrance. 'Stabbed in the neck.' I looked at the slick red patterns on the supermarket tiles, the streaks and smudges where the blood had been walked on, perhaps by the victim himself and the people who helped him. I looked away and leant on the brick wall outside, feeling slightly light-headed.

I did not know anything about the stabbing: who the boy was, why it had happened. I did not even know his name. The ambulance was silent and still, yet inside he was fighting for his life. The crowd were staring at it so intently, they seemed to be trying to see through its neon yellow walls. Watching the boy's friends and family, I felt I was intruding on something private, seeing depths of emotion that rarely rise to the surface. I looked away and hoped, with them, that the boy would come through this.

We went to see the Sergeant at the scene and offered our help, but as the situation had calmed down she told us our support was not required. On the other side of Brixton Road, we could see lines of police vans outside Angell Town. The estate was full of officers looking for the boy's attacker, and our help was not required there either.

I did not want to leave with so much unknown and unresolved, but we turned around and walked back along Brixton Road to the town centre. Looming over us was a gigantic mural, thirty by forty feet, of children with eighties clothes and haircuts. Called 'Children at Play', it had been painted in the aftermath of the 1981 uprising to symbolize racial harmony and celebrate the easy acceptance that young children offer one another.

Looking at the children on the mural, I was reminded of an embarrassing situation at the school where I had taught, when the six-year-old girls splintered into a 'Black Girls Club' and a 'White Girls Club', who refused to play with one another. When we looked into it, it was a product of the friendship groups of the girls' parents. The girls were playing with the girls they played with outside school. It took several sensitive conversations with parents and children to dissolve the clubs and encourage them to play together again.

The good weather had brought people onto the streets and Brixton was heaving with pre-dinner crowds. On Atlantic Road, we spotted two badly parked cars with two IC3 males, late teens, beside them. 'You think you're a bad boy!' one shouted at the other. 'You think you're a bad boy, don't you?' From inside one of the cars, a woman was tugging his T-shirt and telling him to get back in. Passers-by were slowing down. Looking, looking away. There would soon be a crowd. We ran over and told the men to relax.

'My cousin just got stabbed!' the shouting teen replied. 'How are you gonna tell me to relax?'

'In the Esso garage?' we asked.

He nodded and got back in his car.

We walked towards quieter backstreets. The blue sky was darkening, streaked with pink. Passing the steamy windows of the Effra Hall Tavern, I thought again of the buried River Effra, flowing beneath our feet, laced with South London sewage. A call came out: 'There's a crowd of IC3 teenage males in masks and bandanas gathering around the entrance to the Tulse Hill Estate.' We radioed to say we would investigate.

By the time we reached the estate, all we found was a single teenager circling on a BMX; he told us that he had not seen anything. Another call came out: a group of teenagers smoking cannabis in Herne Hill. We cut across the top of Brockwell Park, looking north at the City skyscrapers, lit blue, white and green. By the time we reached the corner where the teens had been spotted, it was empty.

I was often struck by how much time we spent walking to places where something had recently happened, but where nothing was happening by the time we arrived. Trooping from one vacated crime scene to another felt like an underwhelming local history walk.

We looped back towards Brixton. A call came out: more teenagers smoking cannabis. We found two IC3 males in sports gear in a playground. They were out of breath, a punch bag hanging from the crossbar of the swings. 'No way!' one of them told us. 'You can't be smoking when you're training!'

We walked up Brixton Hill, past Olive Morris House, towards my flat. My legs felt heavy, as though the weight of my body had slipped downwards, and my chest and back were covered in cold sweat beneath my stab vest. We had been walking for miles, up and down the hills of South Lambeth. I was about to suggest a break when we spotted an IC1 male urinating in the doorway of Heavenly Hair and Scalp. We approached, holding out our warrant cards.

'What do you think you're doing, mate?'

He looked up, surprised, tucking his penis away and spinning around.

'What do you think you're doing?' we asked again.

'Look, I was trying to piss,' he said, 'but then I couldn't piss. I'm sorry, OK?'

'People live and work here. You're pissing in the doorway of a place where people live and work. Do you realize that? You might think this is a small thing, but it's not a small thing for them.'

'OK, I'm sorry.'

'I don't think you are sorry. There's absolutely no excuse for pissing on someone's door. I don't think you're taking this seriously at all.'

'I am, I am. I'm sorry. Look, I've said I'm sorry. I didn't even piss, you know. I'm guilty of trying to piss, definitely, but I didn't actually piss.'

On our way back down the hill, a call came out: there was a fight in Nando's between two groups of IC3 girls, mid-teens. We ran to the scene, finding the black and white floor tiles covered with broken glass, peri peri sauce and hair extensions. We separated the two groups and spoke to them while they caught their breath and clipped their hair back together.

'What were you fighting about?' we asked.

'I looked at her,' explained one girl, pointing across the restaurant, 'and she said *What are you looking at?* So I said *I can look wherever I want.*'

Walking back to the station at the end of the night, we passed the Tesco Express. The crime scene had been cleared away and there was nobody there. The only sign of the stabbing was a mop and bucket propped against the sliding doors.

The next morning in the Phoenix, I thought about the stabbing and the boy in the ambulance. I thought about the children at the school where I had taught and the tightness in my gut as I had scanned the photos on the wall of the Neighbourhood Policing Office. The headteacher had often talked about Brixton's gangs and the violence on local estates. That was the world some of our pupils' siblings were immersed in, she said, and the future we had to help them avoid.

One pupil in my first class was particularly at risk of entering gang life – the boy who karate-chopped another pupil in my first lesson and said he was King Kong. His older brothers were members of GAS and the police had raided his house a few months before I became his teacher, confiscating bags of cash. Sitting in the Phoenix, I googled his name. I had never imagined googling my pupils, but once the thought had crossed my mind I wanted to check he was all right – or at least that he had not made headlines. Aged sixteen, there was nothing about him in the news, but I spotted a link to his YouTube page and clicked on it. It was mainly a list of his favourite music videos, but among them was a video he had shared of a group of teenage boys standing in a stairwell on a Brixton estate. I put in my headphones and pressed play. To a Grime soundtrack, the boys in the stairwell did gun mimes, waved banknotes and shook empty bottles of rum. At the back of the group, his face now longer and sharper, was my old pupil. He did not do much in the video, just nodded along to the music. He looked slightly awkward. The video was only two minutes long and, when it finished, I looked around the Phoenix and felt uneasy.

I finished my bubble and squeak and thought about the video. I could not comprehend why the boys had decided to create it and share it so publicly.

I opened the video again and followed the links in the sidebar to similar videos posted by young people in my area. The most popular were rap videos uploaded by members of TN1 and GAS – the same young people I encountered on shifts. Generally shot in a single take, in a car park or a cul-de-sac, the videos were rough and homemade, so rough that I could not believe how many thousands of people had watched them. I clicked from one to the next, spotting different corners of Brixton and Tulse Hill, listening to the boys rap, sometimes with real skill and wit, about money, drugs, girls, knives, trainers. Given how evasive the boys were in our interactions with them on shifts, I found it surprising to see them presenting themselves so openly online, without even a bandana to disguise their identity.

Below the most popular videos, hundreds of people had left comments: an eccentric array of voices praising or condemning what they were watching, some interested in the music, some focused on gang politics, others concerned about the boys' well-being. Occasionally someone, probably a Lambeth police officer, would ask whether the boys in the clip had been involved in any criminal activity. 'Fed!' someone would reply, and the discussion would move on.

In the YouTube sidebar, the videos posted by Lambeth's teenagers mingled with CCTV footage of gang fights, and smartphone footage of the police. I found myself following those films around YouTube too. The shaky footage of searches and arrests provided a peculiar mirror for my experiences. As with the rap videos, hundreds of people had left comments, narrating and analyzing, defending or condemning the police.

Some of my colleagues wore body cameras, black boxes clipped to their stab vest, which filmed their interactions. We were constantly creating records about the public. I had not realized the public was creating a parallel database about us. I browsed videos of my colleagues, fleeting interactions that had been viewed by thousands of people. I wondered whether I was on YouTube and how I would ever find out.

I shut my laptop, suddenly exhausted, and caught the bus home. I tried to read a book but my head was full of images of police and teens. I closed my eyes and, without intending to, fell asleep until the evening.

In the van one night, I spotted a blue plaque near the Myatt's Fields Estate in Brixton. The plaque reads:

> Cherry Dorothy Groce, 1948–2011, innocently shot in this house by police which sparked the 1985 Brixton uprising. A heroine to her children, family and community with her spiritual strength, motivation, optimism and love. Her legacy lives on.

Six officers raided Cherry Groce's home on 29 September 1985, searching for her son Michael, and one of them shot her. At an inquest in 2014, Douglas Lovelock said that he and his colleagues believed the house to be a squat and were not expecting to find a family inside. 'We had already unholstered our revolvers and I went in a crouch position and almost immediately there was this figure upon me,' Lovelock said. 'My finger must have been pulling back on that trigger [. . .] I saw the flash and the next thing is Mrs Groce is on the ground. I dropped down to her eyes thinking *I hope to Christ it is shock and I have missed*.'

The bullet hit Cherry Groce in the chest, passing through her lung and her spine, and paralysing her from the waist down. Her eleven-year-old son Lee was asleep in his mother's bed at the time of the raid. 'I remember screaming: "What have you done to my mum?"' wrote Lee. 'I heard my mum saying: "I can't move my legs, I can't breathe, I think I'm going to die."'

Word spread that police had shot an innocent woman in her home. Two days of rioting ensued, more confused and anarchic than the uprising of 1981. Local businesses were ransacked. Fifty-five cars were burned and stacked on their sides as barricades. A press photographer, David Hodge, died after he was attacked by looters outside a jewellery shop.

After being shot in her home, Cherry Groce spent over a year in hospital and the rest of her life in a wheelchair, continuing to look after her family.

Lambeth Council unveiled the plaque on Cherry Groce's home in 2012. To ensure that his mother's story continues to be told, her younger son Lee set up a foundation which campaigned and fundraised for a permanent memorial in the centre of Brixton.

Memorials matter: plaques, statues, murals, gardens, sculptures, street names. They animate the city and bolster our collective memory. They enable an ongoing dialogue between the present and the past. Even when we do not look straight at them, they provide a subliminal reminder of the lives that shaped our lives, of tragedies we must never forget, sacrifices made on our behalf, generosity we should emulate, and mistakes we must never make again.

'Collective memory' sounds warm and organic: something that emerges, not something that is constructed. The reverse is true, of course. Deliberate decisions are made about which plaques to put up, which statues to pay for, which names to give to our streets and parks. And the crux of each decision is that *this* story matters, *this* name should endure. As soon as a decision is made, its validity becomes self-reinforcing. There is a memorial, so we should remember.

I was surprised, on my first visits to Brixton, that twentieth-century figures like Marcus Garvey and Bob Marley had already made it onto the street signs. Over time I discovered many more. Max Roach Park is near Angell Town, next to a housing development called Sisulu Place. Angela Carter Close is just behind the police station. There is a Mahatma Gandhi Industrial Estate in Herne Hill. When a clutch of new cul-de-sacs was built along Shakespeare Road, they were all named after writers, and Brixton now also contains Alice Walker Close, Derek Walcott Close, Langston Hughes Close, Walt Whitman Close, Louise Bennett Close, Pablo Neruda Close and James Joyce Walk.

'[T]here is no such thing as collective memory,' wrote Susan Sontag. 'But there is collective instruction.' For Sontag, our collective memories are simply the stories we hand on, which shape the way we think about ourselves, other people and the places we live. After discovering the 'Do You Remember Olive Morris?' project, I became increasingly interested in local campaigns to challenge or fill gaps in our existing narrative: the Cherry Groce Foundation; the campaign for a memorial to Jean Charles de Menezes; the Nubian Jak Community Trust, which erects plaques across the UK, celebrating significant figures in Black history. Living in Lambeth, I have seen how fraught the battle for a place in our collective memory can become, especially when individuals or events highlight historical violence or injustice. Those determined to remember can find themselves in conflict with those desperate to forget.

It was only after the 2014 inquest that the Met finally accepted they were at fault for the shooting of Cherry Groce and apologized, acknowledging that 'the person who most deserved to hear the apology is no longer here'. The Met's admission came after years of campaigning by Cherry Groce's family. Without those efforts, there would have been no inquest and the facts of her story would have remained inconclusive and too little known.

Over time, new plaques, street names and statues fade into the background of city life, but they never become inert. Even when the details fade and the first-hand witnesses are gone, memorials act as portals to buried histories. The long-fought campaigns are worth it.

There is now a memorial pagoda for Cherry Groce in Windrush Square. People meet there for lunch, run there for shelter when it rains. Her name and story are in the air.

Twenty-four of us were sent to patrol Clapham High Street, walking in twelve pairs, passing the other officers over and over again.

Walking up and down a single street, repeatedly tracing the same line, is unnatural. It smacks of the caged animal. After an hour, I found myself switching off, bored and irritated, then too tired even to feel bored.

We spotted an IC1 male, early thirties, sitting cross-legged inside a phone box, reading a thick paperback. We knocked on the door. 'Come in!' he shouted. As we opened it, he pulled a court summons from his pocket and handed it to us.

'I'm not gonna lie,' he said. 'I've had some problems with drugs, I'm not gonna lie.'

'Why are you sitting in this phone box?' we asked.

'I'm just waiting for my girlfriend to come down from her flat,' he said. 'Just reading, waiting.'

'Good book?' we asked.

He flipped it over and looked at the cover. It was a novel by Rosamunde Pilcher. 'It is, actually,' he said. 'Very good one.'

We kept walking and things kept not happening. There were too many of us. We were too effective. There was not enough crime to go round. It did not feel like time was passing slowly. It felt like time had stalled.

My partner and I left the High Street and wandered Clapham's backstreets, scanning the houses as we passed them. The grids of lit windows played like tiny TVs. We watched couples, families and friends cooking, eating, talking, laughing and watching televisions of their own. We glanced in at hundreds of homes, bright swatches of city interior, shades of yellow, white and blue, hundreds of private worlds, all more or less the same, yet all slightly different.

Turning a corner, we saw a white van with its back doors open. It was the hot-dog vendor arriving for the evening, and a younger IC2 male who, from the way he was talking to the vendor, appeared to be his boss. They were lowering his cart onto the pavement and preparing to load it with sausages, ketchup and rolls. They stopped suddenly when they saw us, eyes wide and mouths open, like children caught with the biscuit tin.

We told them to put the cart in the van and go home. Without saying a word, they did as we asked, although we knew that they would drive to Brixton or Vauxhall and set up there instead.

They did not know it but we had done them a favour. The hot-dog vendor would not have shifted a sausage with twenty-four bored officers on patrol.

We walked back to the High Street and came out next to Barclays Bank. A homeless IC1 male, sixties, had passed out below one of the cashpoints, surrounded by empty Heineken cans. We crouched down next to the man, cradling his head, checking his breathing and pulse. He was thin, with a lined face and a long white beard, wearing biker boots, jeans and a faded leather jacket.

'You're racist, you know that?' said a voice. We looked up and saw an intoxicated IC3 male, fifties, standing over us. 'Racist! The lot of you!' The man walked away and an IC3 male in his twenties walked over to us. 'Don't listen to him,' he said. 'He's an idiot. Honestly, it's times like this that make me ashamed to be Black.'

Although some officers stumbled upon fights and thefts and made arrests, my partner and I had no such luck and just kept walking, listening to the calls coming out of the radio, wishing we were somewhere else.

The shift finished at just after four and I changed in the station basement, glad to remove my boots and walk back outside in trainers. A few early birds were singing as I leant on the bus stop. It was 4.44 and the countdown on the departure board said ten minutes. As a bell tolled five, the bus had not arrived and dew had settled on my hair.

I woke mid-morning. It was raining heavily. I stood outside in our porch, contemplating whether to go to the Phoenix or to type my notes at home. I looked left at New Park Road. A pair of IC3 teens jogged past in raincoats. I looked right at the roofs cascading down the hill, the prison chimneys gothic in the rain.

The hours walking back and forth along the High Street had been punishing. I had experienced a sense of interminability I had not felt since childhood: sitting through long sermons, going on long journeys, lying in bed on light evenings.

When I was seven, my teacher kept me inside for our twenty-minute morning break time. From the classroom window I watched my friends walking to the school field, then sat there with nothing to do. The break seemed endless. I can still feel the strain of it. And now, whenever I feel as if life is passing too quickly, I look back and marvel at the extent of those twenty minutes.

As for the previous night's shift, it was curious; it had felt endless at the time, but already, five hours later, my memories of it felt slim, as though it had passed in a flash. It was as if my mind had compacted the memories to avoid me having to relive them, dulling them as it dulls the memory of pain. Or perhaps the monotony of those hours, the similarity of one minute to another, meant that the memories packed down flat and occupied less space.

I decided to go to the Phoenix and pulled on boots and a waterproof. From the top deck of the bus, I watched crows scavenge in the gutters, dodging the traffic on Brixton Hill. On a rational level I knew that policing's empty moments were as valid as the busy ones – but after an evening mindlessly walking the same half-mile of pavement, I struggled to believe that it had been a good use of time.

The Met's founding principles state that 'the test of police efficiency is the absence of crime and disorder, and not the visible evidence of police action in dealing with them'. Or as a regular I patrolled with put it: 'Success is often quite a boring day really.' I understood what she meant, but it felt dissatisfying. There must be better solutions to our boredom than walking around looking for trouble. There must be ways for success to feel less like punishment.

After six months as a Special Constable, I had to top up my Officer Safety and First-Aid training. I booked onto a course in Kennington, taking a day off work and travelling to the police gym opposite the Jamyang Buddhist Centre. It was a fine morning. The multi-coloured prayer flags outside Jamyang made the street look festive and made me feel as if I were arriving at a celebration, not a day of fighting and bandaging colleagues in a windowless sports hall. I pressed the buzzer and went inside. The gym's breezeblock walls were lined with rubber mannequins – frowning, muscular, topless males. Some had scars drawn on their faces in biro and a couple were wearing woollen beanies. We lined up and prepared to attack them.

An instructor blew a whistle and we did circuits of the gym, battering one dummy after another: hitting one in the thigh with the butts of our batons, pounding the arms of the next with our batons extended, chopping another in the neck with the side of our hand.

We lined up opposite a partner to work on restraints: thumb locks, wrist locks, elbow locks, shoulder locks.

'Grab the hand with a butterfly grip . . . Twist the arm back . . . Step into them . . . Clasp the shoulder . . . Spin your feet forward . . . Roll them down.'

There is an art to these positions. During the initial training at the Crime Academy I was so bewildered by the techniques that I ordered a copy of *Arm-Locks for All Styles*, an illustrated handbook for anyone looking 'to expand, enhance and develop their knowledge of arm-locks'. When I realized, out on shifts, that most officers just grab a limb and hold tight, my anxiety subsided and I left the book unopened in my sock drawer.

We handcuffed one another for a while – rear stack, front stack, back-to-back – then took turns attacking each other with a black rubber knife, slashing and stabbing, underarm, overarm, while our partners defended themselves. It was a simulation, but the attacks were strong and we were soon out of breath. The instructors told us to lie down and protect ourselves on the ground. Our attackers leapt on us and we tried to throw them off and pin the arm holding the knife. Lying on my back, I glanced around the gym at the shouting, straining bodies. There was none of the grace of martial arts practice. It looked like a roomful of people fighting for their lives.

We stopped for lunch and sat in the canteen in our white T-shirts and black jogging bottoms. A regular was talking about his experiences giving first aid – and about the times he had arrived too late to attempt it.

'I'm the small one,' he said, 'so I get put in through the window. That means I'm always first to the body.'

'What kinds of things have you found?' someone asked.

'I once found an old woman who'd died in the bath,' he said. 'Of course, by the time I arrived, she'd been in there so long she'd turned to minestrone. Then there was this time a couple reported water dripping through their light socket . . . Turned out it was the person upstairs.'

An instructor called us into a classroom for a session on how to deal with a stabbing. There were limbless rubber mannequins propped around the walls and we positioned ourselves on the floor next to them. 'The average number of wounds inflicted on a person during a stabbing is seven,' he said, 'and sometimes the person who's been stabbed won't know about all of them. It's your job to check.' We rolled on gloves and patted down our mannequins, then we bandaged their heads, chests and abdomens.

While we worked, the instructor regaled us with anecdotes from his years on the beat. 'I was on patrol with a female officer – and before you ask – yes, I have seen her naked. We were playing strip poker and she had some very bad luck . . . Another time, we were chasing a violent male. This was back when female officers wore skirts, and when my partner apprehended the male, she toppled backwards and we saw *everything* . . .'

I was treating a sucking chest wound on my mannequin's torso. I held the dressing in place and looked around the room. I was not sure how the instructor's banter was going down. We were a diverse mix of gender, age, ethnicity. I spotted a few smiles. Other faces were inscrutable. I wondered what gave him the confidence to share these anecdotes with a group of officers he had never met. Had they just popped into his mind, or was this the patter he always used while teaching first aid? His upbeat delivery implied that we could not possibly object.

We moved back to the gym to practise CPR, kneeling over a mannequin with our arms locked straight, sending our body weight through its taut rubber chest. Another instructor put on some music to ensure we were pumping at the optimal speed. 'We used to play "Nelly the Elephant",' she said, 'but research has shown that that was slightly slow.' She played 'Stayin' Alive' instead and we did synchronized CPR, pausing after every thirty compressions to give two rescue breaths. 'Big Friday-night kiss mouth!' the instructor shouted. 'Don't be shy!' We emptied our lungs into the tight-lipped faces, watching the rubber pectorals rise and fall. 'I don't know if you know this,' she added, 'but there are people out there who find rubber mannequins erotic.'

From the gym we moved back to the classroom to learn how to take care of prisoners, and to hear cautionary tales about times that officers had failed to do so. The instructor emphasized the danger of restraining prisoners face down on the floor. 'Positional asphyxia,' she said. 'When someone cannot get enough air because of the position you've put them in. You've heard about it before. I'm telling you about it again today.'

She showed us CCTV footage of a man having a seizure in a police cell, writhing face down on a mattress while custody officers watch him on a monitor. 'I think he thinks he's swimming,' we hear one of them say. After ten minutes the man stops moving. By the time someone goes to check on him, he has stopped breathing.

The instructor paused the video and looked at us. 'Remember,' she said, 'this happened on a normal day. One minute, nothing unusual was happening. Next thing you know, someone's dead.' We had heard about positional asphyxia in our initial training too, several times, with an insistence that came to seem penitential when I learned more of the Met's recent history.

There were no windows in the gymnasium and when I left, I was dazzled by the late afternoon sunshine. The prayer flags outside Jamyang were flapping in a light breeze. Before the building became a Buddhist centre, it had been a maximum-security courthouse where the Kray brothers were tried. The court-room is now Jamyang's shrine room, with a nine-foot Buddha where the judge used to sit.

I walked to the bus stop, rubbing my forearms. They were covered in bruises from the knife defence session and my wrists were raw from the cuffs. It was warm but I kept on my jacket to cover the marks.

Brixton's third riots, in 1995, were sparked by a death in custody similar to the situations the instructor had told us about that afternoon.

Wayne Douglas, a twenty-six-year-old Black man, was taken into custody after being arrested for burglary. Officers repeatedly restrained him on the ground, face down, his hands cuffed behind his back, and eventually he had a heart attack and died.

Douglas had been living in a hostel at the time, an unemployed postman, reeling from the stillbirth of his first child a fortnight earlier.

News of his death spread and a crowd gathered peacefully outside the police station. As the evening wore on, violence broke out: cars were burned and businesses were attacked. The recently opened Dogstar became a target for locals angered by the area's gentrification. Its windows were smashed, its interior set alight.

When I first moved to Brixton to teach, I noticed a plane tree in front of the police station covered in lanterns, flowers and laminated photos. It commemorated the deaths in custody of two other Black men, Ricky Bishop in 2001 and Sean Rigg in 2008, their deaths entirely avoidable, like those of hundreds of people who have died in police custody across the UK.

Bishop and Rigg died in the same building as Wayne Douglas, face down on the same hard floor, the memory of each appalling death not strong enough to stop the occurrence of the next.

'When we take somebody prisoner,' the instructor had said, 'we assume responsibility for their well-being.' It is our job, she reminded us, to monitor them, to ensure they do not hurt themselves, to seek help if they fall ill. They are in our care.

'There was this one time,' another Special said to me, 'a prisoner told me and another officer, *I've just swallowed a hundred Valium.* It was probably just a blag and the other officer said: *You didn't hear that.* And I said: *Er, I did.*'

'Tonight there are hundreds of people out there with knives,' the Sergeant told us at the briefing. 'We won't even scratch the surface of it. It's the same with firearms. Tonight, eight to ten guns will pass through Brixton. I want to see proactive policing. Stopping people. Hands in pockets. If someone's riding their bike on the pavement without lights, they are involved in criminal activity – it's as straightforward as that. Stop them, see what you find.'

We were going to begin the evening by raiding the Brixton Ladbrokes, where it was known that drugs were changing hands. 'Mid-level stuff,' the Sergeant said. 'We're not going to find more than a bit of cannabis and a few rocks of crack, but we want to keep the pressure on the dealers, let them know we're watching.' The Ladbrokes on Acre Lane is a long narrow room with split leather stools, gum-spotted carpet, a line of fruit machines, a wall of televisions, and a row of employees at the very back, seated behind thick safety glass. We pulled up at the same time as another van and twelve of us bundled out and ran into the betting shop before anyone could leave. It was getting dark and, as soon as we entered, a crowd of passers-by gathered at the brightly lit window, several filming on their phones.

'I'm not getting down. What's going on? Why are you searching me? You've got no right to search me.' We ran our fingers around waistbands and trainer tops, emptied the deep pockets of puffers. 'Is this right? I'm asking you is this right?' We covered the counters in lighters and car keys, tobacco, condoms and phones. 'Tell me my rights. What are my rights?'

'Spit it out! Spit it out!' an officer shouted. The shop fell silent. A tall IC3 male in his mid-thirties had stuffed something into his mouth. The four nearest officers grabbed him and forced him to the floor. Two officers pinned his arms, one held his ankles and another gripped his head, pressing it against the carpet to prevent him from swallowing. 'They're choking him!' someone else yelled. 'Can't you see they're hurting him?' It was a cold evening to be standing around, but the crowd was still outside and seeing the man on the floor they began shouting and hammering on the window. From the brightly lit interior, we could not make out their faces or tell how many people were out there. The other men we were searching began shouting too and some grabbed their phones to start filming. 'You're welcome to film, guys,' an officer announced, 'but your phone may be seized as evidence.'

The man on the floor had opened his mouth but would not lift his tongue. The officers kept him pinned where he was, his head upside down, his arms spread-eagled, his knees tucked under his chest. The hammering on the window intensified, an arrhythmic patter giving way to a steady, coordinated thump that shook the front of the shop. The officers were getting frustrated. 'Spit it out! We're not letting you up until you spit whatever's in your mouth onto the floor.' The man on the floor continued to resist.

'Whoa!' A yelp from the back of the shop cut through the

clamour for a moment. 'Whoa!' A skinny IC3 male walked unsteadily from the betting counter to the middle of the room, drawing everyone's eyes for a moment. He had an unlit roll-up hanging from his lips and a thick wad of cash in his right hand. 'Whoa! I got lots o' money!' he shouted, fanning himself with the notes and walking towards the door, seemingly oblivious of the police, the crowd, the noise.

I turned to the nineteen-year-old IC3 male I was searching. He was friendly and relaxed, our dynamic more like barber and client than officer and suspect. While I patted down his arms and chest, he talked to me about why young people get into drug dealing. 'I'm studying law,' he said, 'but the thing is, maximum I'm going to make is a hundred or a hundred and twenty K. It's not enough! And then the government come and take away half your money. If I want to buy a house for like two, two and a half million, and a car for two hundred and fifty grand, I can't do that with that kind of money. No wonder young people hustle, you know? How else are you supposed to get enough money to get the things you want? And hustling's not easy! People think hustlers just sit around, but they don't. These guys work hard!' I finished the search and passed the young man the things I had taken from his pockets. 'Cannabis isn't harmful at all, you know,' he added. 'The government should just legalize it and you wouldn't have all of this trouble.'

'About bloody time!' an officer shouted. The man on the floor had spat out a sachet of white powder, which the officer picked up with gloved hands and dropped into an evidence bag. The restraining officers lifted the man up. He looked shocked, eyes wide, shaking out his arms. Seeing this, the crowd outside stopped hitting the window but remained where they were while he was arrested and the rest of us wrote our 5090s or Cannabis

Warnings. The raid may have sent a message to the local drug dealers, but it had not been an effective public relations exercise. The crowd outside would go away, post YouTube videos broadcasting our excessive use of force, and talk about how once again we had overstepped the mark in central Brixton, a place where we ought to know better.

We said goodnight to the men we had searched and trooped out of Ladbrokes in one long line. The crowd outside, mainly IC3 men and women a decade or two older than most of the officers, eyed us silently. A boy, about the age of the children I had taught, waved and smiled.

I got home at 5 a.m. When I woke, I went to the Phoenix, recrossing the ground I had walked the night before, memory and vision clashing, memories competing with the sight of young Londoners relaxing with brunch and the weekend papers. Everywhere I looked, incidents flashed before my eyes.

I sat in the corner, watching the tea urn simmer, the coffee machine steam, margarine being pressed into a broad steel bowl, and waited for my bubble and squeak. I watched the manager reciting London's street names under his breath, eyes half closed. Some people coming in for breakfast, or preparing to pay, clearly thought he was praying and hesitated before approaching.

I was two hundred metres from the Acre Lane Ladbrokes, just on the other side of the High Street. Images flickered through my mind of the man restrained on the floor, the crowd rattling the window. The memory burst with colour and motion, like an over-exposed photo. I felt uncomfortable – because of the force, but also because we had been seen using it.

The use of force was perhaps the aspect of policing that felt most alien to me as a former teacher and carer. Although I had occasionally restrained children and adults to prevent them hurting others, I was used to environments where touch was either caring or celebratory. If I touched someone it was to give them first aid or a high five, to help them to shave or to hold their hands and dance with them.

To keep the law, police are allowed to do things that would be against the law for anyone else. Perhaps that is what Egon Bittner was thinking of when he described the police as 'the fire it takes to fight fire'.

Bittner wrote a lot about force. He came to believe that the licence to use coercive force was the heart of the police role, lending 'thematic unity to all police activity, in the same sense in which, let us say, the capacity to cure illness lends unity to everything that is ordinarily done in the field of medical practice'. I found this alarming: if doctors and nurses were defined by their ability to cure people, did it follow that we were defined by our ability to coerce them? It seemed simplistic, even grotesque, to suggest that this was what the role boiled down to. But, as I thought about it, it began to make sense. Bittner was not implying that the purpose of policing was to coerce people, but that this was what made us unique in society.

Use of force became the lens through which Bittner understood policing. In every other public-facing role, if someone refuses to do what you ask, there comes a point when you accept that you cannot make them. If a child refuses to sit down in your classroom, or an adult refuses to stop being abusive in a homeless shelter, there is little you can do there and then. Police work, by contrast, 'is defined by the feature that it may not be opposed in its course'. Whenever people need force to be applied, they call the police.

Bittner saw the police, first and foremost, as the conduit for force in societies that have attempted to abandon force as a tactic. For this reason, they provoke conflicting emotions: the police are a reminder 'that the nobler aspirations of mankind do not contain the means necessary to insure survival'. We may not like coercive force, but we have not worked out how to solve our problems without it.

Bittner believed force was effective only in the most crude, temporary way. The best we can hope is that officers approach the use of force the way that doctors approach surgery. Constables 'must acquire the attitude of physicians who take pride in employing all available means to avoid surgery, and who, when surgery is unavoidable, take pride in making the smallest possible incision'.

In my experience, when we used force, we did not channel the spirit of the surgeon. For one thing, we did not have their expertise. We had a day of training here or there on safe restraint, not years of study. For the most part, with tight faces and beating hearts, we did our best to be careful. I thought about the night before in Ladbrokes. The restraint looked bad, but it had been done by the book; it had stopped a man swallowing a bag of drugs. Without it, he might have choked, or the bag might have exploded in his stomach. He might have died. Nevertheless, seeing the man pinned to the floor triggered a host of unhappy associations, the names and stories of some of those who died in custody in Brixton Police Station: twenty-six-year-old Wayne Douglas who died in 1995; twenty-five-year-old Ricky Bishop who died in 2001, the circumstances still unclear, despite an inquest; and forty-year-old musician Sean Rigg, who died the month I moved to Brixton.

In August 2008, Sean Rigg was going through a mental health crisis and was arrested for behaving erratically in the street. A member of the public called the police to report a bare-chested man attempting to karate kick a passer-by. Detained on the Weir Estate, and restrained face down on the floor for eight minutes, Rigg was then driven to Brixton Police Station.

Dealing with people who are experiencing mental ill health is not unusual for police officers; a third of people taken into police custody have some kind of mental health problem. Nevertheless, when Sean Rigg arrived at custody he was left alone in the back of a custody van for ten minutes, and then carried into the station's custody cage and left face down on the concrete floor, unresponsive, his hands still cuffed behind his back. The Custody Sergeant believed that Rigg was faking unconsciousness and chose not to intervene. By the time a doctor examined him, he had had a heart attack.

Wayne Douglas, Ricky Bishop, Sean Rigg. There was something haunting about the parallels between these deaths, the same mistake again and again. It was as though we did not realize the life-and-death power we had been granted. It seemed, too often, as though we did not care.

A 2012 inquest into the death of Sean Rigg found that the officers involved had applied unnecessary and unsuitable restraint. In 2019, after a decade of pressure from the family, the five officers involved, one of whom had subsequently retrained as a priest, faced a gross misconduct hearing. All five were cleared. 'My question remains,' said Rigg's sister, Marcia, on hearing the verdict, 'if the police acted as they were required, why is my brother dead?'

I finished my bubble and squeak and closed my laptop. It was a beautiful day outside, warm sun and a gentle breeze. I paid and decided to walk to Brixton Police Station, which I had left only seven hours earlier, to visit the plane tree in the station forecourt.

It was strange to be outside the station in the daytime. In

the morning light, the building looked drab and undramatic. I walked over to the tree, with its tangle of lanterns and plastic flowers. Nestled among them were photographs of the men who had died a few metres away. At the moment when they most needed care, they had received the most extreme, indifferent control.

I stared at the faces on the tree and thought about the families who still held vigils there, while four lanes of traffic roared behind me, an unbroken chain of red double-deckers streaming into Brixton.

One of the best-known photos of Olive Morris, used as the cover of the 1979 *Squatters' Handbook*, shows her shinning up a drainpipe onto the roof of a terraced house during an attempt by police to evict her. This was 121 Railton Road, the first house where Olive Morris and Liz Obi squatted in the early 1970s.

There are few signs of it today, but in the 1970s and 1980s Railton Road was the heart of a vibrant squat scene and an epicentre of struggles against racism, homophobia and inequality. A remarkable array of writers, artists and outsiders lived and worked there, including the poet Linton Kwesi Johnson, the writer and activist CLR James and the artists Rotimi Fani-Kayode and Pearl Alcock. Darcus Howe lived just around the corner, on Mayall Road.

At the start of the 1970s, a motorway was slated to pass through central Brixton – the inner ring of a series of five orbital motorways. Lambeth's Development Services saw the arrival of the motorway as an opportunity to transform the town centre: broad expanses of Brixton would be flattened; fourteen fifty-storey tower blocks would be built, seven on each side of the motorway.

Waiting to be knocked down and rebuilt, Brixton became a transitional place, ripe for squatters and activists. Railton Road's squats housed the South London Gay Community Centre, the National Gay News Defence Committee, the Brixton Advice Centre, Icebreakers gay counselling service, an anarchist news service and two women's centres – all along the half-mile stretch between Brixton and Herne Hill.

Having occupied 121 Railton Road, Olive Morris and Liz Obi squatted number 65, enabling 121 to evolve into the Sabaar Bookshop, as well as a meeting space for gatherings of the British Black Panthers. When the Race Today Collective needed an office, Morris secured them a squat at number 165.

Olive Morris left her trace all over Brixton. Jon Newman from the Lambeth Archives describes how she took on 'an enormous burden of activism' in this period, involved with 'the Black Workers Movement, the Anti-Nazi League, the Brixton Ad-Hoc Committee Against Police Repression, Black People Against State Harassment, the Campaign against Overseas Students Fees, the Organisation for Sickle Cell Anaemia Research, Sussex African Students Association, the Socialist Union Internationalist, the "Scrap Sus" Campaign'. In the words of her old friend Diane Watt, 'Olive is the type of person that was everywhere.'

A motorway was never built through Brixton. But the idea of the motorway created a lacuna within which an alternative Brixton developed – with Olive Morris and Railton Road at its heart. In April 1981, Railton Road became the front line of the first Brixton uprising. The community response to police abuse was formidable – in part because Railton Road was already a powerful site of resistance

The Sabaar Bookshop later moved from Olive Morris's first squat on Railton Road into a unit on Coldharbour Lane. While there it became the home of the Black Cultural Archives, a collection documenting the experiences of the Afro-Caribbean community and the long, rich history of Black lives in Britain.

Archives, writes the cultural historian Saidiya Hartman, dictate 'what can be said about the past and the kinds of stories that can be told'. 'Archival silences' are the gaps, the spaces where under-documented lives should be, and they are rarely innocent omissions. The silence of the archive, Hartman writes, is also 'the violence of the archive'. The Black Cultural Archives grew out of the violent silence that followed the New Cross Fire, intended as a site where young people could see themselves and connect their existence to a known and valued past. For a quarter of a century the collection expanded until, in 2014, the Black Cultural Archives opened as a public museum in a handsome Georgian hall on Windrush Square.

With initiatives like the Remembering Olive Collective, the process of capturing significant, but overlooked, lives continues. When Brixton's local currency, the Brixton Pound, was launched, Olive Morris – shouting into her megaphone – was selected as the image on the one-pound note.

Spring gave way to summer and we were deployed to the South Bank for the evening, patrolling the most popular and iconic stretch of the Thames. After long nights in Brixton, Clapham and Vauxhall, it sounded like a glamorous assignment, giving directions to tourists, smiling for photos and chatting to the human statues.

When I got to the station, the rosy-cheeked Sergeant presented me with a new white shirt, the latest design. I removed it from its plastic bag and was about to take it to the changing room when he gestured at an ironing board in one of the offices. 'But no one will see the creases,' I said. He smiled and pointed at the ironing board again.

It was a fine evening and, for the first hour, we walked back and forth between the London Eye and the National Theatre. Tourists smiled, took photos and asked where things were.

A call came out: 'There's a woman beating a man with a chain by the skate park on the South Bank.' We were moments away and ran to the scene.

When we got to the skate park, we found an IC1 male, fifties, curled on the concrete, rocking and moaning. His left hand was outstretched to shield his face, the right was cradling a can of beer against his chest. A woman, IC1, fifties, stood over him, swinging her dog lead high in the air before landing blow after blow on his back. A pit bull stood panting at her side.

The skateboarders had stopped and a group of tourists had gathered to watch. A couple of people, with tight faces and springy knees, were hesitating on the verge of action. Others were filming the scene. Among the skaters and smartphones, the scene looked ancient and out of place, like the whipping of a drunken sailor.

'Police! Cut it out now!' We charged through them all, shouting at the woman to stop, grabbing her arms and locking them behind her back.

'It's all right,' the man said, standing up slowly. 'Let her go. She's my girlfriend.' Another pair of officers arrived and we took the man to one side to check he was OK and take a report. He shook out his arms, massaged his temples, and told us he did not want to press charges.

'You've just been badly assaulted,' we said.

'It's OK,' he said, 'just leave us alone.'

We took down their details and ran name checks. When the checks came back clear, we let the couple go. The woman clipped the lead onto the dog's collar and put an arm around the man's shoulders. The man put his arm around her waist and the three of them walked away along the river, a blissful silhouette.

I thought about the bystanders at the whipping who looked ready to act, who would surely have intervened if we had not appeared so promptly. Seeing them reminded me of times I had found myself on the edge of violent situations, wondering what to do.

One evening, in the town where I grew up, I came out of

a shopping centre and saw two men fighting outside a bar, one pinning the other against a wall, trying to land a punch. There were people with drinks nearby, clearly uncomfortable. Without thinking I shouted: 'Oi! People are watching!'

At those words, the men stopped fighting. They turned their heads, stared at me in silence, then drifted apart. They looked dazed, like subjects who have been woken by a hypnotist.

Afterwards, I wondered why those were the words that had come to me. 'People are watching!' Not 'Stop it now!' Not 'What do you think you're doing?' Not even 'I'm calling the police.' The message I most urgently wanted to convey was that they had an audience. As the men looked around at us, it was clear that this message was the right one, appealing not to reason or morals, but to the fact that we could see them.

The gaze of others is one of the most powerful forms of policing there is – which is why those who seem unaffected by it attain a kind of power and are often considered 'off their heads' or 'out of their minds' by people around them: like the woman whipping her husband, oblivious to the crowds.

Further along the South Bank we encountered an IC1 male, fifties, sobbing and shouting: 'Tie me to the bed! Just rape me will you . . . Raaaape meeee!' It was not clear whether he was appealing to one imagined listener, or to the hundreds of tourists streaming past. Everyone acted as though he was not there. The strangeness of his howls, and the completeness of his solitude in such a busy patch of London, made him look as much like a performance artist as the human statues who surrounded him.

The crowds knew what to do about the woman whipping her boyfriend – even if they were nervous about doing it. Nobody seemed to know what to do about the howling man.

–

A call came out: a violent male was being restrained by bouncers outside The Thirsty Bear, a couple of streets away, after starting a fight with another customer. When we arrived the man, IC1, mid-twenties, was being held on his back on the pavement, his legs and torso pinned by the bouncers' knees, his arms by their hands.

We knelt down and lifted him up. As we did, he gasped for breath, his chest heaving, his eyes wide, as though we had just fished him from the bottom of a swimming pool.

'What's your name, mate?' The man told us and we were part way through running a name check when he admitted it was fake. 'I'm just shittin' yer,' he said. 'I'm just shittin' yer.'

He gave us another name. While we were checking it, he admitted that that was fake too. 'It's all right,' he said. 'I'm just shittin' yer, it's all right.'

This kind of thing is not uncommon – we were told in training that Billy Nomates and Fuckyou Cunts both have entries on the Police National Computer. We asked the man to show us some ID.

'Conor, the man you assaulted says if you'll give him twenty pounds for the ripped shirt he'll leave it at that and won't press charges.'

'Twenty fuckin' quid! Are you taking the piss? Twenty fuckin' quid! Right, goodnight gents, I'm off.'

'You aren't free to leave, Conor.'

'Right you are, gents. Goodnight, I'm off.'

We took out a pair of cuffs and Conor agreed to pay for the shirt.

—

When the bars closed and the tourists drifted away we returned to the van. I felt invigorated by the wide-open space of the Thames, the big sky above it, the breeze along its banks. Driving back to the station, I felt like I was returning inland, to noise and normality, small skies and tight streets.

While we paused at a red light in Stockwell, an IC1 female, late thirties, knocked on the window. Her name was Tiffany and she was heavily intoxicated.

Tiffany had got off a bus believing she was in Stratford, where she was planning to catch a train. When she realised that she was not in Stratford, not even close, she had gone to a cashpoint to get money for a taxi. While standing there, someone had taken both her card and her cash. Now she had no money, no way of getting money, and she was not sure how she was going to get home.

Tiffany slumped on the lip of the open window and began to sob, massaging her cheeks with her fingers. She lived a long way away, at the very top of the Northern Line. It seemed unlikely she would make it home safely without assistance, so the Sergeant opened the side door and invited her into the van.

We drove through Kennington, across Vauxhall Bridge, around the side of Buckingham Palace, along Park Lane and past Marble Arch. Leaving Lambeth far behind, it felt like we were absconding, escaping our responsibility for the domestics and the stabbings, navigating streets that were someone else's problem.

We were dedicating a lot of time and resources to helping one woman get home. Was that appropriate? How many other drunks in London would benefit from a lift? But Tiffany was the drunk we had bumped into; she had been robbed and, in the absence of anyone else, we had taken responsibility for her.

It made me think of something Egon Bittner wrote, about the positive things police do whose effects are invisible. 'The drunk whom the patrolman escorts home, knowing who he is and where he lives, will be neither the victim nor the perpetrator of an assault. How should one measure credit for the prevention of relatively rare and unforeseeable contingencies?'

We helped Tiffany phone her bank and freeze her debit card. As we drove to the far north of London she told us about her life and her work as a postwoman, walking as many miles in a shift as we did.

After an hour, we pulled up to a suburban terrace. Tiffany climbed down and tottered along her front path. She unlocked her front door, turning to wave and smile before closing it behind her. Our driver swung the van round and began the long ride south.

I could not square my reactions: on the one hand, it seemed a phenomenal waste of our time to spend two hours driving one drunk person home. On the other, those two hours felt more straightforwardly worthwhile than so much else we often did.

I was surprised by the regulars' willingness to do it. No one would have known if we had just left Tiffany to find her own way. Perhaps it was because this was a problem we could solve, its complexity calibrated to our capacity. We could feel useful, we could be kind. It was all, for that moment, very simple.

After eight months with the police, I signed up to visit the mortuary at a coroner's court. It was an optional extra, a chance to learn how bodies react to death and how we react to dead bodies. Just as surgeons need to become accustomed to sights that might frighten or disgust others, police officers need to train their reactions to extreme situations.

In our initial training, we were shown videos of officers dealing with house fires, terrorist attempts, drowning children, and through them given a foretaste of the panic we might feel. We were shown photographs of children who had been physically abused: the shape of an iron burnt onto a leg, the blank stare of a head injury victim. But one situation it is challenging to prepare for in training is a sudden death. For this reason, the mortuary visits were scheduled.

A dozen of us met beforehand at a greasy spoon, ordering big breakfasts. Talking and laughing over coffee and rolls, there was the atmosphere of a school trip. A colleague described a previous mortuary visit where he was shown the body of an elderly woman who had choked on her dinner and died.

'Just think,' he said to the mortuary technician, 'you live your whole life and then you choke on a piece of chicken.'

'Something's got to kill you,' the technician replied.

—

The coroner's court was a brown-brick building surrounded by shops and cafes. Nothing about the exterior hinted at the ninety-eight refrigerated alcoves within. It was a perfectly underwhelming municipal structure which happened to contain the bodies of local people who had died suddenly, violently or unexpectedly and required further investigation.

We filed inside and put on blue overshoes and transparent green aprons. A jovial mortuary technician greeted us and gave a quick overview of the day's inventory. Then he ushered us into a long room and gestured to a grid of square metal doors along one wall. 'Most of the refrigerators are set at four to five degrees, normal fridge temperature,' he said. 'These ones here are reserved for infectious bodies, and these ones over here are set much colder, minus twenty degrees, to preserve bodies involved in crime. Sometimes we have to hold onto those ones for weeks. Let's have a look, shall we?' The technician began opening one door after another, pulling out the long sliding shelves, unzipping the body bags, telling us the story of how each person had died and pointing out the changes to the bodies since their death.

A fifty-year-old IC1 male had had a heart attack. A brown bruise on his chest marked where CPR had been attempted. A seventeen-year-old IC1 female, a foreign exchange student, had cut her wrists. Brown curls were matted around her narrow face, her arms and hands twisted, frozen in a position of pain. Her skin was creamy white and perfectly smooth, uncannily like polished marble. 'She arrived in last night,' the technician said. 'We still haven't managed to get through to her family.' An IC2 male, forties, was a triple-murderer who had slit his throat in prison using a glass shard from a fire alarm cover. 'He was on suicide watch. He'd been trying to kill himself by headbutting his cell door.' A silver-haired IC1 female, seventies, had carried a dining chair onto her balcony, climbed onto it, then jumped over the rail. She had been in the mortuary a long time because they could not identify any family or friends. 'Alone in the world,' the technician said. An IC1 female in her sixties had died in her flat and had not been found for several weeks. In the intervening period, she had been eaten by her starving dog and her face was missing its lower jaw. Her body looked ancient, as though it had been preserved in a peat bog centuries ago. An IC3 male, seventies, had died four months earlier and was only discovered when a passer-by smelt something and saw flies at the windows. His body was shrivelled and black, like a fruit forgotten at the bottom of a bag.

In her film *Dreams of a Life*, Carol Morley tells the story of a woman who died alone and unnoticed in a flat above the Wood Green Shopping Centre. Joyce Carol Vincent was thirty-eight when she died in December 2003. She was not discovered until bailiffs kicked down her door in January 2006. They were there to collect unpaid rent and found the remains of Vincent's body on the sofa in front of the television, which was still on. This kind of death is reasonably common in London, although people tend to be found within weeks rather than years. The isolation can be so complete that certain people cease to be connected to anyone.


The technician closed the doors and invited us to watch a post-mortem. 'There's no shame in feeling faint or uncomfortable,' he assured us. 'You're not made to watch this kind of thing . . . If you need to leave, just walk out – the toilets are over here.

If you do faint, try to get up quickly – our team do a stocktake every half-hour.'

We crammed into a small tiled room, a windowless cube with a low ceiling, a stainless-steel worktop along one wall and a stainless-steel table at its centre where the body of an ICı male, late twenties, was lying, his head propped on a block, a square of white gauze over his loins. His partner's name was tattooed on his neck, his son's name and date of birth were tattooed over his heart. 'Look at it like it's a mannequin that hasn't been dressed,' the technician said. 'We think he took a deliberate drug overdose last night. The suicide notes are in a bag on the counter behind you.' There were twelve of us standing in a ring around the table while the technician prepared his instruments. The room was modern and clean, with its strip lights and brushed steel, but the atmosphere was from another time, as though we were a crowd attending a public dissection. The aim of this dissection was to prepare the body for a pathologist, who would be coming later that morning. And so, for ninety minutes, we watched the young addict being split into his constituent parts, ready for inspection.

Perhaps the most shocking moment in a post-mortem is the initial incision, the slice from throat to abdomen, the sense of a wholeness violated as the two sides of the chest pull away from each other, revealing the layer of fat between the skin and the muscle, spongy and yellow, like the insulating foam between the inner and outer walls of modern houses. Once the body is open there is no going back.

The work of a mortuary technician requires a remarkable combination of brute force and delicacy. There is no genteel way to cut through a ribcage or saw open a skull, but great care is required to separate the organs and to bring them, pristine, out of the body. The technician's contact with the body reflects this and looks, by turns, violent and tender. The technician's language expressed a similar contradiction. There was a constant negotiation between respect for the deceased and the irreverence required to gain distance from the task at hand. 'Any of you like macaroni?' the technician said, pointing at some tubes. 'Talk about dying for a pee,' he said, lifting up a sagging bladder. 'You won't get a closer shave than that,' as he peeled back the skin from the forehead. Throughout the dissection he cracked jokes about the things he was showing us and recounted his favourite anecdotes: 'Nobody could find his car keys. I found them wrapped around the large intestine . . . One person I opened up had 147 bags of drugs in their stomach . . . I found a cup handle inside one person. I mean, how do you swallow that?'

The technician had been working in the mortuary for over twenty-five years. 'Whenever someone new starts working here,' he said, 'one of us will arrive early and sit one of the bodies upright to surprise them. Sometimes when a body comes in there's air still trapped in the lungs – it makes a sort of groaning noise when it comes out. Frightens the life out of you first time you hear it.'

Prior to the visit, I had not realized that the dead human body has a specific smell, not rotten or meaty, but dry, dark, almost gamey. We were invited into a room where seven bodies had been prepared for the pathologist, their chests and heads hollow, brains and entrails in tubs by their feet. The smell made it hard to enter, not just because it was unpleasant, but because our bodies seemed to resist it, tugging us in the opposite direction. It was not so much revolting as repellent and it took us several attempts to get inside and stay inside. 'That smell will stay with you for three days now,' the technician said as we removed our overshoes and prepared to leave. 'It lingers in the hair follicles in your nose.' And it did, although I wondered whether his remark was a tease and I was just imagining things. The smell surprised me several times in the coming days, while I was answering emails, standing at a cashpoint, chopping salad, lying down to sleep.

5

## YouTube: *The Murder of Zac Olumegbon – CCTV*

167,149 views

### George Springfield

LOL THIS MAN ARE EDIATS THEY GOT SCOPED BY
CCTV AS SOON AS THEY LEFT THEYR YARDS
JOKERS

#### Professional Bob

Lol, try going anywhere in London and not get seen
by atleast one CCTV camera . . .

#### cee cee6

thats there getaway car, the driver got 12years

### GorgeouslyReal T.V.

Sucks to see him running for his life . . . so sad.

#### PsyQo

R.I.P Zac

**leonoflondon**

How can you hate someone you don't really know enough to kill them? Stupid.

**king davy**

why did they kill a little boy

**Zetsu**

zac was in TN1 gang they've killed him for a reason not saying it was right but he wasn't a innocent kid like everybody say he is

**Kieron Hyde**

Live by the knife then you die by the knife

**wayne foster**

I am a Londoner now in my 40's. I ran with a gang called the Tudor when I was young. Yes we protected our manor (In South West London) but we respected our Manor, old folk's & people on the Manor. We didn't carry blades or guns. We didn't need to. If someone from another Manor came onto ours & started a fight we fought back with our fist's & if they went down we stopped. No need to stab, no need to shoot, no need to take life. We also respected the old bill & in turn they respected us. Yes it was them & us but each knew where we stood. Time's have changed in London.

**Krilzz Menace**

looool pusyio

**Jumbbo222**

Krilzz Menace Bruv man can't even spell fam, shut it rudeboyy. Man up there got a point. maybe u should listen and learn a few things.

**Bog Wang**

wayne foster it's just the culture. Much nicer over here than many countries ofc

## SUNDAYSCHOOLTEACHER

I watched this last night; I cannot remember anything making me feel as sick in a long time. How can people so young be so COLD and RUTHLESS? What has happened to the human heart?

**MaryAnne Samir**

so sad. no one has the right to take some ones LIFE!! and cut short their time!! sick bastards if the people dont get them, karma will

**shane kambiri**

y u paigons hating on gas gang lil zak wernt a good yout fuk da h8er free maggy clicka mad h y sneaky n shak

**James**

i agree, free maggy free mad h free clicka free jj

I was posted to the Lambeth Gangs Taskforce for the night. I had wanted to go out with them since I began policing, but their shifts were popular and hard to get onto. The taskforce office is a large square room with headshots of known and suspected gang members taped to the wall, row upon row of young IC3 males. Beneath the headshots was a 'Wanted' poster for a smurf with an eye mask and a swag bag. 'There's this one young robber who wears blue all the time,' a taskforce officer explained. 'Looks just like a smurf.' Above one of the desks was a row of funny animal photos: a duck with a quiff, a squirrel riding a bike, a roadkill fox. 'One of the guys is interested in wildlife photography.'

Another taskforce officer was on the phone, describing the suspect in a fatal shooting the night before. 'Cut left side nose . . . Tattoo left calf: *Faith, hope and love* . . . Upper right incisor white gold . . .' Two TN1 members had gone to Angell Town, spotted a member of GAS and attacked him, unaware that twenty of his friends were just around the corner. The TN1 boys were badly beaten up and retreated to Tulse Hill. The following day, one of them went back with a gun.

'What do the taskforce do?' I asked, once the call had finished. 'We hunt,' an officer replied. 'We hunt criminals, arrest bad guys . . . Drugs, robberies, gangs. We don't do domestics, road traffic accidents, any of that stuff.' The Gangs Taskforce drive unmarked cars and hang around on estates in hoodies and jeans. They get closer than anyone to Lambeth's gangs, but they still seemed mystified by the young people involved.

'Why do they join?' I asked.

'Belonging? Protection? Money?' an officer replied. 'I've been doing this job for eight years and still, whenever I get into an interview room with these kids, I ask them why they get involved . . . But they can't explain it properly either. We arrested a thirteen-year-old recently and I asked him: *What are your aspirations?* He just shrugged, and I said: *It's to get to fourteen at the moment, isn't it?*'

Our first stop was the kitchen of an IC1 female, early twenties. Her iPhone had been snatched by someone on a bike and she only got a good look at the robber's hands. The best description she could offer was IC3 male, grey hoodie. With such limited information, the team were not optimistic. 'Your phone, worth three or four hundred pounds, will be sold for ten, maybe twenty pounds,' they explained. 'Then it'll go abroad where it's not locked and it'll be sold on. For the robber that stole it, the money they make will buy maybe one rock of crack.'

We left the young woman's kitchen and went hunting, touring popular corners, alleys and play areas, trying to flush the gangs from their hiding places. A boy on a BMX cycled up to our car and our driver rolled down the window.

'All right, Shakir?'

'Why you lot flooding the area tonight?'

'You hear about the shooting last night? The managers are shitting themselves about it.'

Shakir nodded.

'Do you know what it was about?' our driver asked. 'A girl? No, wait, people use knives when it's a girl.'

Shakir shook his head and cycled away.

Over the radio, we heard a CCTV operator say she had seen an IC3 male, mid-teens, standing on Brixton Water Lane with a knife. He had stashed it behind a wall and was chatting to some friends. We drove over in two unmarked cars, flicking on the blue lights just as we pulled up next to them. The group starburst immediately, each boy running in a different direction, but we got hold of the boy who had hidden the knife and recovered the blade from its hiding place. The lights on our car were still spinning as we searched him and the boy began to move in time with the pulse, rolling his head, waving his arms, flexing his hips. 'Yeah! Disco!' shouted an IC1 male walking past.

We cuffed the boy and waited for a van.

'You're looking thin, Phil,' said one taskforce officer to another.

'Maybe he's thin because he's only been eating my spunk for two weeks,' replied a third. 'Phil, are you not getting enough protein from my manhood?'

We drove to the Kebab Company, picked up pittas, and drove back to the station. We were mid-kebab when a firearms call came out: an anonymous caller had seen an IC3 female hand a gun to an IC3 male in red trousers before he entered Hootananny, on Effra Road. Without talking, or even looking at one another, we scrunched our pittas into their greaseproof paper and jogged to the car.

We were the first unit to reach Hootananny and an Inspector radioed to tell us to stay put and not rush into anything. We parked around the corner from the club, out of sight of the entrance, and went to check the phone box where the 999 call had been made. There was no one near the booth so we returned to the car and awaited further instructions while firearms units surrounded the building. Five minutes, ten minutes, fifteen minutes passed. The tension in the car dropped from intense to high to tolerable and then seeped away altogether. Finally, a CCTV operator radioed to say that they had looked at the footage from the last hour and could not see anybody entering the club in red trousers. 'All units stand down,' said the Inspector. 'We're not going to disrupt the club over an anonymous call.' She called the CCTV operator: 'Keep an eye on the entrance and let us know if anyone matching that description comes out.'

We were disappointed but not surprised. Anti-climaxes are a routine feature of police work. At first, I assumed that the quantity of non-events must frustrate regular officers, but this did not seem to be the case. Most officers exhibited a child-like optimism whenever a dramatic incident came out of the radio – and a child-like ability to move on if that prospect evaporated.

We drove into the Tulse Hill Estate, parked up and got out to wait for the officers who had arrested the teen with the blade earlier on. They had finished at custody and radioed to ask where we were.

'We're in the car park at the entrance to the Tulse Hill Estate.'

'Mate, your radio sounds muffled.'

'Sorry, mate, your mum's tits are muffling it. How's that? Any better?'

It was gone midnight and the estate seemed calm. A couple of officers smoked while we waited for something to happen. Someone handed around a packet of Percy Pigs. 'We look like a gang, hanging around like this,' another officer said. 'The biggest gang in London!' another replied.

'What would it take to sort out all the gang stuff?' I asked.

'A bomb,' someone replied. 'One here, one down in Angell Town, and one around Coldharbour Lane. That would sort it.'

A call came out and two of the officers, one male, one female, got back into their unmarked car. The driver turned on the engine, but instead of reversing out of the parking space he began pumping the accelerator with the handbrake on. The car bounced on its suspension, as though they were having sex inside, and everyone laughed.

Another robbery call came out, an IC1 female attacked on her way home in Clapham, and we drove to her address. 'This kind of thing's typical. Gang members pick off the weakest people,' our driver said. 'Drunks, women walking alone.' The front door was opened by a tearful woman in her twenties wearing black leggings and a leather jacket. 'It's so frustrating!' she said. 'I got a cab home, but I told him to leave me at the end of my street, and then, when I was walking to the door, someone pushed me really hard from behind. I didn't even hear any footsteps. I fell over and he grabbed my handbag and phone and ran off.' As the robber fled, she had shouted after him, begging him to drop her handbag, which was empty except for her UK residence card, appealing to his goodwill moments after he had attacked her. 'I screamed at him, screamed at him to drop my bag, I told him there was nothing valuable in it. Then I walked up the road to see if he'd dropped it, but he hadn't.' Our driver suggested she sit down and he knelt down next to her, asking if she needed a drink of water and whether she wanted us to clean her bloody knuckles. She was in shock and each time it seemed she had calmed down she would burst into sobs again. 'It's terrible,' he said. 'You should be able to walk home without this happening.' In the car afterwards his tone was the same. 'That's not right,' he said, shaking his head. 'It's not right.'

We wove around the adjacent streets in case we spotted the robber. A DV call came out of the radio, a woman beaten up by her husband. Nobody answered. 'I need somebody to take this,' the operator said. More silence, then a response unit called in to claim it.

There were female victims of violence we wanted to help, and others we preferred to ignore. The inconsistency was bewildering.

I thought about the sex joke in the car park, which somehow felt related to this picking and choosing: another instance of male officers defining the terms on which they would interact with women. A lone female officer, out with ten men, was expected to laugh at a gag at her expense. Which she had – perhaps up for it, perhaps used to it, perhaps used to putting up with it. It looked harmless, like friends messing about, but I struggled to imagine an equivalent moment in any other social profession. For teachers, social workers, carers and health professionals, swapping sexual banter while working would seem grossly inappropriate. Crossing a boundary stated by a colleague would be grounds for the most serious complaint. Saying 'She'd get fucked' would be career ending. What was it about policing that made this feel so everyday? We were doing related work, so why should our approach, our intentions, our standards be different?

'Do the kids in gangs grow out of it?' I asked.

'Maybe some do,' our driver replied. 'Some distance themselves from it gradually. But a lot just move up the ranks and off the streets.' He paused. 'Some of them make a clean break. There's one guy used to be a proper little shitbag. Now if he sees us he stops the car for a chat.'

We drove back to Brixton along quiet roads, most of the houses dark around us, lights still on in some upstairs windows. 'I arrested a fourteen-year-old yesterday,' he continued. 'Picked him up in Angell Town near where the shooting took place. Later, when I heard about the shooting, I said to him: *You know, there's been a shooting around Angell Town. If we hadn't arrested you, that could have been you.* He just looked at me and said: *So?*'

We came across a group of IC3 teenage boys and girls standing on a dark corner. We drove past them slowly, then immediately looped round and drove past them again, not stopping, just letting them know we were there. The second time, the boys walked right up to the car, leaning close enough to look in and grin. Their faces swam past the windows, dim and strangely distant, as though separated from us by thick aquarium glass. We drove away from them and, when we were almost out of sight, the boys began jumping up and down, waving their middle fingers.

'The parents'll tell you they can't stop their kids going out at night,' said our driver. 'Mind you, you see some of these kids' flats and you can see why they'd rather be out on the streets. I wouldn't let my cat live in some of those flats.'

We were driving through Tulse Hill and spotted a car that seemed to be trying to avoid us. We pulled it over and asked the driver, IC3 male, early twenties, to turn off the engine and step onto the pavement. 'All right, Elliott?' shouted one of the older taskforce officers. Elliott looked up and gave a shy half-smile, like a child meeting an uncle he does not see very often. 'Me and Elliott go back,' the officer explained. 'I used to chase him round Clapham when he was a teen robber.'

He walked over to Elliott. 'What you up to now?' he asked.

'Working,' said Elliott. 'And this.' He pointed through the window at a baby asleep in a car seat. The officer laughed and ushered the rest of us over. We clustered around and pressed our faces to the window, just able to make out the pursed mouth and closed eyes of Elliott's six-month-old son. The checks came back clear and we said goodnight. 'I hope I don't see you for another seven years,' Elliott said as we were leaving. 'Don't take that in a bad way obviously.'

I went for breakfast in the Phoenix, leant back in my chair and felt a wave of exhilaration wash over me. I felt as though I had returned from doing something illicit, the way I imagine an urban explorer might feel after a night of trespass. Then I felt guilty. I had got a high hunting teenagers.

My coffee arrived and I took my laptop from my rucksack. Perhaps policing *was* a kind of urban exploration, I thought. It offers the kind of boundary-crossing it is difficult to secure legally. Or perhaps my feelings were a natural response to the way we policed teenagers. Out with the taskforce, it had felt as if we were on a mission. It was risky. It was fun. It was us versus them.

I had been waiting to go out with the taskforce since I began policing. It was why I had signed up in the first place: to get closer to the challenges for young people in my area, to get a sense, however partial, of the world that might be awaiting some of my pupils.

Sitting with my coffee, I felt just as confused as before about Brixton's gangs. Perhaps what shocked me most was the shared bewilderment of the officers who interacted with these young people every day. They were uniquely positioned to address this issue – but beyond cleaning up after robberies and stabbings, they did not seem to have a plan for making things better – or even believe they could make much of a difference.

When we had encountered the big group of teenagers on a corner, and had done a slow drive past, what were we achieving beyond shoring up their group identity and adding some excitement to their evening? As the boys had stared through our windows, I had felt terribly vulnerable and, with a jolt, realized how frightened I was of these young people, even though I cared about them, even though I worked in education and was constantly talking to teachers about how to support their most at-risk pupils. My fear made me uncomfortable. I wished it were simply concern. Perhaps my emotional confusion, this cocktail of protective and self-protective urges, mirrored gang members' own internal contradictions: their vulnerability fuelling their aggression; their aggression masking their vulnerability. And perhaps the fear was justifiable. The damage was real. The toll of woundings and killings kept rising. In 2011, two members of ABM ran into Stockwell Food and Wine to hide from two assailants from a rival gang. Shots were fired – hitting a customer and the five-year-old niece of the shop's owners. The girl spent a year in hospital and was paralysed from the waist down. It was appalling.

According to Donald Winnicott, teenage 'aggressiveness is not something to be cured; it is something to be noted and allowed for'. Policing gangs, we dealt with its deadliest extremes. If adolescent behaviour becomes 'unmanageable', Winnicott continued, 'we jump aside, and the law takes over'. That was us. We were the law, but we did not seem equipped for this challenge. Our institution was not designed with children in mind, and yet every day we interacted with the most vulnerable young people at their most vulnerable moments.

I thought about the boy dancing during the search. It reminded me of the way children sometimes played to the crowd while they were being punished at school. I remembered doing it myself as a child, flashing a grin at the class while my maths teacher was telling me off, an act that enraged the teacher far more than my initial transgression. And I remembered punishing those acts of defiance as a teacher myself. The boy dancing almost seemed to be inviting us to discipline him, to react the way a teacher would. As it was, we did not care. It made no odds to us whether he danced or complained or ignored us completely.

Thinking about how differently I would have dealt with that behaviour as a teacher, I saw more clearly than ever that discipline is not a police officer's job. Teaching is perhaps seen as the milder profession, but it involves a far more serious engagement with misbehaviour. Both jobs involve reacting when people break rules, but police officers can, if they choose, deal with situations without feeling much responsibility for the outcome. If they fail to bring about a calm, positive resolution, they still have sufficient power to come out on top. If a situation spirals out of control, it may be their fault, but it is not their problem. They can restrain, search, arrest and move on. There is no equivalent for the teacher, whose success and satisfaction are intertwined with the success of their pupils.

Faced with challenging situations, teachers have to achieve calm and compliance without force. Doing this without bullying or scare tactics involves gravitas and skill: enabling pupils to back down without losing face; defusing or deferring stand-offs; gaining respect without disrespecting the children they work with. Teachers need genuine moral authority – the credibility to hold pupils to account, and to make that feel like an act of care, not control.

As a police officer, with my uniform and my baton, I did not need moral authority to get people to do as I asked. However, when I thought about the best police officers I had seen, they reminded me of the best teachers: warm, authoritative, holding people to high standards because they had their best interests at heart.

Egon Bittner noted the overlapping skills required in policing, teaching and a host of other occupations. 'Waiters, psychiatrists, cab drivers, and teachers know that the handling of uncooperativeness is a necessary part of their occupational skill,' he wrote, 'and it is not too much to expect the same of policemen.'

The licence to use force poses a significant threat to the development of a police officer's craft. It is always there to fall back on, and officers sometimes use it to punish people for their own ineffectiveness, venting their frustration that people will not do as they are told. But, as teachers know, discipline without care backfires. Trust erodes. Relationships break down. Everything gets harder.

The best teachers and the best police officers give people respect and agency while providing clear boundaries and consequences. They get to know people. They enable people to think differently, to act differently, to see themselves differently. Perhaps great policing, I thought, is not only similar to great teaching; it could itself be thought of as a form of teaching.

In our initial police training we were told about the importance of body language. Likewise as a new teacher, I attended a body-language workshop in Lambeth Town Hall. 'Watch out for where your feet are pointing,' the instructor told us. 'The direction of your feet gives away your intentions.' She got us all standing up and walked around critiquing our posture. 'Watch out for self-hurting,' she said, 'twisting the fingers and so forth. And self-comforting – touching the neck, hands, or face. Children are expert interpreters, and all these things give you away. But above all, think about what you're doing with your shoulders. Your shoulders are the most expressive part of your body.' I struggled to bring everything together in the body-language workshop. Just as I got my shoulders right, I realized my knees had sagged, or my hands had come together in a self-comforting clasp.

As a teacher and education researcher, I saw that what really makes a difference is not impeccable poise but trusting relationships. A certain skill in body language is useful in establishing credibility, but beyond that relationships are what count – not just for behaviour but for supporting young people to succeed in every way, for knowing them well enough to know what they need and notice when something is wrong, to be trusted enough for them to talk to you.

The taskforce encountered many of the same young people day in day out. I suspected that if I saw the officers in a less performative mode, one on one with a gang member, I would have seen the power of relationships there too. For all the bravado, they clearly wanted the best for the young people they worked with. They wanted to solve the problem of teenage gangs, even as it confused and eluded them.

—

I was keen to find out more about TN1 and GAS. I had encountered many of their members out on shifts, but my sense of the gangs' structures and stories remained vague. Looking online, I found Wikipedia pages, Reddit threads, whole websites dedicated to London's street gangs, charting their rise and fall like the dynasties of an ever-evolving empire. I was amazed at how thoroughly and publicly documented they were. I read blogs, BBC articles, *Guardian* features, *Evening Standard* profiles. But the more I read, the more inconsistencies I noticed. It was difficult to tell which details were fact-checked and hard-won, and which had been invented, intuited or cannibalized from elsewhere. The more I read, the less able I felt to differentiate between fact, rumour, supposition, myth.

One detail that recurred and was beyond dispute was that Sneakbo, one of the stars of the Grime music scene, had grown up on the Angell Town Estate and been involved with GAS. He had been in deep and come out the other side. That was clearly an achievement. 'I always say you never realize how deep you are until you're too deep,' said an ex-gang member quoted in a report I had read, 'because it is only when you start doing things to people that you start thinking *I do not want to do this any more* and you're too deep then.'

On YouTube, as well as his slick recent videos, there are lots of shaky recordings of Sneakbo rapping in and around Angell Town. 'Everything I went through was mainly in Brixton,' he said in an interview. 'I was just in Brixton. Clapham was far for me. Clapham is ten minutes to me now.' Asked about the young people in the gangs today, he said, 'they don't have a clue what they could be doing'. In 2018, Sneakbo released the album *Brixton*, a dramatization of the world of his youth.

A subsequent album was called 9 *Lives* because of a long-standing rumour that Sneakbo once went into the toilets in Brixton McDonald's and transformed himself into a black cat. He is frequently asked about it in interviews. 'No way, that's never happened in my whole life,' he told one interviewer. 'McDonald's would have had a video of it.' The rumour helped Sneakbo's burgeoning career. By the time he released music, he was already well known as the boy who turned into a cat.

I closed my eyes and saw faces and places from the night before. The exhilaration had gone. I felt flat and exhausted and even more confused.

Finishing my breakfast, I thought about an afternoon in Brixton years earlier, when I was still working as a teacher. I had taken a bus along Brixton Road and a group of IC3 teenage boys sitting at the back began to throw pieces of chewed gum at my head. I ignored them, hoping they would get bored, picking the gum out of my hair without turning around. I could feel the toothprints on each wad as I shook it from my fingers to the floor.

I did not know whether to tell them off like a teacher. I did not know whether to reason with the boys or to smile and make a joke of it. I did not know these boys and did not know how they would react. They threw more and more balls of wet gum at my head. The frustration in my gut – the mix of fear, irritation, and concern – was similar to the impotence I had felt policing gangs the night before.

The boys on the bus were trying to get a reaction. At the time, it felt as though the most powerful thing I could do was to ignore them. I got off the bus before they did and I did not look at them once.

But in retrospect, I could see that my decision not to react was also an attempt to absolve myself of any responsibility. Their behaviour was their problem, not mine. Instead of showing the boys that there was a community of firm, caring adults around them, people who would push back when they overshot a boundary, I showed them another adult who was afraid, or annoyed, or indifferent, an irritated man who would not even acknowledge their existence.

The question of how to work with young people caught in cycles of violence was on my mind when I went on a school visit for my education research job. In extreme circumstances, what is the relationship between care and control? Can control be a form of care if it prevents serious violence? And might certain forms of care remove the need for extreme control?

I was visiting a primary school that had descended into chaos eighteen months earlier and then been taken over by a chain of schools who had promised to turn it around. Before the takeover, the school was not just failing academically, it was violent and unsafe. Now, only one school year later, it had some of the highest test results in the area. The amount and speed of the change were almost impossible to believe.

The first thing I noticed when I entered the school was how quiet it was. 'SILENCE IS GOLDEN' said the signs on the corridor walls. I was shown into a classroom of immaculately behaved seven-year-olds, sitting with perfectly straight backs and their hands clasped identically on the desks in front of them. The children did not turn to look when I walked in. They sat silently, their eyes fixed on the teacher. Taking a perch at the back, I saw that their chairs had been silenced too: tennis balls, slit open like clown noses, had been attached to the bottom of every chair leg.

I walked around the classroom and stopped at the timetable by the door, my eyes drawn to the timings: 9.10–9.21 . . . 9.21–9.27 . . . 9.27–10.03. The precision set the tone for everything that followed: lessons where every moment was pre-planned and where the children were told exactly how to move, what to do and when to do it. Even when the children were invited to speak, they could only do so using the sentence structures tacked onto the wall. I did not see a child do or say anything spontaneous that morning – except one boy, seated alone at the back of the room, slumped with his head on one arm, shuffling in his seat, sighing and glancing around with a look of desperate pent-up boredom.

At lunchtime I went to the dining hall so that I could eat with the children. I had arrived before them, I thought, as I pushed open the door of the silent hall. But inside I was surprised to find, not empty benches, but two hundred children seated and eating in perfect silence, teachers stationed around the hall watching. I asked when I would have chance to talk to the students but was told that it would not be possible. The children had no break times and lunchtime was silent. If they were good they would be given five minutes of 'Talk Time' at the end of the day, but I would be gone by then.

My guide for the visit, who had been to the school before, told me to look at the children's feet. 'Look at them and tell me what you notice,' she said. I scanned the hall and spotted a peculiarly large number of undone laces trailing on the floor. 'Don't they know how to tie them?' I asked. 'It's not that,' she said. 'Think about it: they have no play time, they are punished in the classroom if they don't look at the teacher all the time, they are punished if they move their hands off their desks, they are punished in line if they don't keep their hands by their sides. They have literally no opportunity in the day to bend down and tie their shoelaces.'

The turnaround had succeeded by controlling everything, down to where children put their hands and when they could bend their knees. The new team had removed every opportunity for self-initiated speech or action, and in the process created the silence and space to impose a new set of expectations.

Can control be a form of care if it prevents harm and violence? It was extraordinarily impressive that an environment in which children were unsafe had been replaced, in the blink of an eye, by calm productive classrooms. It was a remarkable insight into what top-down command and ruthless consistency can achieve.

Still, I have never felt so conflicted by a visit to a school. I was upset to see small children silenced, their every word and movement policed. I thought about the simmering energy of the children I had taught – how keenly they needed to speed around the playground in break times, how much they needed the gaps between lessons when we would jump up and sing. I thought about how much they had to say: their imaginations working faster than their mouths, words tumbling out when they entered the classroom in the morning. How were the children at the turnaround school bottling that up and holding it in? How much does it cost a seven-year-old to submit to that kind of coercion?

Taming mayhem, the new team had made trade-offs and compromises at every turn. They had met one extreme with another, using coercion as a route to care. Now they knew that they needed to find a middle ground.

I wondered whether a focus on care in the first place might have removed the need for extreme control – treating the children as partners in the process of transforming the school. I knew this was easier said than done – I had stood at the helm of a chaotic classroom – but I asked myself if another approach was possible: focusing on the relationships with children, making school joyful and fun, showing young people you believe in them. Ultimately the message of silent corridors, no break times and detention for slouching is *We don't trust you.*

The children I had taught would play football in the playground every day with tennis balls, or sling them to one another, holding contests to see who could throw them the furthest.

I wondered whether the turnaround school had ordered sacks of tennis balls to have enough to put four on every chair, or whether they had decimated the school's existing supply, knowing they would not need them. I imagined the teachers sitting in a circle with Stanley knives, puncturing the hide of each ball and prising it open.

I had been policing for nine months when I stopped counting my shifts, and the things that happened on them began to merge in my memory. The nights in Brixton, Clapham and Vauxhall started to feel like one long night. The people we stopped, searched or helped were starting to meld. The specifics of individual situations were fading, and I realized that, without my notes, I would struggle to disentangle them. One thing I remembered with perfect clarity, however, was where things had happened, and whenever I passed places the details came flooding back. Rather than a place reminding me of something, it was as though I stumbled upon the memory itself, intact and immovable. Travelling around Lambeth, this made for an unsettling kind of double vision, with remembered scenes often more vivid than present experience. Sitting in my flat on New Park Road, everything blurred.

When I arrived for my next shift, the regulars were talking about a stabbing earlier that week, in an alley less than a minute away from the station – so close that several of them had sprinted straight to the scene to help. 'There was nothing anyone could do,' I heard someone say. 'Honestly, it was hideous.' The boy had received multiple serious wounds and they had not been able to save him. 'Do you know what it was about?' an officer asked. The others shrugged.

I was assigned to the station's front office for the night, while the other Specials walked out into a warm late summer evening. Brixton's actual front office was being refurbished, so a replacement had been set up outside in a static caravan. For reasons I could not fathom, the caravan windows had been mirrored, so that people could look in, but we could not see out. It was stuffy, the heat of the day trapped inside and the windows sealed shut. The caravan's radio was tuned to London Heart, playing 'Disco Inferno', 'Hot Stuff' and 'The Rhythm of the Night'.

There was a steady stream of visitors for the first five hours and we fielded concerns and requests of all kinds.

'I'm here to sign in – it's for my bail' . . . 'Our friend's run off. She's drunk' . . . 'I left my bag in the station – in one of the domestic violence interview rooms' . . . 'My friend's been arrested. Can I bring him some clothes, shower gel? What about prawn cocktail crisps?' . . . 'My ex-boyfriend and his family keep insulting me, grabbing me' . . . 'My iPhone's been stolen from my handbag' . . . 'Where can I get a minicab?' . . . 'Where does the 133 go from?'

After the pubs closed, the queues dwindled and I sat at a computer and looked at some CCTV stills of crimes being committed on buses. The pictures were regularly emailed to us – threats, assaults, harassment, thefts – in case we recognized the offender. The blurred bodies, paused mid-action, looked guilty, whether or not they were.

I wondered how many hours of CCTV footage were filmed on London's buses every day. Then I tried to guess the quantity created in the city overall. Millions of hours, most Londoners filmed by dozens of cameras daily. Under the Freedom of Information Act, if you are captured on CCTV, you have a right to request the footage. If you felt so inclined, you could watch a significant proportion of your life on film.

Most CCTV footage is never seen by anyone. Thousands of crimes must be caught on camera every day without anyone realizing, and incriminating evidence must be deleted every day, unseen. I wondered whether we would detect more crime trawling CCTV day and night than we did patrolling the streets.

It was 2 a.m. and I felt tired and cooped up in the caravan. I surfed the Met's intranet, clicking on a link to the Metropolitan Police Glossary: a gargantuan list of all our acronyms – over one and a half thousand of them, each bewilderingly similar to those around it. ABA, ABC, ABD . . . CSR, CSS, CST . . . It felt like staring at a very detailed paint chart, the gradations so subtle it is impossible to focus on any individual shade. FAW, FAWA, FAWAA . . . I closed the glossary, awed by its extent. Impressed, too, by how many acronyms I recognized after only nine months.

When I began policing, I was daunted by the number of linguistic codes and registers I had to absorb. As well as its technical jargon, the Met has its slang. Policing is 'the job', an arrested suspect is 'a body', blood is 'claret', criminals are 'slags', meal breaks are 'refs'. But just as a person learning a new language reaches a point when they no longer consciously translate what they are hearing, there was a moment in the first few months of policing when my mind integrated the acronyms, codes, conventions and slang, and they ceased to stand out.

Wear the uniform often enough, spend enough time steeped in the culture, and it starts to seep inwards. I found myself internalizing ways of thinking and seeing I had not intended to adopt. I had noticed that I was starting to think in terms of police identity codes, even off duty, using them to label people I would not previously have labelled: IC1, IC2, IC3. Perhaps it was because I had started observing streets, buses, parks with a police officer's eye, scouring them for signs of misbehaviour. Perhaps it was the language of policing overwriting my own. Either way, it was unsettling to be constantly defining people by their appearance, looking for what was generalizable rather than individual.

Police procedures are predicated on people making assumptions. We need rough descriptions that will allow us to find someone. Identities are shrunk to a presumed gender, age and ethnicity. But what did it do to us, this habit of attaching labels and working off assumptions? On the beat, we privileged first impressions to a degree that would be unthinkable in most occupations. Doing that dozens of times a day was bound to affect our outlook.

An IC1 male, thirties, in a white shirt and blue chinos, came in and staggered to the desk, steadying himself on the caravan walls. 'Is there a toilet?' he asked. 'I need to clean myself up.' I said no, we were in a caravan, and there was no public toilet. 'Look, mate,' he said. 'I've shat myself. I don't know where else to go.'

We were put on the beat in Kennington, not far from Brixton, Vauxhall or Clapham, but another little world unto itself.

Walking the beat, beating time, beating the bounds of a patch of North Lambeth. As we walked, I thought about what a strange term 'beat' is for walking the streets: a word that suggests rhythm, violence, exhaustion, competition, the pulsing of a heart. I was not sure what it had to do with police officers doing the rounds, walking miles in a confined area, miles that would have taken us from one side of London to the other if walked in a straight line.

Originally, a constable's beat would have been compact: an early Met pamphlet states that a constable should be able to 'see every part of his beat at least once in ten minutes or a quarter of an hour' and should 'possess such a knowledge of the inhabitants of each house, as will enable him to recognize their persons'. The only people who came anywhere near that now were the Neighbourhood Policing Teams – and they were an object of scorn, doing a job most officers would not touch: slow, dull, mired in dilemmas and disputes that would not go away.

The experience of a volunteer officer, encountering dozens of unknown people on each shift, could scarcely be further from the Met's early vision. I felt like a sightseer. I found the contrast with teaching stark too. As a teacher, I had focused on thirty children for a year. The thrill and frustration of policing was the constantly changing cast of characters. As a new Special, I found it difficult to keep track of the other officers, let alone members of the public.

We passed a funeral director's, a barber's, a pharmacist, a nail bar, and then a serious-sounding call came out of the radio. There had been a fight between fifteen IC3 teens at the centre of an estate just off Kennington Lane and one boy had been seriously stabbed. We radioed to say we were en route, as did several other units. It took us twenty minutes to walk to the scene and, by the time we arrived, the paramedics had been and gone and the victim had been taken to hospital. Two rival gangs had been fighting with metal poles, another officer told us. At some point, someone had pulled out a kitchen knife and stabbed the victim several times in the stomach. When the other boys saw what had happened, they ran, leaving the victim to be discovered by the estate's residents, who pressed a beach towel to his wounds and called an ambulance.

The scene had been cordoned off with plastic tape and, while we waited for the Scene of Crime Officers to arrive, some of us went door knocking, asking for witnesses. The neighbours sounded more frustrated than surprised, shaking their heads and saying that it was out of control. While some officers took witness statements, the rest of us were sent to man the cordon that had been stretched around the estate's exterior, prohibiting access to the courtyard where the stabbing had taken place. The SOCOs arrived in their overshoes, face masks and white protective suits. From where we were standing, we could see them taking photographs, dusting for prints and inspecting blood spatters, difficult to make out on the estate's red-brick paving.

Crime scene investigation is archaeology without the digging. SOCOs reconstruct the past by examining objects and the arrangements of objects, teasing out latent information. Their relationship with a crime scene is similar to the archaeologist's with a dig site. Both are treated with the utmost care and acquire an almost sacred character. When they are sullied, there is a sense that something pure has been irreparably corrupted, and that something that might have been known has now been lost forever. Crime scene investigators make no assumptions. They log and gather everything, not knowing which details will be significant, knowing that some pieces of evidence may not reveal their significance until years after the event.

For three hours we stood at our designated points along the blue and white tape, cold and bored, casting giant shadows across the silent flats behind us. There were no updates on the boy who had been stabbed. We did not know how serious it was. The SOCOs were working slowly and thoroughly. We kept an ear on the radio while we waited for them to finish. Among the bar fights and domestic violence calls, we heard a report of a 'drunk male stuck at the bottom of a rubbish chute outside his flat'.

'Just to confirm: there's been a report of a *trashed* male, over?' someone replied.

'The male is drunk, yes,' said the operator.

'I'd really like to *refuse* this call,' said another officer.

'I know that, but I need someone to take this.'

'Do you know where he's *bin*?' asked a third voice.

—

When the SOCOs had scoured the scene, they told us they were leaving and asked us to bag up the victim's clothes. We ducked under the outer cordon, then the inner, rolled on gloves and squatted in the doorway where the boy had been stabbed and where a mound of clothes was now lying. We picked them up, one item at a time, and placed them in large brown paper bags: his trainers, a slashed black puffer, blood-soaked jeans, the T-shirt he had been cut out of, white with a palm tree on it, someone else's jacket thrown over him for warmth, and a neighbour's bloody beach towel. We sealed the evidence bags, signed the sticky labels, and taped them up to make them tamper-proof.

It was gone 1 a.m. Time to close down the scene. This space, untouchable minutes earlier, was no longer important. We began reeling in several hundred metres of cordon from the lamp posts and bollards. After hours guarding the scene, I felt protective. It felt as though there ought to be a deconsecration ritual, not this unceremonious stamping about and scrunching of plastic tape.

In the Phoenix, my legs felt stiff after standing on the cordon for so long. My breakfast arrived but I felt queasy and unsettled by the stabbing and from bagging up the blood-soaked clothes of a boy I had never met.

Sitting there, I remembered something from my last term as a teacher. It was July, the children were relaxed and excited about the holidays, glowing after sports day and the school summer fair, at which they had paid money to pelt me with wet sponges. I kept the door onto the playground open while I was teaching, and gusts of warm air would blow the worksheets off the tables. In the midst of this warmth and contentment, I heard about the murder of a boy at a nearby secondary school.

The boy was called Zac Olumegbon. He was fifteen, attending a school for pupils excluded from mainstream provision. He was a member of TN1, trying to leave the gang, and he was stabbed outside his school, first thing in the morning.

I read accounts of the murder as they emerged. Zac had arrived at school early and asked to talk to a senior teacher. While he was waiting in the school reception, he saw a group of boys from GAS outside, looking for him. Instead of staying where he was, or running further inside, Zac ran out of the school to evade his attackers, sprinting down a cul-de-sac opposite. The boys chased him, stabbed him four times, and left him to die in someone's front garden. It was this detail that had particularly hit me: Zac's killers came looking for him at school, and Zac had left a place of safety in his attempt to escape. There is no doubt about who murdered Zac. Four boys – known as Clickz, Mad H, Maggy and JJ – were caught on CCTV, tried at the Old Bailey and received life sentences.

The day before his murder, Zac had attended a conference for London's Youth Violence Board, talking about his experiences to an audience of 150 people. I listened to a low-quality recording on YouTube, in which a man asks: 'What do you feel the risks are, just on a daily basis, of serious violence in the world that you live in?'

'Daily basis?' Zac replies. 'Get stabbed, shot, die, school day, any time.'

It was busy in the Phoenix. I felt worn out and grim. I waved at the manager and ordered another coffee. A lot of young people had been killed in London since I moved to Brixton. Part of what made it so upsetting was how difficult it was to feel really upset. I had got used to it. When I picked up the *Evening Standard*, I almost expected to read about another death. It began to feel inevitable.

Zac's murder was the first gang stabbing I felt fully aware of and affected by. It transformed an abstract phenomenon into something that happened at a school down the road. Everybody was horrified. He was a local child and his death made the threats feel close and real for the children we worked with.

–

I could not shake the feeling that Zac's death, and other teen murders, were like children's games gone dreadfully wrong. They contained so many of the gestures I remembered from my own childhood – the running, the fighting, the rivalries. But the weapons were real. I could not fathom how the motions of late childhood had acquired such lethal consequences.

The manager of the Phoenix was reading his London A–Z again, mouthing street names. He paused when he saw me stand up and prepared my bill.

I wondered about the boy who had been stabbed the night before. Who was he? How was he? At my next shift, with a different set of officers, no one knew, and I never found out.

The patch of Clapham Common next to Holy Trinity Church, with the old Temperance Society water fountain in the middle, has something of the village green about it. People cluster there day and night. The calm of the Common, the anonymity of the darkness, is a relief after the hustle of the High Street. The lamp posts are sparsely placed and there's plenty of shadow for anyone wishing to avoid attention. The issue with trying to avoid attention, however, is that you attract it. People who linger in dark places invite suspicion.

We were on foot patrol in Clapham, criss-crossing that patch of grass, hoping to smell cannabis. Each time we passed a group in the shadows, we inhaled deeply. Cannabis might not provoke outrageous behaviour, like alcohol, but it was easy to detect and it also brought people into our orbit. A cannabis search could be a gateway to further policing, and we were always alert for its distinctive aroma.

We passed three IC3 males, twenties, huddled together in the darkness, talking softly. We smelt cannabis, although we could not see the glow of lit spliffs. Perhaps they had just finished them.

We followed the men as they moved towards a street light. As they walked below it, we saw a glint on a glass phial one man was handing to another. It looked drug-related, so we called to the men, stepped into the light, and stopped them for a search. The three men were smartly dressed, and we slid our hands inside the collars of their polo necks, padded down their tweed jackets, skimmed the tops of suede shoes. They were compliant, but from their stiff limbs and set expressions, we could see they were unhappy.

Our stop was legal. We had smelt cannabis and seen a suspicious object in a known drugs hotspot. But from the men's demeanour, it was clear they saw things differently. We tried to keep the search friendly, asking what they were up to and where they were going. 'Nothing much . . . Meeting friends.' They could not bring themselves to ignore us completely, but they said as little as they could.

There is a sort of doublethink to a search. We treat people as potential criminals, while acknowledging that we may be wasting their time. We accompany actions implying guilt with words implying innocence. We try to make it feel like the security check at an airport: a reassuring inconvenience, a minor humiliation in service of a greater good. But, as in airports, everyone knows that certain groups of people are stopped more often than others.

We did not find any cannabis on the men, and the glass phial we had seen was an aftershave miniature. We wished them goodnight and thanked them for their time.

A minute later, we spotted a figure crouching by a tree – an intoxicated IC1 female who had wandered onto the Common and was rummaging through her handbag, looking for her phone. We knelt down next to her, checked that she was OK, and nudged her back towards the tube.

–

On the radio, we could hear somebody pursuing a runaway. We could not tell what he was wanted for, but we could hear an officer's breathless directions. 'Venn Street! He's gone down Venn Street!' We sprinted in that direction, on the lookout for an ICi male, twenties, in a blue suit and a red striped shirt.

It took us almost five minutes to run to Venn Street. When we arrived, there were several officers there already, pulling a man from beneath a car, dragging him by his tan leather shoes. The runaway had punched somebody in Infernos, been detained by a bouncer and arrested by police. Then, as he was being walked to the custody van, he had done a runner. He should have been cuffed, but he was wearing a suit and looked tame, so the officers had decided not to. 'I think I dropped my phone while I was running,' the man said. 'Can you go back and look for it?' The arresting officer smiled. 'No, I think it's time we went to custody now, mate.'

It was a hot night, and after all the running, I wished I could remove my body armour. We walked back to the High Street and I tried to ignore the sweat running down my spine. As we were passing an Italian restaurant, the manager handed us something. 'A guy just come in and give me this,' he said. It was a black business card with a phone number and a pile of diamonds on it. 'He said to call him if we wanted drugs.' We took a description – IC3 male, early twenties, black jeans, brown leather jacket – and circulated it on the radio.

An IC3 female, late teens, walked past crying.

'Are you all right?' we asked.

'You couldn't even understand, you know,' she replied, without breaking her stride.

Outside Infernos, a woman was dancing in the road, an ICi female, sixties, not much over five foot. She was doing a wild jig, shuffling her feet, waving her arms above her head, and darting at cars as they tried to weave round her. We ran over and asked the woman to return to the pavement. She sat down in the road instead. 'I do what I like,' she said in a thick French accent. 'If I want to dance, I dance.' With horns beeping and a crowd watching, we persuaded her to get up.

We were ready for a break. On our way to the Kebab Company we spotted the hot-dog vendor outside the Picturehouse and told him to go home. 'You got nothing better to do?' he asked and pushed his cart away from the High Street. We placed our orders in the Kebab Company and while we waited I leant on the counter, hypnotized by the kebab meat revolving on its spit, watching its reflection spin next to it in the window.

As we left the Kebab Company, we heard that the man distributing the business cards had been spotted nearby and had bolted when an officer approached him. We sprinted along the High Street, ears pressed to the radio. He was running west, past Roosters Spot, past Snappy Snaps. A pair of officers caught him at KFC and were searching him around the corner when we arrived.

'We think he dropped something while he was running,' the searching officer said. 'Maybe a bag of cocaine.' As she was emptying the pockets of the man's leather jacket, she pulled out a stack of black business cards, identical to the one we had been handed.

The dealer had been running along the crowded High Street, where there was nowhere obvious to stash something valuable. We walked back along the route he had taken, scouring the pavements, checking the doorways. There was no sign of a bag of drugs, but there were people crowding the pavements so we could not be sure. We presumed the man would have dumped the drugs somewhere he could recover them. The most obvious place was the bin outside KFC.

While our colleagues finished their search, we rolled on latex gloves and began digging through the rubbish. It was midnight and the air still held the day's warmth. The bin was full to the brim and we dug through the evening's cartons and cans, lunchtime's wrappers and rinds, all the way to the morning's coffee cups and coffee-soaked newspapers. The bin contained the same things it probably contained every day. Tomorrow this batch would be gone, and an identical haul would take its place.

Picking through the layers, observing the effects of moisture, compression and heat on throwaway things, the search felt faintly archaeological. I tried to sift the contents systematically, shifting the rubbish from one side to the other, but it kept caving in on itself and covering the sections I was trying to reveal. By the time I reached the bottom, I was bent double, in up to my armpit. We did not think the drugs were in the bin, but without emptying it onto the pavement it was hard to say for certain.

It was a beautiful morning and I decided to have a coffee outside Rosie's Deli in the covered market, looking across at the Neighbourhood Policing Office on Coldharbour Lane. I needed to type up my notes, but first I sat back and enjoyed the sun and the breeze around my ankles. I watched people pass by in shorts, string vests, strappy dresses.

I felt drowsy and happy in the sunshine, closing my eyes while I waited for my breakfast. But my good mood jostled with a sense of unease. I felt uneasy about searching the three IC3 males on the Common the night before. Or perhaps that was not quite right. I felt uneasy imagining what they were thinking about me. I wanted the chance to justify myself. I was not sure I could.

In 'Walking While Black', the essayist Garnette Cadogan describes his experiences moving through cities, and how he makes himself less of a target for police:

> No running, especially at night; no sudden movements; no hoodies; no objects – especially shiny ones – in hand; no waiting for friends on street corners, lest I be mistaken for a drug dealer; no standing near a corner on the cell phone (same reason).

Cadogan's movement is theatrical, a 'pantomime undertaken to avoid the choreography of criminality', involving exaggerated gestures to both police and public. 'I would see a white woman walking toward me at night and cross the street to reassure her that she was safe.' If we had been able to see the three men clearly the previous night, perhaps we would not have stopped them. They had assembled what Cadogan calls a 'cop-proof wardrobe': smart attire that short-circuits easy assumptions.

Thinking about our search, and many others like it, I sensed that they were less about fighting crime or disrupting the drugs trade, and more about keeping ourselves busy. If you drop hundreds of people in uniform into a city centre without a clear brief, they will find some way to occupy themselves. We are not like teachers with a class or social workers with a caseload. Out on the beat, we are essentially invisible to the state who has sent us there. We turn this way or that, trying to find or generate something to do. The distinctive scent of cannabis is a gift – a trail that always leads somewhere.

In his essay, Cadogan notes that none of the officers who stopped him 'thought an apology was necessary'. Leaving the three men the previous night, we had not apologized either.

I left the market and walked towards the tube, joining a crowd outside Iceland who had gathered to watch a steel band playing 'Quando Quando Quando'.

Whenever I hear steel pans I am transported back to the classroom where I taught. Every Wednesday afternoon there were steel-band rehearsals in the music room across the play-ground. On summer days like these, when all the doors were propped open, the music drifted over and soundtracked my lessons – the deep bouncing bass lines, the shimmering melodies, the long-held notes that rolled and rolled. Often the school band would practise the same fragment repeatedly, imperceptibly perfecting it, and it was as though life was on loop until they cracked it and moved on.

The band started playing 'Red Red Wine'. In the crowd, I felt close to the people around me, these bodies I did not know but which were resonating next to mine. I closed my eyes, soothed by the sound of the pans, breathing in the dust, sweat and incense hanging in the air.

I arrived to find the station abuzz with the story of a female officer who had single-handedly broken up a fight between two large groups of drunk IC1 males, running between them with her baton raised, shouting at them to back off, which they did. 'She's got more balls than the rest of you put together,' a Sergeant said.

At the briefing, we were given a pile of arrest warrants for people who were wanted or had breached their bail conditions. It would probably take most of the evening to round them up and get them booked into custody. 'Nice easy bodies,' the Inspector said. 'Go to their houses, grab them and bung them in Brixton nick.'

Our first warrant was for a thirty-year-old IC1 male with a string of robbery convictions. He was well known to the regulars, having spent most of his adult life in jail, on bail or on trial. The pattern was so well established it was difficult to imagine it changing, except perhaps for the worse. We surrounded the man's house and knocked on the front door. He was electronically tagged and was supposed to be at home. When there was no reply, we knocked on the back door and cupped our hands to the unlit windows. The man's warrant was for breaching his bail conditions. He was clearly still ignoring them.

The next suspect was known for drugs and violence against police and lived on the Angell Town Estate. Four of us stood poised around the entrance and knocked loudly. The door was opened by a short, softly spoken IC4 female in her forties. When we told her why we were there, she picked up her handbag from the hall table, pulled the door closed behind her and shuffled out to be arrested. We called the custody van and two colleagues took her back to the station.

Just before 9 p.m. we pulled up at a mock-Tudor terrace. Tekeysia, IC3, fifteen years old, was watching cartoons in the front room with her two little sisters. All three were curled on the couch in matching pink dressing gowns, faces flickering in the dark. When we knocked, their foster mother invited us in, turned on the big light and muted the TV. Tekeysia had breached bail earlier that week, we announced, and we were there to arrest her. We stood between the sofa and the television and explained that Tekeysia would spend the night in a cell in Brixton Police Station and face a magistrate in the morning. The three girls stared up at us, motionless, as though we were just a different channel. Above the top of one of Tekeysia's pink slippers we could see a thick black bangle: an electronic tag, fitted after she had been convicted for taking part in gang robberies, a digital ball-and-chain that kept her at home every night from 7 p.m. to 7 a.m.

The arrest warrant showed that earlier that week Tekeysia had arrived home an hour after the start of her curfew. 'I was at a meeting that ran over,' she told us. 'It was with my YOT worker. That's the reason I got back late. It actually wasn't my fault.' We explained that, regardless of the reason, we had a warrant and were compelled to arrest her. 'But I was with my YOT worker!' she insisted. Her Youth Offending Team were aware of her bail conditions, we told her, and we had no choice.

The point of Youth Offending Teams is to help young people navigate the legal process and to steer them away from crime. If what Tekeysia said was true, this was an unfortunate slip on their part. The experience of interacting with multiple agencies can be confusing for young offenders, being cared for one moment, disciplined the next, protected by a society that is also trying to protect itself from them. For police officers, teachers, youth workers, social workers, the experience can be confusing too. Confronted with complex needs, we often struggle to do our job, making it more difficult for others to do theirs. Unresolved issues are handed from one institution to the next, looping and growing until both state and individual are caught in a vicious spiral.

I arrested Tekeysia in the living room, sitting with her sisters on the couch, her foster mother in the doorway, cartoons playing silently behind me. 'You do not have to say anything,' I said, 'but it may harm your defence if you do not mention when questioned anything which you later rely on in court. Anything you do say may be given in evidence.' Saying those words, reeling them off like the terms and conditions on a radio advert, I felt freshly aware of the different sanctioning styles of the teacher and police officer. As a teacher, I dealt out minor punishments with a punitive tone. As a police officer, taking away a child's liberty, my tone was flat and functional.

'It's not fair!' Tekeysia shouted. 'Why are you taking me away for? I told you I had a meeting! Phone my YOT worker! Phone them and they'll tell you I had a meeting!' She went upstairs to change and we waited in the hall, talking to her foster mother. 'I understand, officers,' she said. 'We all want the best for her.'

Tekeysia came back downstairs slowly, landing heavily on

each step. At the bottom, she told us she was ready to go and swung a studded black handbag over one shoulder. With her hair up, in a leather jacket and leather boots, she was dressed for a night out.

At Brixton Police Station we presented Tekeysia to the Custody Sergeant and checked in her belongings, emptying her bag onto the counter and listing each item. Purse, keys, phone, hair clips. Gum, Oyster card, tampons, lip gloss. Headphones, a biro, some strands of braided plastic. We were about to log a loose cheesy Wotsit when Tekeysia told us to throw it away. We sealed the handbag and its contents into a clear plastic sack and handed it to the Sergeant.

We had almost finished at the desk when an IC3 female, forties, in handcuffs, was escorted into the custody suite. She looked over at Tekeysia. 'Keep smiling, girl!' she shouted. Tekeysia smiled at the woman, who then looked away and began muttering, 'She's just gotta keep smiling, gotta keep smiling, gotta keep smiling,' before bursting into a hysterical drunken cackle. We could hear a skirmish outside, a prisoner kicking off, an officer trying to calm him down. 'Stop struggling. Stop struggling! Why are you covered in shit? Is it your shit?'

We got Tekeysia some blankets and water and left her in her cell.

Walking to the Phoenix, I passed a pair of children outside KFC throwing fire crackers under the feet of passers-by, laughing each time one exploded and an adult jumped. I approached a man I presumed to be their father, IC1 male, forties, to tell him what the children were doing. He looked at me and laughed. 'Scared of kids, are you?' he said, then turned away.

I pushed open the door of the Phoenix, waved to the manager and took a seat at the back.

I thought of Tekeysia and wished there had been a solution to her situation that did not involve her spending a night in a police station, a child experiencing a system built for adults, getting used to thinking about herself as someone who spends time in those spaces.

My bubble and squeak arrived. It was strange to think that she was probably still in her cell, a few hundred metres away, waiting to be taken to the Magistrate.

I felt rattled by that encounter. On the couch in her dressing gown, Tekeysia had looked like a child. It made me realize how often the police see and treat teenagers – especially Black teenagers – as though they are older than they are. If they suspect a teenager of breaking the law, many officers treat them as a problematic young adult, not a vulnerable child, a category shift that represents a devaluation, as though those young people have outgrown the possibilities and protections of childhood, forfeiting the care and understanding that is owed to them. They may be children, but the label no longer applies. The role of the police is no longer to shield them from harm, but to shield others from them.

On the way to the station I had asked Tekeysia how school was going, and she told me, with pride, how well she was doing in art and how much she liked her teacher, chatting about a project she had just finished. It was exactly like the conversations I had in my educational research job, only in the back of a police car.

Policing gangs, we rarely interacted with teenage girls. This was not because girls were not involved. They were, but they were less visible. In 2020, only six of the 3,000 people on the Gangs Matrix, the Met's database of suspected gang members, were women and girls. We barely noticed them – a fact that increased their value to gangs and their vulnerability to abuse. I thought of the young woman who had confronted us while we were searching the boys from ABM, or the young woman alone in her car in Tulse Hill, both known to police for hiding weapons. The girls in gangs appeared on the periphery, hardly mentioned. A boy stabbed on the street is unignorable. We rarely found out about the harm girls endured, much of it hidden behind closed doors.

I ordered another coffee and thought about Tekeysia waking up in a police cell. How would that experience affect her? I wondered what they served for breakfast in Brixton Custody.

We were going out on patrol in the van, early autumn, the pavements covered with leaves that still looked half alive. The Sergeant flicked through the briefing deck and we stared at the faces of robbers and sex offenders. She paused when we reached the Top Five Burglars, a mixture of IC1 and IC3 males, twenty years older than the Top Five Robbers.

She cocked her head and stared at their mugshots. 'They're not bad guys really,' she said. 'They're just misunderstood, that's all. I reckon they weren't loved as kids.'

We had only been in the van for a couple of minutes when a call came out: 'A thirteen-year-old girl has glassed another girl outside a youth club in Myatt's Fields'. The victim was described as an 'IC3 female, thirteen years old, white trainers, blue hoodie'.

We arrived to find two dozen young people standing in the road, about half of whom matched the description we had been given. 'This is the problem if you don't ask for a detailed description,' said the Sergeant. 'You've got to ask people to be specific, or things like this happen.' She shook her head and scanned the crowd in front of us. 'You get a call: *Suspect is dressed as a clown*. And you think, all right, that's easy, I don't need more information than that. But what if you get there and there's a clown convention going on?'

We asked around and found the girl who had been assaulted standing next to her mother at the entrance to the youth club. We asked her how she was and where she had been hit. 'I'm OK,' she said, 'it wasn't that hard.' We inspected her head, lifting her braids to check for cuts.

The bottle the girl had been attacked with lay unbroken on the pavement and we could not see any marks on her skin. 'Yeah, look, it's fine. I'm fine,' she said. 'It's my mum who called the police.' While the Sergeant took her details, and the attacker's, I went to chat to a group of teenage boys who were waiting nearby.

'What have you been doing this evening, guys?'

'Shooting guns.'

'Shooting guns?'

'Yeah, we just hid them over there.'

'You're too honest for your own good. What have you actually been doing?'

'That's it. Shooting at cop cars.'

'What would you do if I got a gun and put it to your head?'

'Yeah, what would you do?'

We drove past Brixton McDonald's and one of the regulars spotted a bike he believed to be stolen, in the possession of an IC3 male, forties. We pulled up and two regulars got out to confiscate the bike and arrest the man.

'What are you arresting him for? It's his bike, it's his bike!' shouted the man's wife, IC3 female, forties, gripping the handlebars and trying to take it back. A group of passers-by gathered around us, several filming on their phones.

'Look, calm down,' the regular said.

'It's his bike! Let go of it!'

'That's enough,' the regular said, trying to lift off her hands.

'Don't touch me,' she shouted. 'Get your hands off me! You're racist!'

'You're drawing a crowd now and you'll get nicked if you carry on like this.'

'Go fuck your mother! Go fuck your mother! You're racist!'

The woman withdrew and the regular wheeled the bike to the van. He popped his head through the open door and smiled. 'I still get that treatment, even though I'm Black,' he said. 'It's nice that people don't discriminate.'

We ran a name check on the man we were arresting and discovered he was wanted for burglary.

Driving up Brixton Hill, the Sergeant spotted a crack addict she knew at a bus stop near Olive Morris House, an IC3 female, late forties. The woman was boarding each bus as it pulled in, trying to blag a ride.

'Hello, how are you?' said the Sergeant.

'Oh, hello, I didn't see you there. How you doing?'

'I'm good. How you doing, all right?'

'Yeah, normal, not too bad . . .'

They chatted for a while about what they had each been up to, talking about people I did not know, teasing each other and laughing.

'Right, I'm going to try this bus,' the woman said, as a 133 pulled up.

'OK then. Take care.'

The Sergeant wound up the window. 'Right, let's get away in case she causes any shit. She should try spending her money on an Oyster card instead of crack.'

We sped away before we could see what happened next.

It was curious – the Sergeant was the one who had spotted the woman and made us pull over. Then the Sergeant was the one who made us rush away. I did not know whether this was motivated by a reluctance to deal with anything that occurred, or a desire not to witness something we would have to react to. She had sounded genuinely pleased to see the woman, so I suspected the latter. That was the bind of being a law enforcer: your desire to check in on someone could end up with you arresting them.

We circled the backstreets behind the prison, passing a mural on the side of a house: a watermill with children swimming in a river beside it. It had been painted in 1984, when local residents requested a scene that would distract them from the Thatcher government and the Cold War. The river represents the Effra.

We drove over to Tulse Hill, to the address of an IC1 male whose wife had reported him to the police for slamming her against a wall. We had an arrest warrant, but the man was not there. An IC3 teenage male drove past on a moped without lights. We followed him into the Tulse Hill Estate and parked up.

Two IC3 females, mid-teens, were leaning on a wall and greeted the boy as he removed his helmet. We stepped out of the van and walked up to them.

'Do you realize you were driving without lights?'

'No,' the boy replied.

We took his details and ran a name check while one of the regulars inspected his moped with a torch. The girls looked away and lit a cigarette.

'Did you know the tank is leaking?' said the regular.

The boy looked over at the girls. 'Didn't I tell you this thing's been eating up petrol?' He walked over to the moped and knelt down next to the regular, looking along the torch beam. The regular was a traffic specialist and gave the boy some advice on how to get the moped mended. 'Nice one, thanks,' the boy said as the regular stood up and walked towards the van.

We wove from Tulse Hill to Brixton Hill, eating Percy Pigs in silence. I sensed we were all ready to call it a night, but it was not yet time, so we kept driving. We were metres from my flat. My wife was asleep in our bed. I leant my forehead on the window.

A call came out: a group of IC3 teenage boys were letting off fireworks on the New Park Road Estate, rockets bouncing off walls, landing on balconies, exploding in bins. A wave of relief passed through the van. Something was happening. We accepted the call, turned on our siren, and raced over there, passing the end of my road and stopping a moment later. When we pulled up, we could see shadows behind railings, figures running hunched. I felt uncomfortable – we were right on my patch, going after boys I shared a corner shop with. But running after them, chasing shadows, it felt like a game, and I noticed I was moving in ways I had rarely moved since I was a child myself. As we entered the labyrinth of narrow passageways, I could hear our driver shouting after us. 'Doors! Someone shut the fucking doors!'

After we left the New Park Road Estate, we went back to the
station. When I had changed, I took a bus back to New Park Road
and rushed from the bus stop to my flat, wary of meeting the
boys we had chased, alone and without my radio, baton or CS.

In my flat, I undressed in the dark and climbed into bed.
I lay on my back in a state of maximum exhaustion and
maximum wakefulness, the two sensations somehow occurring
in parallel. When I finally fell asleep, I dreamed that I was at
a gala dinner in a derelict warehouse near the Thames, dressed
in black tie and walking drunk through white marquees. I
stumbled outside and flagged a taxi home to Brixton. When the
meter was on £20 the taxi driver stopped by an estate and told
me that I had to walk through it and he would meet me on the
other side. It was late and drizzling and I walked along the
narrow brick passageways that led into the estate. It was abandoned and I continued through a couple of courtyards until I
came across a group of IC3 teenage boys. When I saw them, I
doubled back and changed direction, but immediately encountered another group. I turned a corner and spotted the way out
of the estate but saw that twenty or so IC3 teenagers had assembled along the path. I walked towards them, determined to get
out. A boy, who could not have been more than fourteen,

approached me and, as he did, I began beating him with a rolled-up umbrella, hitting him repeatedly on the side of his neck. When he fell to the ground, I ran at full pelt towards the main road. I escaped but I could not find my taxi anywhere.

I woke a few hours later with a dry mouth and the dirty feeling that accompanies a dream you wish you had not had, a dream whose atmosphere is stronger than that of the room you have woken up in. I needed to get out of the house, so I dressed without showering and left.

Walking from my flat to the bus stop, I paused on New Park Road and looked past the local primary school to the brown-brick estate where I had chased a group of teenagers eight hours earlier. I caught a bus down the hill, flashing my warrant card at the driver as I boarded, and went for breakfast at the Phoenix.

As I ate my bubble and squeak, images of the chase and the dream flashed through my mind, bleeding into one another. We were rarely called to the New Park Road Estate and regulars never mentioned it. It was small compared to Tulse Hill, Angell Town or Myatt's Fields. I never went into it off duty either, even though it was just round the corner from my flat.

The estate is famous now. While we were living nearby, some of the teenagers on the New Park Road Estate were developing a new form of British rap, which would spread from a patch of Brixton Hill across the country and around the world. New Park Road is the birthplace of UK Drill, and the 67 Drill Crew, from the estate, were the pioneers, taking a sound that originated in Chicago and blending it with the raw energy of Grime which came out of East London in the noughties. Drill builds on Grime, but its sound and content are darker, the violence more graphic, the basslines sparser.

Brushing shoulders with local teenagers, I had no idea I was living in the middle of a major cultural moment. But if I go onto YouTube, my local streets are the backdrop to 67's performances. '#WAPS' was filmed outside Airy Food & Wine, a hundred metres from my old front door. I probably stood at the bus stop with Drill's leading producers and MCs. I might have stopped and searched some of them.

There are always discussions about whether art reflects or creates violent realities, but this question has been posed particularly forcefully in relation to UK Drill. Since its emergence, it has been caught in a bind – hailed as an artistic breakthrough and condemned for its ultra-violent lyrics. When Jeffrey Boakye broaches the issue in *Hold Tight*, his book about Grime, he grinds to a halt and writes:

> [Insert nuanced essay on the intersection of urban
> social decay and fictionalised crime, exploring the
> psychological appeal of violence alongside Grime's
> chicken-and-egg relationship with aggression . . .]

Boakye then offers nine aborted attempts to write this section of his book, each grappling with the circularity and stereotypes that the question evokes: that music is sometimes part of the problem, sometimes part of the solution, and sometimes just a soundtrack.

For the writer Musa Okwonga, Grime's abrasiveness, and its illegibility to those in authority, is its power. 'Grime is the story of survival not only against the odds, but in contempt of them,' he writes. In the same way, UK Drill is an assault on the ethics and eardrums of the uninitiated, goading you to take it at face value.

The Met has a troubled relationship with Grime and Drill.

They were accused of hijacking the Grime scene by requiring venues to complete a risk assessment before upcoming gigs. Form 696 gathered performers' names, allowing the Met to spot events, such as Grime nights, that they believed might pose a risk of violence and advise that they be cancelled. In 2017, after protracted lobbying, Form 696 was scrapped. Now the Met's focus has shifted to UK Drill.

The Met monitors Drill videos closely, strange as it is to imagine police staff watching teenagers rap for hours on end. In 2018, the Met asked YouTube to remove over fifty Drill videos. The same year, they applied for a Gang Injunction for Skengdo and AM, two rappers from 410, the Angell Town Drill Crew, to prevent them performing music that incites violence. After a major London gig, Skengdo and AM were deemed to have breached their injunction and the two rappers, neither of whom has been convicted of any violent crime, were given two-year suspended jail sentences: the first time British courts have issued a prison term just for performing a song. 'There's a root problem,' AM told Channel 4 News. 'Music or not, there's a problem in this area . . . The fact that people are being allowed to live in it – and live it day to day and experience it – that's not a problem. However, making it known – saying it, saying it in music where it's public knowledge – that's the problem.'

Dimzy, from the 67 crew, has expressed similar frustrations. 'Drill music has positively changed my life in so many ways,' he wrote, describing it as 'an outlet and a form of therapy to those that create it'. Dimzy is credited with importing Drill beats from the USA to London in the first place. 'Who, what, and where influences your creativity?' he was asked in an interview. 'New Park Road,' he replied. 'That's our home. That's where we grew up, that's what made us men.'

But that morning, as I sat in the Phoenix, the day after a night chasing teenagers around the New Park Road Estate, UK Drill was yet to become a phenomenon. I was unaware that my young neighbours were furiously writing, rapping, and filming metres from my door.

I thought about going home to sleep, but my bad dream still felt fresh and I needed distraction. I walked to the Ritzy and bought a ticket for a matinee and spent the afternoon sitting in the dark.

We were going out in the van for the evening. While I was sitting with some other Specials before we set off, the rosy-cheeked Sergeant walked past and waved. I waved back.

'You know he was the one in charge when someone died in Brixton Custody?' another Special said. 'Everyone knows about it.'

'What? Who?' I asked.

'Sean Rigg,' she replied. 'Left him face down on the floor for too long.'

'Sean Rigg?'

'Yep. He was the Sergeant in charge.'

I watched the rosy-cheeked Sergeant disappear along a corridor, then stared at the other Special, my mind racing, my head swimming from the shock of what she had just told me. The man who had welcomed me into the Met, who helped me search for stray bits of kit, who was always smiling and always had time for me, was the Custody Sergeant who had left Sean Rigg on the floor to die.

The month I moved to Brixton, while I was decorating the walls of my classroom, the rosy-cheeked Sergeant was down the road in the police station with Sean Rigg. He was the one who declined to seek medical help while Rigg lay unresponsive on the floor of the Custody cage. He had decided that Rigg was 'feigning unconsciousness'. He had held off summoning a doctor. I wondered what would have happened if Rigg had not been bare chested, had not shown signs of mental health issues, had not been an IC3 male. Would a smartly dressed, forty-year-old IC1 female have died the same way?

Years later, he was still a Sergeant. He was the person supervising volunteers who had never policed before. What's more, he was such an upbeat character. Was that warmth and exuberance his natural style, or was it a manner he had adopted to cope with the fact that everyone knew a vulnerable man had died on his watch? Did he like working with new Specials because we did not know what he had done? Every time he left the police station, Sean Rigg's face was there to greet him, among the lanterns and the flowers on the plane tree in the forecourt.

6

YouTube: *Kenz TV – G.A.S Gang J Kidd Sneakbo (SW9).flv*

### xJordyboi

Wastemans tried to catch lil Zack slipping after he quit he said he wanted to change so u shanked him on a school day . . .

### REDEMPTION

I understand where youre coming from but thats not how it works with gangs.

### Cherry monroe

once your gang ur always gang no quiting

### mary jones

even tho zac was in TN1 they didnt deserve to stab him to a point where they kill em . atleast punch him up or something less than killing the yute.

**MightyScenester**

RIP Zac.

**Tekashi 6ix9ine**

Little did they know this music was going to be evidence they were associated with gang 😊

> **Deez Nuts**
>
> looool that must of been awkward as fuck to be shown in court

> **Luca**
>
> Shame. These guys had talent. Now 4 of them have a life sentence

**jack jacob**

has JJ, Maggy, and them only kill zac before and no one else?

> **SRP**
>
> Fed😊

**MissPreach**

I proper vibe off this, can't lie. Who else see the man on the wall near the end, clock the skankin lol love it

> **ooglies boo**
>
> The boy with the crash helmet looks like a octopus

**best of the best**

Lol there gangsters but wear safty bike helmets

**FRisky james**

what the fuck is safty, and why would they not wear helmets.

**best of the best**

There in a fucking gang they risk getting shot but wear helmet for riding a bike lol

**Eric DeVito**

Have TN1 retaliated yet? Don't let Zac's death slide fam.

**Shit Life Syndrome**

Why do gangs get so fiercely protective over such shit areas. I mean, Tulse hill!

I was in the Phoenix. Across the road I could see a queue outside the Duck Egg Cafe, where, for a pound, you could upgrade your hen eggs to duck eggs. There were queues all over Brixton on weekend mornings now. Brunchers came from miles around for coffee and avocado at Federation, Seven, Brick Box, Burnt Toast or one of the other new places that had opened in the market. When they failed to get a seat, or could not stomach the wait, they spilled over into the older haunts: the Ritzy, the Express, San Marino or the Phoenix.

Brixton has changed a huge amount since 2008. My friends and I moved there at a hinge point in its recent history, a moment that felt static but when in fact it was changing faster than it had for decades. The following years saw squat clearances, new public spaces, a crackdown on the dealers outside KFC, the opening of a Starbucks, a Costa and a Pret A Manger, the construction of numerous blocks of flats, and the appearance of a retail park made of shipping containers.

What accelerated everything was the gentrification of Brixton Village Market, a stately 1930s arcade where businesses were closing and footfall was dwindling. When I moved to Brixton, the market was threatened with destruction. As an experiment, the council offered twenty of the unoccupied units rent-free for three months to anyone with a good idea. Artists, tailors and coffee grinders popped up between the existing grocers, record shops and fishmongers. There was a Winter Menagerie, a Memory Exchange, a Communist Gallery and a Cabinet of Curiosities. It was exciting. People who would not normally come to Brixton came to see it. The new crowds attracted new cafes, shops and restaurants. Over those three months an irreversible process was set in motion.

Although there were some raised eyebrows from other young professionals when I first moved to Brixton, people warning me it was 'stabby', within five years I was considered discerning. A landmark came in 2013 when Speedy Noodle, the cheapest and best eatery on the High Street, was replaced by a branch of Foxtons estate agents. When it opened, the words 'YUPPIES OUT' were sprayed across its window. In 2015, its window was shattered during a 'Reclaim Brixton' protest. Other estate agents appeared along the High Street and Coldharbour Lane, preparing to house the wave of well-paid twenty-somethings who were now eager to live there.

I had a sudden flashback to one of my night shifts, talking to an IC3 teenage boy during a search.

'It's changing a lot around here, isn't it?' I said.

'It hasn't changed at all,' he replied.

The new bars and restaurants, the young professionals crowding the morning bus stops, did not seem to have impacted Brixton as he knew it. What I had presumed would be a point of connection served only to highlight how differently we experienced the area.

I finished my bubble and squeak and looked out at Coldharbour Lane. Directly opposite the Phoenix was a gift shop called Joy, which had recently closed down. The premises had been taken over by squatters and the insides of the windows were covered in newspaper. 'The London Queer Social Centre', read a handwritten sign. 'A space for LGBTQ people and our friends, allies and fellow Brixton activists'. It positioned itself as a successor to the Railton Road collectives of the 1970s and 1980s, proud to be opening in the place 'where queer & radical squatting in London began – where the Brixton Faeries opened their squatted Gay Community Centre in 1974, where Olive Morris fought the police and cracked squats for black families, where squatted women's centres offered space for feminist activism and refuge to women and kids fleeing domestic violence, where the squatted Sabaar Bookshop hosted Black Panthers meetings and the anarchist 121 Centre put on Queeruption, where whole streets and blocks of flats were reclaimed and turned into homes and community spaces'. From the street you could hear the hum of music and conversation on the other side of the glass. Brixton's radical spirit may have been tamed in recent years, but it remained close to the surface.

Brixton was busy, and I watched the people passing by: young parents trailing toddlers; determined-looking grocery shoppers; a butcher in a white smock pushing another pig in a shopping trolley; twenty-somethings, slow walking and sated, drifting towards the tube, or twitchy and frustrated by the lack of seats and coffee queues.

In a van circling Brixton, a lively sounding call came out of the radio. An IC3 male was making violent threats to an IC3 female outside the Angell Town Estate. We turned on the blue lights and dashed over. It was a popular call and we were the fourth vehicle to arrive, parking our van behind three response cars.

The cars had all left their blue lights on, each set spinning out of time with the others, creating a jerky cross-rhythm that pulsed behind the scene, reflected and multiplied by the shop windows and the windows of passing cars, multiplied again as the shop windows reflected the car windows and the car windows reflected reflections of themselves back onto the shops. Everywhere I looked there were points of blue light. 'Look at you!' a bystander shouted, an IC3 female in her forties. She had her phone out filming. 'You got fifteen police officers for two people! Is that right? Is that right? That's why we can never, never trust you. Because you're all the same. All of you are the same!'

The nearest officers separated the man and woman who had been arguing so that they could question them. The other officers, seeing there was little to do, were standing in small groups chatting. 'You think you're above the law in your black and white,' the bystander continued. 'You think you're above the law, but Black people don't know your law.'

We drove north, the streets colder and harsher now the trees were bare. Someone passed around the Percy Pigs. 'There's Phizzy Pig Tails or normal ones,' they said.

We saw a white Transit van with a brake light out on Stockwell Road. The man driving it, IC2, twenties, had been lent the van for a few hours to move house. We stopped it 400 metres from his destination, discovered that he was uninsured and seized the vehicle. The driver called the van's owner on his mobile and passed us the phone. There was a frustrated voice on the other end, complaining, suggesting, pleading. 'Couldn't we just. . . . How about . . . Isn't there any . . . This is so . . .' The slowest part of the seizure was taking an inventory; the van contained all of the driver's possessions: toiletries, tools, appliances, pillows, a duvet, a gym bag full of DVDs, four bin bags stuffed with clothes, a six-gallon demijohn full of copper coins.

I felt freshly attuned to the significance of these traffic stops because I had recently received a court summons to give evidence against a man I had written a ticket for months earlier, an IC1 male in a trilby, who was driving without due care and attention. He had not paid the ticket, so I would be seeing him in a few weeks in a South London magistrates' court.

A call came out: the theft of a handbag in a cocktail bar in Brixton Market. The suspect was an IC2 female, mid-fifties, in white jeans and a red vest. We raced to the scene and spotted a woman who matched the description outside Fish, Wings and Tings, but not the white leather handbag she had been seen stealing on the bar's CCTV. We arrested and cuffed her at the Coldharbour Lane entrance to the market. 'My daughter! Oh my god, that's my daughter,' the woman said, ducking behind us. 'Please don't let her see me.'

The woman's name was Martina. The custody van arrived and we helped her into the cage at the back. In the middle of the van, where the arresting officers sit, a sword was rolling around on the floor, a polished steel sabre with a gold hilt. Someone radioed my partner, requesting our support. 'Can't, we've got a body,' he replied.

When we got to Brixton Custody it did not seem too busy and we went straight into the holding cell nearest to the desk. 'Won't be long,' we said to Martina. But we were. There were clearly some complex cases ahead of us, because we were waiting in the holding cell from half past nine until eleven o'clock. Martina was calm and upbeat to begin with, talking about the football game she had been planning to watch on TV that evening, telling us about her early life in South America, but after three-quarters of an hour her mood dipped. She started to need the toilet. She started to find the cuffs uncomfortable. She wanted to call her family.

'They're going to be worrying about me.'

'We understand you're frustrated,' we said, 'but these things take as long as they take.'

All three of us were ready to leave the small square cell when our turn came. It felt as though we had been standing in a lift for ninety minutes. We walked Martina to the desk, presented her to the Custody Sergeant and checked in her property. Keys, purse, phone, a toy car, a job seeker's card. I glanced around while the Custody Sergeant filled in the necessary paperwork. 'PCs: If you need to wash blood off your handcuffs,' read a sign behind the desk, 'please don't do it in the kitchen sink.' On the other side of the counter we could see the hot-dog vendor, a blank expression on his face, in for ignoring his fines and failing to appear at court.

Aside from the female constables and custody officers, Martina was the only woman in the custody suite. That was not unusual. Only about 15 per cent of people arrested are female. 'If men behaved like women,' wrote the criminologist Barbara Wootton, 'the courts would be idle and the prisons empty.' Martina said again that she was eager to let her family know she was OK, but we told her that as we had not found the stolen handbag, and she would not tell us where it was, she would not be allowed to phone home until we had searched her flat.

Once Martina was booked in, my partner and I left custody to join our unit in the van. We drove south from Brixton, up the hill, past Olive Morris House and the prison, and onto a quiet residential street. It was 1 a.m. and there was no other traffic around. There were speed bumps every few metres and the Sergeant accelerated towards them. He hit each bump as fast and hard as he could and we flew over them, all four wheels leaving the road, the van's undercarriage shuddering. We spun round a corner and parked outside Martina's flat.

'Look, what are you all doing charging in here in the middle of the night?'

'Are you Martina's daughters? She's been arrested.'

'For fuck's sake. This is just like her!'

Even in a small flat, there are a lot of places to hide a handbag. We split up and searched the five rooms, in two of which small children were sleeping. We searched the kitchen and living room, then dug through the overflowing wardrobes and toy boxes in the five-year-old's bedroom. The Sergeant popped his head in. 'Found anything? No? Well get the fuck out then,' he whispered. 'We don't want him to wake up and find his room full of coppers.' The officer searching Martina's twenty-year-old daughter's bedroom leaned into the corridor and rattled a pair of heart-shaped handcuffs at us. 'Boys, do you need these?' He disappeared for a moment then peered out again. 'Do you need this?' he said, waving a silver vibrator. 'She was pretty fit, wasn't she?' he said, back in the van. 'I bet as soon as we left, she was straight back in her room, strumming herself.'

We did not find the stolen handbag. The outrage on her daughters' faces also suggested it had not been dropped off there. We could only assume that Martina had been working with somebody else or had panicked and dumped it in the market.

In the Phoenix the next morning, I thought about Martina's grandchildren waking up and wondering where she was. I thought about how strange it was to have the power to demand that a family let you into their sleeping children's bedrooms in the middle of the night. We demanded such pure and total trust from the public.

Listening to the breathless excitement of the officer who found the vibrator, his delight that the call of duty had called him to the bedroom of a twenty-year-old woman, I felt as if I was back in a teenage changing room again. I was reminded of the banter of the most confident, athletic boys at my school, the boys who successfully and repeatedly struck up relationships with teenage girls.

And as I remembered those boys, I also recalled the rumours: tales of consent only half-given, of consent skilfully procured, of consent unrequired because a girl was so drunk, of acts that were right on the perimeter of rape. The rumours were shared like jokes. *He did it while she was being sick in the toilet. He tied a flag around his neck and phoned me while he did it, shouting, 'I'm doing it for St George!'*

Looking back, I could not believe I had heard a story like that and not told anyone. It had felt like it was nothing to do with me. These were boys I did not like, taking advantage of girls I did not know. More than anything, though, each story was just one story, and there were often others rumbling in the background.

In Year 8, I was picked as the reserve for the English Schools' Athletics Championships and found myself in a white minibus, not dissimilar from the police vans I would sit in fifteen years later, with a group of boys I would never normally socialize with, including the boy who would later do it for St George. I sat near the front and no one spoke to me for the entire day. During the long journey south, the boys at the back papered the van's windows with tabloid nudes, drank energy drinks and threw the glass bottles onto the motorway, where they shattered beneath the wheels of the oncoming cars. At the time, I thought the teachers could not see what was happening and agonized over whether to tell them. I now realize that they must have seen everything and had chosen to ignore it. At the contest, I was drafted into the 400 metres and the long jump and came last in both.

A coffee appeared in front of me. I sat up straight and looked around the Phoenix. I was pleased to see the manager chanting above his A–Z and Brixton alive outside the window.

The officer who found the vibrator was not a teenage boy. He was a professional contracted to work with vulnerable people, people in distress. His behaviour was a violation of trust and privacy – of his duty as a police officer. I wondered again how such a moment had become possible within the Met. There were plenty of workplaces where it would be highly risky to use the language and behaviour I had witnessed. In the Met, it sometimes felt riskier to opt out.

Was it simply cooped up men enacting a misogyny rife in

society? Was it something to do with the police role itself, with the raw, unrelenting exposure to other people's trauma? Cynicism, emotional numbing, avoidant behaviours, difficulty empathizing, minimizing violence. These were known effects of trauma, and they were all things I had noticed in some of the regulars I worked with. Had they been traumatized by their work? Was that what lay behind the normalization of violent sexual language and casual misogyny?

I had been troubled by all of this from day one. Yet each time I encountered overt sexism or sexualization, I did nothing more than write it down on a notecard in the dark. I knew that if I had encountered overt racism on a shift, I would not have hesitated to report it. So what was it about casual misogyny that seemed less worthy of escalation? The answer was the same as when I was a teenager: these moments were the product of a culture so evident and accepted that it seemed pointless to point it out. Senior officers must know, so why tell them? I wondered whether that was how some officers had felt in the face of overt police racism across the preceding decades.

Instead of complaining, I came to the Phoenix and I typed up my notes. My response was weary disgust, not urgent concern, underpinned by a belief that I was so peripheral to events it was not up to me to report them. As a teenager and as a police officer I underestimated the danger of what I was seeing. I left the complaining to the victims.

The appalling can sometimes become habitual. Values warp, big things seem small, abuse presents itself as entertainment. And out of the everyday, extreme violence can arise. Policing showed me this again and again in the situations we dealt with – gang stabbings, domestic violence – but I did not turn the lesson back upon policing itself.

Casual sexism co-existed in the Met with what seemed to be a sincere attempt to stamp out racism. Yet the night before, we had still been accused of being racist. I thought about the call to Angell Town, about the IC3 male threatening the IC3 female, and of the bystander shouting at us, telling us we were all the same. I understood her bewilderment at the sight of fifteen police officers surrounding two people, but I still felt needled.

*You're all the same.* Such a simple formulation, such a neat denial of individuality and agency. It reminded me of a comment by James Baldwin in *The Fire Next Time*: 'all policemen have by now, for me, become exactly the same', he writes. 'I cannot risk assuming that the humanity of these people is more real to them than their uniforms.'

*You're all the same* did not mean that we were literally all identical. It meant that, after decades of racist policing, we had forfeited the right to be seen in a more nuanced way. For Baldwin, for the bystander, it was a deliberate, political refusal of nuance.

The police are often accused of treating certain groups of people as if they are all the same: addicts, the homeless, and especially young Black males. The bystander's comment projected our inability to see people as individuals back onto us, stereotyping the stereotypers. Prior to becoming a police officer, I had never felt the sting of being stereotyped. After a year in the Met, I had an inkling.

The thrust of the bystander's comment was that nothing had changed: we were as racist as ever. Linton Kwesi Johnson made a similar remark in 2020. 'Our relationship with the police is one thing that has not changed one iota,' he said. 'My grandson experiences the same harassment that I experienced.' By contrast, the Met believed that it had changed immeasurably since the trial of the Mangrove Nine, Swamp 81 and the Brixton uprising. I did not know what to make of this disconnect.

In my trawl for books about the police, I had come across John Benyon's 1986 book, *A Tale of Failure: Race and Policing*. Early on, Benyon details the experiences of Mark Bravo, an IC3 male who bought a motorcycle on his sixteenth birthday in 1982:

> During the first week he was stopped by the police on seven occasions and this began a pattern which continued for several months. His mother kept a record of his encounters during a two-week period in April 1982: 2 April: stopped four times; 4 April: stopped once; 5 April: stopped twice; 7 April: stopped seven times; 8 April: stopped twice; 9 April: stopped twice; 14 April: stopped five times.

Until the Macpherson Report declared the Met institutionally racist in 1999, after the myriad failings in the investigation into the murder of Stephen Lawrence, the leaders of the Metropolitan Police maintained that race was not a factor in the way their constables policed. In 1978 the Commissioner Robert Mark described the Met as 'an outstanding example of a happily integrated and harmonious multi-racial organization'. The police were not, he wrote, responsible for the 'problem of alienated black youth', which had been 'dumped on their lap without any means to resolve it'. Nevertheless, his officers' efforts to engage with these young people had been 'one of the most admirable chapters in their history so far'.

In his memoir *A Search for Belonging*, Michael Fuller

describes the decades of subtle and explicit racism he experienced as a Black police officer, and the way that his confrontations with prejudice often backfired on him. 'Police racism was an ugly beast in the corner which I didn't want to poke,' he writes. Fuller persisted and went on to develop the Met's action plan after the Macpherson Report. He later became Chief Constable of Kent Police, then Chief Inspector of the Crown Prosecution Service.

From my time inside the Met, I could see that the overt racism of the 1970s and 1980s had gone. Racism was condemned openly throughout recruitment and training. Officers policed one another's language. I believed that most officers had rejected it in theory. But I could also see that intentions and outcomes did not match up: Black people were almost ten times more likely to be stopped and searched than white people, and more than twice as likely to die in police custody. Principle and practice were running on separate circuits. Many officers were acting against their stated beliefs without even realizing it. In 1970, Egon Bittner remarked that 'police activity is as much directed to who a person is as to what he does.' He was writing about the police in the USA in 1970. He could have been writing about the Met today.

'My view is that on occasions we work on stereotypes,' said Chief Superintendent Victor Olisa in 2016, the most senior Black officer in the Met at the time. 'That stereotype of Black men being more aggressive, more confrontational, is a stereotype that plays on some officers' minds and that can lead to a different level of policing style and force being used on a Black suspect than it probably would do otherwise.'

My bubble and squeak arrived, along with a second mug of coffee. Even if present-day policing were perfect, I thought, there would still be the past to contend with. How should the Met come to terms with the lives it ruined, and the abuse it doled out to communities it had pledged to protect? The need to reckon with the past jostled with the impulse to forget, ignore, downplay and move on. What James Baldwin said about white America could be said about the Metropolitan Police: 'They are, in effect, still trapped in a history which they do not understand; and until they understand it they cannot be released from it.'

When I began policing, I struggled to understand the depth of the distrust and anger still felt towards us by certain sections of the community. As I heard the stories of Cherry Groce, Wayne Douglas, Ricky Bishop and Sean Rigg, it began to make more sense. How could we expect people to presume the best when they saw another IC3 teenager being searched, or four police vehicles descending on one Black couple?

For Baldwin, reckoning with a dark past is a constructive process, something that strengthens those who do it. 'To accept one's past – one's history – is not the same thing as drowning in it,' he wrote, 'it is learning how to use it. An invented past can never be used; it cracks and crumbles under the pressures of life like clay in a season of drought.' Painful and counter-intuitive as it might feel, I wondered what would happen if the Met embraced the most uncomfortable aspects of its recent past and placed them at the centre of the story it tells about itself.

I looked around the Phoenix and nobody looked back at me. I was glad to be out of uniform, to be just one more person having breakfast.

'Me and Jamal are waiting here because that girl took down my number plate,' said Darren. 'We're nothing to do with this and that's why we're here – to tell you that we didn't do nothing.'

A group of IC3 teenage robbers had put their victim in a headlock, unclipped his three-thousand-pound Rolex, then jumped into a silver hatchback and driven away. They had known exactly what they wanted and had not even bothered to ask for money or phones. The victim's girlfriend was with him during the attack and she had noted down the getaway car's licence plate – and Darren's too, because his car was parked nearby and he and Jamal had appeared a few moments after the incident.

We were on Arodene Road, just off Brixton Hill. It was gone midnight and bitterly cold, the kind of biting early-winter night that keeps people indoors. My partner was talking to the victim and his girlfriend, an IC1 couple, late twenties, who lived near the site of the robbery. I was standing a few metres away with Darren and Jamal, a pair of IC3 males in their late teens. While they were explaining what had happened, another response car pulled up and three officers got out. They surveyed the situation and, as they did so, Jamal walked away from me to Darren's car to get his chips from the front seat.

'Step away from the car, mate,' one of the new officers shouted.

'No, man, I'm just getting my chips,' Jamal replied.

'Step away from the car,' the officer repeated.

When Jamal did not comply, the officer ran over and yanked him backwards, causing the polystyrene tray to spin from his hands. 'My chips!' Jamal shouted. Another officer joined the first and they walked Jamal to the side of a house and pinned his arms behind his back, so that his torso and the right side of his head were pressed against the brickwork. Darren walked over to them. 'Hey! Get off my friend!' he said. 'You need to get off my friend. We haven't done nothing!' The third response officer withdrew his cuffs, clipped a bracelet on Darren's left wrist and, with a well-practised motion, pulled the right wrist in to join it. 'What are you doing?' said Darren. 'Can you see what he's doing?' he shouted to the empty street. 'I ain't done nothing and he's putting cuffs on me!'

All of this took, perhaps, forty-five seconds and it was only when Darren and Jamal were both pinned against the wall that we had the opportunity to explain the situation to the three response officers. They nodded as we talked, relaxed their grip on the pair and unlocked Darren's handcuffs. We told Darren and Jamal they were free to go.

'Have a good night, guys,' one of the officers said.

'Have a good wank!' said Jamal. 'You go home and have a good wank!'

'You know, I might just do that,' the officer replied.

We took a description of the robbers from the IC1 couple, circulated it on the radio, then took them on a drive-around of the neighbouring streets, in case the robbers were still at large. We found the getaway car in the middle of the Tulse Hill Estate. According to our checks it was a rental vehicle. We called a forensic team to come out and dust for prints.

The Friday before Christmas, thousands of office parties, the most drunken night of the year. Vauxhall was overrun. On Goding Street, making the most of the occasion, we found the hot-dog vendor. We dismissed his customers and ran a name check on him. When we had confirmed that he was not currently wanted, we told him to pack up and go home. 'What's your problem?' he said. 'You got nothing better to do?' But he scraped the sausages into a box and wheeled the cart away.

This was going to be one of my final shifts. My wife and I were moving to South America with her work. I had handed in my resignation to the Met and in a few weeks' time I would return my uniform and warrant card.

It was going to be a lively evening. Already, at half past eight, the atmosphere was raucous.

An IC3 male, early twenties, ran up to us shouting, 'Listen, listen, three Black guys down there took my money. I was trying to buy drugs, I gave them twenty pounds, and they just walked off!' We were taking down his details when his friends ran up to pull him away.

'Mate, what are you doing telling them you were buying drugs? Mate, come on!'

'No, no, I want my money back!' the young man persisted.

Looking around, crowds everywhere, people shouting and running, I felt overwhelmed. It was chaos. I knew, though, that my bewilderment was really a form of illiteracy, an inability to sift and decode what I was seeing. I was patrolling with an experienced regular, and when she looked at Vauxhall – the clubs, the Pleasure Gardens, the thousands of people streaming in and out of the bus and train stations – she saw what the urban activist Jane Jacobs called the 'organized complexity' of big-city life. She could see patterns and abnormalities invisible to my eyes: troubling behaviour, simmering tensions, people in places you would not expect them.

I observed the way she approached people, pausing for short, friendly interactions with anyone sitting or standing around, from the homeless IC1 males in the park to the laughing crowds of IC3 females gathering before entering the clubs. Interaction by interaction, my colleague gauged the way the evening was shaping up, what was happening where, which issues to anticipate.

Great policing is a mysterious blend of knowledge, skill, judgement and values that can be difficult to pick apart. I asked the regular about her approach. 'I genuinely believe in prevention rather than cure,' she replied. 'If you talk to someone early on in the evening, they're much more likely to get on with you if you pull them out of a club later on. I joined the job fourteen years ago and, in all that time, I've never been assaulted. Policing is all about getting on with people, and not enough officers think like that.'

She kept pausing to chat to people, conducting short stops, but without them feeling like stops. She was intelligence gathering, but she was also just being friendly. She was like a diplomat working the room at a cocktail party, moving seamlessly from one group to another. Over the early part of the evening, she must have greeted several hundred people, imprinting our presence onto their minds, affecting their outlook and behaviour in small but significant ways. 'Cheers, we'll be around all evening,' she said at the end of each interaction. She was assertive, while still sounding warm and sincere.

Robert Peel, the founder of the Met, wanted his new police to offer 'individual service and friendship to all members of the public'. 'Service' made sense, but 'friendship' surprised me. I would have imagined it being a secondary concern, or even something to be avoided. But Peel was clear that the 'power of the police to fulfil their functions and duties is dependent on public approval' and that constables needed to be not just professional, but friendly and affable.

Watching the way my partner policed, her easy open manner, her genuine interest in what people were saying, and watching the faces of the people she spoke to, clearly happy and surprised to be having a laugh with a police officer, Peel's focus on friendship made sense.

Some of the regulars I had worked with seemed suspicious of the public and saw themselves as separate.

'I hate the public,' I heard one regular say.

'I hate to tell you,' his partner replied, 'but you kind of are the public sometimes.'

Robert Peel founded the Met on the 'historic tradition that the police are the public and that the public are the police'. His new police constables were simply members of the public paid to give full-time attention to issues that concern everyone. The best officers I encountered embodied this ethos. They acted like part of the community. They treated the uniform as a passport, as a device for getting closer to others.

My partner did not seem to think she was doing anything particularly remarkable. Egon Bittner noted something similar among officers on Denver's skid row. He was struck by 'the unanticipated high level of competence of some police officers in the handling of problems of obviously high complexity, seriousness and importance', and he was even more struck that the 'the officers themselves did not seem to be cognizant of their remarkable capabilities'. The officers did not think they were doing anything special, even while resolving thorny situations, preventing crime and offering the public care and respect.


A call came out about an IC3 teenage male loitering outside a building site a few streets away. We accepted it and went to see what was happening. When we got there, we found the boy wearing a pair of headphones, leaning on a fence.

'You OK, mate?' my partner said. 'What you up to?'

'Just waiting for a friend,' he replied.

'Doing anything nice tonight?'

'Just chilling,' he said. 'Go to a friend's place, listen to some music, eat some pizza.'

'All right mate, you have a good one,' she said, and we walked away.

'Why didn't you search him?' I asked.

'What for?' she said. 'Just because someone sees a young guy standing on the street and phones the police? He was relaxed, he didn't seem to be hiding anything. I'm going to need more than that before I make him turn out his pockets.'

'I don't know that young man,' she continued, 'but for things like stop and search, it makes a real difference when you know the local crowd. If you don't know the place, the people, what's going on, you end up searching any old person. And that's when people get pissed off. You search them, but what are your grounds? You search them and they're standing right outside their home address, minding their own business. It's not on.'

We were walking back along Goding Street when we saw a car with a window wide open. On the back seat was a red leather handbag, the kind of deep, plump bag that clearly contains the coordinates to somebody's entire existence. If we did not do something, it was unlikely to be waiting there for its owner at the end of the evening. My partner leaned into the car, pulled the bag out and rootled around for the owner's ID. She found a name, but not a phone number, so she began calling the numbers on the back of various cards in the purse. After several fruitless phone calls, she got hold of the doorman of a hall of residence and persuaded him to call the bag's owner on her mobile phone and tell her the police were waiting by her car. We stood by the car waiting, whippits gleaming by the kerb beside us, laughing gas canisters inhaled for a quick high. Five minutes later a pair of IC3 females, early twenties, came around the corner. 'Did I leave it like that?' one of them shouted. 'I can't believe it! Oh my days, I am so embarrassed!'

Policing can be a route to status and power, to care and service, to action and thrills – or some blend of the three. Each officer has their own reasons for being there, which play out in their interactions with the public.

The role attracts a curious blend of characters, but it

demands the same of all of them: police officers need deep and enduring empathy for vulnerability, pain and loss; and, at the same time, they need to embrace their role as guardians of order, and as a vehicle for coercive force. Police officers need genuine humanity, and they need to be willing to pin someone to the floor. The potential for cognitive dissonance is high. Add to this the challenge of responding effectively to domestic violence, mental ill health, homelessness and teenage gangs, and cynicism and disillusionment are ever-present risks.

It is not a big step from failing to solve a problem to thinking that a problem cannot be solved. It can be difficult to maintain empathy with people who do not seem to want you there, or people you cannot seem to help, or people in situations you have seen so many times that they have come to seem inevitable. It takes resilience to turn up every day at Brixton Police Station, optimistic, empathetic, with a belief in your ability to make a difference. 'Are you thinking of joining the job?' regulars would often ask Special Constables on patrol with them. The Specials usually said yes. 'Don't,' the regulars usually replied.

I asked my partner how she saw her colleagues. 'Fifty per cent of officers are good,' she said, '25 per cent are truly excellent. And 25 per cent are in this job for all the wrong reasons, and they're the ones that the public remembers.'

Outside Chariots Roman Spa, we spotted an IC3 male, late teens, wearing a white apron and setting up an oil-drum barbecue. On the pavement around him were packets of napkins, bottles of water, polystyrene cartons, plastic cutlery and Tupperware full of jerk chicken. He was busily laying out his wares, getting ready for the crowds that would come pouring out over the coming hours. We walked over and explained that it was illegal to sell food on the street without a licence. The young man was silent for a moment, then looked at us.

'I'm at college. I've done all my health and safety and stuff.'

'That may be,' my partner said, 'but you can't sell food on the street without a licence.'

'I'm just trying to make some honest cash. Look at this: it's jerk chicken, not crack. I've got all my stuff ready . . .' He paused, his facial expression changing several times in quick succession, his mouth opening then closing as his desire to argue battled with his hope that not arguing might improve the chances of us leaving him to it. 'Look, I've got literally 300 chicken thighs I need to cook tonight . . .' He went quiet and waited for us to say something. My partner took out her phone and showed him the local council website explaining how to register as a street trader.

'This is no judgement on your cooking,' she said. 'We admire the entrepreneurialism, but you need to pack up. The regulations are there for a reason.'

The young man disassembled his barbecue in silence and loaded the napkins, water, cartons, cutlery, and tubs of raw chicken back into the boot of his car.

'Shame that,' my partner said, as we walked away. 'I hate to crush a young person trying their best.'

'Why not turn a blind eye?' I asked.

'Slippery slope,' she said. 'The rules are there for everyone. They exist for a reason. That chicken could be full of salmonella. Probably not. But it's not impossible. Then you've got a mass poisoning, just because we wanted to be nice to someone.'

—

I found that it was not that difficult to do police work – to turn up and go through the motions. Relative to teaching it is a forgiving profession. As a teacher, working with the same children every day, you are accountable for their progress, and for the quality of the relationships in your classroom. You cannot disguise your failure or success. As a police officer, there are endless fresh starts. When we sour a situation, we just move on to the next. We are not accountable for the well-being and growth of the people we interact with. In fact, the convenient paradox for police is that the less effectively we respond to complex social issues, the more necessary we seem. More teen violence, more mental health crises, more disorder look like justifications for more assertive policing by even more officers, even though they may be sending the opposite message entirely.

I found, however, that it was very difficult to do police work well. In no small part, because I simply did not know what that meant. I thought about the hypothetical poisoning we had prevented, the hypothetical bag theft we had prevented, and all the hypothetical fights and drug deals and robberies my partner had prevented by being so proactive at the start of the evening. Policing was strange work. Great teaching makes good things happen. Does great police work simply stop bad things happening? Were the things we prevented our greatest achievements?

I wondered how much further police work could go and whether we could get close enough to communities to see a real connection between our work and improvements in the lives of the people we worked with and for.


It was just gone eleven. An intoxicated IC1 male had swung an empty vodka bottle at one of the bouncers outside Barcode. The bouncer, a foot shorter than his assailant, had knocked the man to the ground and we ran over to help, with a couple of other officers, the broken bottle crunching beneath our boots. 'Get me up! Just get me up, all right?' the man on the floor was shouting. 'I'm going to complain!' He was flailing and at risk of hurting himself, so we crouched down to restrain him, one officer on his legs, my partner and I pinning his arms, and another holding his head. 'My willy's hanging out!' the man said. 'Get me up! Can't you see my willy's hanging out!'

Once the man was cuffed, we left another pair of officers to do the arrest and went to chat to the bouncers outside each of the clubs to check how things were going, starting with the bouncer who had been attacked with a bottle. He laughed when we asked how he was. 'It's because I'm short,' he said. 'People think they can have a go.' Everything was peaceful at Union, Lightbox, Fire, the Hoist, so we went for a walk across the Pleasure Gardens.

A call came out. An IC1 male, forties, was walking around St George's Wharf menacing passers-by with a golf club. Officers were in pursuit but needed backup. The man had beaten up another IC1 male with the golf club in the middle of Vauxhall bus station, the boyfriend of a woman with whom he was also involved. There were blood spatters the length of the concourse and, while a group of officers ran to St George's Wharf, we were instructed to cordon off the entire bus station until the Scene of Crime Officers had inspected it.

Vauxhall bus station is long and narrow, with bus stops on both sides, and a sleek stainless-steel roof suspended above it. We jogged around it with rolls of blue and white tape, wrapping it around poles and bins, until there was almost nowhere buses could stop or people could wait. Buses arrived, hovered wherever they could to let passengers off, and then pulled out again, often without picking anyone up.

We stood there for two hours, while SOCOs examined the scene in their white suits and police dogs nosed around the traffic island between the bus station and St George's Wharf. A dozen of us were needed to keep the full length of the cordon secure as confused clubbers, spotting their bus home, tried to cut the six metres from one side of the cordon to the other. We sent them running around the cordon's 400-metre perimeter instead, generally to find that their bus had gone by the time they reached the place where they had seen it.

My partner and I had hoped to be outside the clubs keeping the peace, dealing with drug dealing, robberies and drunken altercations. Instead, we were stuck in one place, shouting at men urinating on the wheelie bins outside the *Big Issue* office, and flagging buses for desperate passengers.

From where we were standing, we could see across to the nightclubs in the railway arches. On the spot where the jerk chicken chef had been setting up, I could see the illegal hot-dog vendor, selling to people leaving Union, Barcode and Chariots Roman Spa. With all of us on the giant cordon, there was nothing we could do about it. We stood guarding the scene for three and a half hours until a voice shouted, 'Take down the tape!'

Out in the Phoenix the next day I was typing up my notes and thinking about Egon Bittner again. The previous night's shift, patrolling with my partner, had given me a sense of what excited Bittner during his nights on skid row: the promise of good policing, its beauty when enforcement and empathy mesh.

In certain ways I felt a kinship with Bittner. He was a sociologist who had happened upon policing as an object of study. He had simply begun going out on night shifts with officers and his work evolved from there. It all started 'in a quite unplanned way', he wrote, 'and remained throughout its duration an entirely open-ended ethnographic adventure'.

Part of what attracted me to policing was the fact that I had never been attracted to policing – and yet the police interacted with so many themes that I cared about. I also embarked on my night shifts unaware of what I would find, and I treated it as open-ended research and, yes, adventure too.

Bittner's interest was piqued by the realization that we know very little about the police. The police are 'the best known and least understood institution', he wrote. Everyone in a society is acutely aware of them, knows how to behave around them, and yet popular beliefs about what police do are often limited to notions of crime fighting and law enforcement. Bittner's fascination developed when he observed 'the immense richness and scope of police work'. Law enforcement was a facade that masked a far wider and deeper role in society. The 'range of police responsibility was virtually unlimited', he realized, and yet the police's reach and influence was little acknowledged, even by police officers themselves.

In London today, the shortcomings of the police seemed to be due to a shortage of imagination as much as a shortage of money or talent. If we embraced 'the immense richness and scope of police work', what might the role become? We spent so much time driving and walking around and so little time discussing how we should be spending it. Even looking at good policing, I could not help asking myself: *Is this it?* Faced with exclusion and isolation, with cycles of violence, damage and pain, was this the best we could come up with?

I had now read a lot of Egon Bittner's work, had grown to like and admire him, and yet I still knew very little about him. I had searched for obituaries, newspaper profiles, anything that contained biographical information, but I had found nothing of note. I was about to look for the email addresses of his former colleagues, when I came across a special issue of *Ethnographic Studies* dedicated to Bittner, a memorial publication full of tributes from his students and peers. This was more promising. Most of the pieces were scholarly appraisals of his work, but among them I found a surprise cache of reflections and memories.

Egon Bittner 'was a man of obvious depth who exuded a kind of passionate soul', one person wrote. Another described the 'mischievous spirit in his otherwise somber melancholy', and another his 'wonderfully whimsical sense of humor'. The comments tallied with the wry half-smile in his photo and the flair and idiosyncrasy of his writing.

I read through all of the personal recollections from his students and colleagues, accounts of what he was like as a teacher and friend. It was all very pleasant and urbane: scenes of intellectual sparring in armchairs, seminars and serene university meeting rooms. Then I read something that stopped me short. 'We all knew that Professor Bittner was a Holocaust camp survivor,' one of his students had written, 'the tattooed numbers on his wrist were there for anyone to see.'

I paused. I had known that Bittner had emigrated to the USA after the Second World War. But nothing I had read had hinted that he had suffered directly at the hands of the Nazis. As far I knew, Bittner did not mention this in his writing anywhere.

Another student went into detail:

Egon (and his wife Jean and her two sisters) had
(independently) all been Holocaust survivors. I learned,
for example, that he had been a (cub?) reporter for a
small newspaper in Krakow, Poland in 1939 when the
Nazis invaded. Egon was arrested and incarcerated for
all of World War II. As we became better acquainted,
he gradually revealed some of the details of his
concentration camp life, especially what it was like to
exist in a constrained and often brutal bureaucracy.

An obituary by a colleague, George Ross, tried to make sense of the man he became:

Egon Bittner was born in 1921 in Silesia, a part of
central Europe which was then in Czechoslovakia, but

which at different moments in Egon's youth had been
Polish and German. Egon was from a Jewish
community decimated by the Holocaust, and he was a
rare survivor. It is hard to know whether his
extraordinary generosity, compassion, modesty, and
ability to recognize and live with difference and
diversity came from this upbringing or this horrible
experience.

Bittner grew up in contested territory, lost his family in the
Holocaust, married a fellow concentration camp survivor and
emigrated to the United States. He suffered and witnessed
horrific atrocities, enabled by an appallingly efficient bureaucracy. And he went on to become one of the greatest scholars
of bureaucracy – of the way states channel and apply force, and
of the ethical dilemmas faced by those who wield it. There was
still much I did not know, but I was no longer surprised by the
unique lucidity of his insights.

Bittner described the development of the police as part of
'the rise of the sustained, and thus far not abandoned, aspiration
of Western society to abolish violence and install peace as a
stable and permanent condition of everyday life'. Bittner's
impassioned scholarship, his lifelong project to improve
policing, now looked less like diligent criminology than a
personal and political mission. He dedicated his life to shaping
societies in which the violence he experienced could not recur.
He understood that, left unchecked, the police would likely
enact our worst impulses. Set up correctly, however, they might
enact the best.

Better policing could lead to a better, more peaceful world.

On patrol in Brixton town centre, a cold Friday in early January. Some people were starting their night out, others were still making their way home. There was a long queue at the cash-point outside Sainsbury's and crowds at a dozen different bus stops. There was an incense vendor outside Iceland, a man begging outside Morleys, a woman buying flowers. There were boys on bikes, smokers outside the tube. There were several dozen people standing still and several hundred in motion, their places taken by others as soon as they moved out of sight. It was a standard Brixton scene, busy but unremarkable. We walked down Atlantic Road, then turned right onto Coldharbour Lane.

As we were passing Bookmongers, a call came out about a stabbing outside McDonald's. We radioed to accept it, ran past the Ritzy, across the High Street and were the first at the scene, arriving in under a minute. We looked around, ran left and right, but there was no sign of a stab victim and there were no witnesses waiting. Nobody standing outside McDonald's had seen a stabbing, not even the door staff in their hi-vis jackets. It was not clear who had made the call and we could not see anything untoward. We radioed with an update. It must have been a prank or a false alarm.

We continued along the High Street. As we were passing NatWest, an IC1 female, mid-twenties, in business attire, walked briskly up to us and said that an IC3 male, medium height, late teens, had just passed her holding a wad of bloody tissues to his face. We ran in the direction she was pointing, turned down Brighton Terrace and spotted two people on a street corner behind Morleys. The victim, Louis, was an IC3 male, late teens, wearing black jeans, a black puffer and a black leather cap. Blood was seeping through the napkins he was holding to his jaw and there was a trickle of blood running down his left cheek from his eye. With him was an IC3 female, mid-teens, calling an ambulance and passing Louis fresh tissues. I had never been the first responder at a stabbing before and I had always imagined that the experience would be noisy and horrific. Louis seemed so calm, applying pressure to his own wound, that the situation felt strangely undramatic.

'This guy just came out of nowhere,' Louis told us. 'I thought he'd punched me in the face but then I realized I was bleeding.' He lifted up the napkins to reveal a gouge on his right cheek an inch wide, which went down to the bone. He had been punched by somebody holding a shard of glass. From the shape of the wound, and the amount of flesh ripped out, the attacker must have twisted the shard before pulling it out.

Did Louis know the man who had hit him? He did not. Could he describe him? Nothing detailed, just that the attacker was an IC3 male with a scar on his face. I remembered learning in first-aid training that stab victims do not always realize that they have been stabbed, believing they have been punched, and may not be aware of all the wounds they have sustained. I patted Louis down, my gloved hands travelled methodically from head to toe, checking the rest of his body for injuries, checking the palms of my gloves for blood after each pat. It was like a slow-motion stop and search, the same gestures for different ends. It was like a surreal extension of all of the times I had patched up children in the playground, muttering reassurance, wiping grit from their grazes.

A response car pulled up and an officer stepped out with a full first-aid kit. She pressed a thick dressing onto the wound and wrapped a bandage around Louis's head, under his chin and over his scalp, around and around, until it looked as though he was wearing a wimple and his jaw was so tightly clamped that it was difficult for him to talk. Louis placed the bloody tissues he had been holding on top of the hedge next to him. We kept telling him how well he was doing and that he was going to be fine, although he did not look as if he needed the reassurance. Perhaps he was calm because he had not seen the wound and did not know how severe it was. Perhaps his composure was actually shock. As more officers and an ambulance arrived, passers-by crowded around us, standing on tiptoe to see. 'Wow, mate, nice safe area you've brought us to!' we could hear. 'Typical Brixton. See what a lovely area we live in?'

When we found Louis, the girl looking after him told us that she had seen what had happened. But when we looked for her after Louis climbed into the ambulance, our only witness had disappeared. Meanwhile, back at McDonald's, on the stretch of pavement leading up to the Acre Lane Ladbrokes, some regular officers had found blood spatters and cordoned off the area. My partner and I walked over there and took their places on the tape.

Scores of people walked past us, most walking around the cordon without looking at it, some pausing to ask what had happened. I called to a group of IC3 males, late teens, sitting outside Ladbrokes, and asked whether they had seen anything.

'We ain't seen nothing. Now move along, officer,' said one.

'It's not our job to tell you what happened,' said another. 'It's all on CCTV. Shouldn't you be looking at that?'

We stood on the cordon, rocking backwards and forwards on our heels, frustrated we had missed the blood spatters, embarrassed we had lost our witness. I played events over in my mind and stared at the five-way crossroads in front of me, hypnotised by the shifting red and green lights, watching the haphazard changes resolve into a clear and orderly system, watching the buses and cars stream up Brixton Hill, along Effra Road, Acre Lane, Coldharbour Lane. How was it always so busy here? Where were all these people going? Was there ever a moment when this crossroads was empty? I thought of the River Effra passing unperceived below all the movement and noise.

We had been standing on the cordon for forty minutes, when our lost witness walked up to us. 'Do you remember me?' she said with a smile. 'I was the one who was with him!' I could not believe it and I smiled and thanked for her coming back. We took down her details, her account of events, and a full description of the suspect. It turned out she had not been out with Louis that evening. She barely knew him. She was passing by when he was attacked and had stayed to check he was all right. She told us that an older IC3 male, mid-thirties, had smashed a brown beer bottle against the wall of an off-licence, then punched Louis in the face outside McDonald's with the broken bottle in his hand. Louis had then dashed around the corner, his blood spattering the pavement where we had set up the cordon, and over to the young men we had spoken to outside Ladbrokes. 'He's definitely involved with drugs and things, like all of them,' the girl said, 'so that's probably why he got stabbed.' She said that the attacker had followed Louis and it looked as if he was going to hit him again. At that point, she had started shouting and the older man had run away. She had then grabbed a fistful of napkins from McDonald's and walked Louis to the quiet corner behind Morleys where we had found them. The girl was bubbly and upbeat as she recounted the incident, seemingly unfazed by what had happened. We asked if she was willing to be contacted by the police and she said that she was.

The girl's talk of smashing and shouting made it even more peculiar that nobody we had spoken to had noticed the stabbing. Was it possible that a person could be stabbed in the face at eight in the evening outside McDonald's, without any of the hundreds of people present realizing? It made me think of the murder in Antonioni's film *Blow-Up*, which the photographer-protagonist inadvertently captures on camera while he is out taking pictures in a London park.

'I saw a man killed this morning,' he tells a friend.

'How did it happen?' the friend asks.

'I don't know, I didn't see.'

The photographer blows up his photos as large as possible and pegs them around his studio, but in the enlargement, the images become incomprehensible abstracts. 'That's the body,' he says, pointing at a smudge at the bottom of a blur. He goes to the park that night to test his theory and discovers that he is correct: there is a dead body beneath a hedge. But when he returns to his studio, the prints have been stolen, and when he returns to the park in the morning the body has gone. At no stage does the photographer seem tempted to involve the police. He appears to be more interested in the distance between what he perceives and what is actually happening, between the records he creates and the reality they record. I wondered whether anyone out in Brixton, snapping a selfie or a photo of friends, had inadvertently captured the stabbing.

One thing the girl's report established was that our cordon was in the wrong place. We had blocked off a section of pavement that Louis had bled onto, but not the crime scene itself, which had now been walked across by hundreds of people for almost an hour. When we looked around the corner, at the spot where Louis had been attacked, we found the remains of a smashed brown bottle on the ground.

I went out for breakfast in the Phoenix the next morning. Although Louis had seemed calm about the attack, I felt shaken. I thought about Zac Olumegbon again, and all the other young people who had been killed and would be killed within a mile or two of my front door.

One thing seemed clear: the gang violence in London made no sense to anyone, not even the young people involved in it. But it was happening, and its senselessness did not diminish its impact. Something had been set in motion and now it was playing out.

'Why would a young person that is fifteen, sixteen, seventeen years old want to pick up a knife and just stab someone at random that they've never met before?' asks the criminologist Craig Pinkney, who investigates the causes of youth violence. 'Why would someone want to pick up a gun just because someone lives in a different postcode and be prepared to shoot it? Why would someone be prepared to kill a child on a school bus just because they're looking at them for ten seconds?'

I had heard versions of these questions time and time again. 'Do all nations produce teenagers willing to kill each other over virtually nothing?' wrote Akala. 'Because I promise you that the vast majority of the stabbings in London are over almost nothing: a wrong look, a perceived disrespect, a silly comment, getting caught in a rival postcode.'

The irrationality of the violence was staggering. Pinkney pointed to factors such as poverty, austerity, family dysfunction, racism and a sense, among some young people, of being 'invisible, unseen, unheard', as he tried to untangle why young people attack one another. But even taken all together, these factors could not provide a satisfactory explanation, and it was the very irrationality of the violence that Pinkney zeroed in on. These were not rational acts. They were not the result of cold calculation. They were the products of intense stress on developing brains, the cortisol overload that comes from knowing 'when I step out of my house I might die'. They were the product of experiencing, and never processing, major trauma. 'Violence is a public health issue,' Pinkney writes. 'Violence is a disease, it's contagious, it spreads.' To look for logical explanations was to profoundly misunderstand it. The parallel reality of gang life was not just about living by different codes, it was about being in an altered state.

From working in education, I knew about the effect early experiences have on later life. I was aware of the effects of stress on children's brains, the way it can affect their ability to pay attention and control their impulses. I had thought a great deal about the impact of stress on children's performance and behaviour in the classroom. I had not confronted the fact that the state of children's brains could be a matter of life and death. Children who grow up in poverty, experiencing chronic stress, peril and adversity, are quite literally not in their right minds.

I thought about my own teenage years, and what a mind-addling experience those years are for even the most secure, well-supported young people. Writing about adolescence, Jane Jacobs described how easily, without the right accompaniment, it can become 'a form of outlaw life' – even before you add in trauma, daily peril and toxic stress.

Some former Brixton gang members support young people caught up in the gangs today. One such figure is Jaja Soze, formerly of the PDC gang, who was an important influence on Sneakbo. PDC became a local success story after it transformed itself from a gang into an entertainment business. 'All the violence can be stopped,' Jaja Soze says. 'I want to show people you don't have to disassociate from your friends. You can turn your gang into a gang of property developers or solicitors. You can change the energy into positive stuff.'

Another is Karl Lokko, formerly known as Lox, leader of the OC gang on the Myatt's Fields Estate. OC, which stands for 'Organized Crime' or 'One Chance', were long-time allies of GAS and the precursor of the 410 Drill Crew. They provided another template for transformation, after Mimi Asher, a local pastor, took it upon herself to coax OC's leaders out of gang life, when her son joined. She welcomed Karl Lokko and others into her home, mentoring and caring for them.

Lokko describes gang life as a form of addiction: 'Like any addiction,' he writes, 'those who are addicted can see that the lifestyle they are leading is self-destructing but are almost powerless to change their circumstances.' The gang mentality is a closed circuit that makes no sense to those outside of it, but it has an internal logic which is incredibly difficult to escape. Looking back on a life in which he was once 'totally entrenched' and in which he 'used to carry a firearm going to the chicken shop', Lokko wrote, 'I don't even know how a man can have the capacity to inflict harm on another man in a way of stabbing or shooting – the thing for me is grotesque at the moment, but it wasn't always the case – it's just where your head is.' He described what he experienced with Pastor Mimi as 'therapeutic rehabilitation'.

Driving to a secondary school on an ordinary morning, chasing a fifteen-year-old and stabbing him to death in someone's front garden, made sense to five teenagers in summer 2010. A lot of horrific acts had made sense to a lot of young people in London. In due course, many of the survivors snap out of it and wonder how on earth they had thought that way.

Thinking about my nights chasing and searching teens, I did not feel we had treated gang violence as a health issue. I was not even sure what that would look like. We squared up to gang members as though they were our opposite numbers, shoring up their sense of identity. We were appalled by what these children were doing to one another, but we enjoyed running around after them. They gave us permission to regress, and we joined them in their distorted, deadly role play. Youth violence is the perfect storm for police officers: Pinkney, Lokko and others suggest that we need to meet vulnerability with care; we wanted to meet aggression with force.


Force often springs from frustration. When I began teaching, struggling with behaviour, the teachers I saw succeeding were the most forceful. Children were told there were hidden CCTV cameras around the school, children were stood up in front of the entire school and shouted at, children were told God could see what they were thinking, children were screamed at and demeaned. 'Look at you. You think you're a little prince!' a senior teacher screamed at one of my pupils when he would not be quiet. 'You think you're a prince, don't you? Well, you're not! You're just a little boy, a tiny little boy! Now don't you dare say another thing!' The scorn in her voice, the disgust on her face, were as cutting as her words; the boy was sobbing by the time she had finished.

I did not like what they did, but the forceful teachers looked strong. Only looking back can I see that they were struggling, that their methods were the product of deep frustration. Nothing worked for long. Children became immune to their tactics. They could only retain control if they continually escalated their threats, if they constantly reinforced their ferocious persona. They had probably never imagined treating children the way they did. But we were in Brixton, they reasoned, our children were tough, what else could they do?

I saw the same frustrations in the school staff room and the police canteen, and I saw the way that all sorts of things can come to feel normal within the closed culture of a school or a police force.

A few weeks into my first term, I began to notice the teachers who somehow achieved control without force, who were assertive and authoritative, but who never screamed, and never played mind games. Theirs was the more difficult approach – it wasn't clear, as a new teacher, what I should copy – but what they achieved was profound: it looked like control, but really it was consent, cooperation, even, in the best classrooms, community. It was similar, perhaps, to what the best policing could achieve.

Talking to regular officers, I could see that they were exasperated by their inability to get through to local teenagers, that they did not have a better approach. Our tools were bravado, sarcasm and force. Although those things might earn us a kind of grudging respect, they did not seem to make things better. We chased, we stopped, we searched. We felt good when we took a knife off the streets. But we were caught in a game we did not really want to play.

Force is the cheapest form of power and the easiest to wield. It works. And because it works it is tempting to use more and more of it – as a teacher, a police officer, or anyone trying to control anyone else. But using force is like fishing with dynamite. You catch the fish, but what have you damaged in the process?

Sometime after finding Louis behind Morleys with his face gouged open, I read Roger Robinson's poetry collection *A Portable Paradise*. Many of the poems are set in Brixton and in one of them, 'Citizen III', a description of gang violence jumped out. Robinson describes the terrible absurdity of boys killing one another when they have so much in common and would surely, in other circumstances, be friends:

> you don't want no one round your way,
> especially if they look like you
> . . .
> you defend it,
> stand by it, and areas become ends
> to be defended from people who look just like you.

When I had typed my notes, I left the Phoenix and crossed the High Street to McDonald's. The blood spatters were still on the flagstones, sharp and clear in the morning light, although not so prominent that passers-by paused to look at them. I walked around the corner, to the street behind Morleys. Louis's bloody tissues were still on top of the hedge. They would probably never be cleaned up. They would stay there until it rained and they mulched into the leaves.

For the poet Roger Robinson, the River Effra, buried beneath the streets, provides an image for Brixton's submerged memories and the complexity of the community's relationship with its recent history: the challenge of both remembering and moving on, without one impulse overpowering the other. '[E]ven though the river calls, / things have moved on here', Robinson writes in his poem 'Walk with me'. 'Brixton is not its history / and neither should we be / though we hear the call of the past.'

When rivers flood, the height of the water is sometimes marked on a building or bridge. At Lambeth's southern limit, on Elder Road in West Norwood, there used to be a marker on one of the buildings, showing the level the Effra reached when it flooded in 1890. This kind of record-keeping keeps the past present, makes the intensity of an overwhelming moment visible on calmer days. We learn that extreme things happened in that place – and could again.

One of Brixton's high-water marks is commemorated by a brass plaque on the side of Iceland, on Electric Avenue: the site of the 1999 Brixton bomb, a racist attack which injured forty-eight people. But many other public records are absent. There is nothing to mark pivotal sites in the 1981, 1985 and 1995 uprisings. Nothing to mark the deaths in custody at Brixton

Police Station. Perhaps in time the names of those who died under the protection of the state will be stamped on the police station's facade, like the brass lines stamped on the stones of old bridges.

The area outside Brixton Police Station was redeveloped in 2016. The lanterns, plastic flowers and photographs of those who died in custody were removed from the plane tree outside. A public square was created, with six circular cast-iron plaques cutting across the middle, each marked with the words 'The hidden River Effra is beneath your feet.'

7

**YouTube:** *FTL (Yung Krimz, Yung Skeng, Timzy & Bee) – Dey know*

281,068 views

### Jordan YS

looool these man are like 12 stop acting like you man do road go do your homework

#### TamaraJadee

Loool bunch of little joke boys look like their in year 8 haha

#### Richard Losonczi

if you listen closely, you can hear their mums calling them in for dinner

### Savage G

Who's kids are these LMAOOOOO! I shouldn't be laughing cos these kids think road life is something good, sad really. But I have to say they flow better than some man tho lol

**Money Wise**

primary school kids rapping yeah

**Chris Powell**

Worst rapping I've ever heard . . . puberty might help

**Anastasia Snow**

tunes alright yu kno. It bangs. plus some of u are peng 😳 ☺ but the other ones need to pay for some plastic surgery with that paper they claim they make. xx

**jay.11s**

tht tall black guy (the second one) was good for his age ✓. little less on the skeng talk though. It's becoming a bad habit in these vids

**Ian2**

How you man talking about skengs when you're not old enough to even buy scratch card from shop LOOOL stay in school you man

Although it was a cool evening, there were a lot of people out and there was a lively mood on the streets. The Sergeant split us into pairs and put us on patrol in Brixton town centre.

We patrolled back streets: Rushcroft Road, Saltoun Road, Kellet Road. An IC1 male, thirties, walked towards us. 'Don't hurt the kids', said the slogan on his T-shirt. 'No, seriously, they have guns now.'

Walking past Morleys, we bumped into a pair of regulars and decided to pop into the Acre Lane Ladbrokes to keep the pressure on the local dealers and maybe do some searches. There were only five people in the betting shop when we arrived, IC3 males in their forties and fifties, sitting silently at the fruit machines. The floor was covered with betting slips, chicken bones and scrunched McDonald's bags. The red leather on the stools had been picked away and patches of yellow foam showed through. We said good evening and left them to it.

We walked down to the McDonald's and took in the scene, all the life of Brixton High Street, Coldharbour Lane, Windrush Square. 'I've had enough of this,' one of the regulars said. 'I've got to get out of this shithole.' His partner nodded. 'Let's head up the hill,' he said, 'away from this cess pit.' They walked up Brixton Hill in the direction of Olive Morris House and the prison.

My partner and I crossed the road and paused outside KFC, where only five years earlier dealers had openly offered skunk and weed to passers-by, muttering under their breath when you got within a metre of them, as though you had triggered a sensor. There had been a major crackdown a couple of years after I moved to Brixton, which drove the trade into the shadows. An IC3 female, late teens, walked up while we were standing there. 'There's someone taking drugs in that phone box,' she said. We walked over and opened the door. There was an IC3 male, forties, squatting on the floor. His beard was yellow, his fingernails black. He stepped out and we searched him, finding a homemade crack pipe down the front of his trousers, a cognac miniature with a hole in the base.

The man's name was Anthony. We ran a name check and learned that he had an ASBO preventing him from carrying drug paraphernalia, so we arrested him and walked to Brixton nick, carrying the crack pipe, a pack of Rizlas, two lighters and a mobile phone in an evidence bag. On the walk to the station, Anthony's phone rang repeatedly. 'I need to answer that,' he said. 'Can I have my phone? I've come here to collect money. The man calling owes me money. Just let me have my phone and I can answer. Look, if I don't, he's going to leave, he's going to just give up and leave the area.'

We entered the yard at Brixton Police Station, where two of the hot-dog vendor's confiscated carts were rusting after weeks in the open air. There was a long queue at custody. It was prime time on Friday evening and we waited for over an hour in two consecutive holding cells before we reached the counter. 'You've got no right to arrest me, you know,' said Anthony. 'My ASBO says I can carry a crack pipe. Call up my local police station and they'll tell you. Call them. Why won't you listen to me? You're not even looking at me! You think all drug users are the same, that's what it is, that just because we've got a problem with drugs we're all the same.' As we waited, his phone kept ringing. 'Just answer it, please,' he said. 'Tell him not to leave!'

Eventually Anthony's phone stopped ringing. The silence upset him more than the missed calls. He grew agitated, rocking backwards and forwards, sighing heavily. His neck and temples were tense. His cuffed hands rode up and down his back.

'I swear, when I get out of here I'm going to stab up a policeman, right in the neck!' he said. 'You'd better watch out. I'll be looking for you and I'll kill you. I'm definitely going to kill a policeman.'

'We're not going to talk to you while you're like this,' said my partner and Anthony went quiet for a while.

'I've got an itchy nose,' he said. 'Can you itch it? Excuse me! I've got an itchy nose! Can you itch my nose, please?'

We were called to the desk. The Custody Sergeant authorized overnight detention and a strip-search, so we uncuffed Anthony and took him into a search suite, a tiny beige room, empty except for a black plastic chair and a red emergency push-bar, mounted on the wall like a dado rail. We instructed Anthony to remove the top half of his outfit and we searched each item thoroughly as he handed it to us, then we told him to put the top half back on and repeat the process for the bottom. We searched his shoes and turned his socks inside out, then as he was taking off his trousers, Anthony leaned on the emergency bar, setting off an ear-splitting siren. We opened the door, shouted, 'False alarm,' and the siren stopped. Anthony stood up, dropped his underpants and held them open so that we could see inside. Then we asked him to lift his penis and testicles so we could see beneath them, then to turn around and squat down. Anthony completed each step quickly and methodically, without any signs of awkwardness.

He knew the drill, I found out later. It was his seventy-seventh arrest.

Often while policing, we are not solving people's problems, we are just interacting with the vicious cycle they are trapped in. Sometimes we interrupt the cycle momentarily. Sometimes we make it worse. Arresting Anthony, I was uncertain what impact we were having. None of the previous arrests had helped him get his life back on a surer footing, yet here we were, still arresting him. Did we think this time would be different? Seventy-seventh time lucky? Or was it pure cause and effect: one drugs offence equals one more arrest? It felt as if we were locked in as much of a vicious cycle as Anthony.

My partner and I went to put a CRIS report on the system. He slumped in a chair, puffed out his cheeks, and sighed. 'This is the worst bit,' he said, logging onto a computer. We sat together at the terminal and filled in box after box, writing out everything that had happened in minute detail, knowing that hundreds of hours had already been dedicated to documenting Anthony's offences and that nothing we were doing was making a difference.

Perhaps we did not think it was our job to make a difference. But if not us, then who? Who else saw Anthony as often as we did?

Leaving the station hours later, I caught a bus travelling straight into the rising sun. A pair of gulls glided along next to us, beating their wings slowly.

I watched the first market traders setting up on Electric Avenue, a pink sky above a quiet town. I saw the silhouettes of chimneys, a church tower, a line of trees climbing Brixton Hill.

The clock on the town hall struck eight as I passed. It was such a beautiful morning it seemed a shame to go to sleep.

Climbing into bed, I put on an eye mask, blocking the warm light around the edge of the window. I lay still for a long time, my feet tingling, my mind alert.

Walking along New Park Road the next morning, I was surprised to find a boy, perhaps ten, sitting on the kerb, his legs stretched into the road. He was on a bend and cars would have to swerve to avoid him. I crouched down and asked the boy if he was OK. He shrugged. 'Are you all right?' I asked again. 'Because this isn't a very safe place to sit. You could get hit by a car.' He looked straight ahead and said nothing. 'Do you live near here?' I said. 'Are you waiting for someone? Let's find a safer place to wait.' The boy continued to ignore me.

Unsure what else to do, I said: 'Look, I'm worried about you. If you don't want to move, I'll have to call the police.' At those words, the boy jumped to his feet, crossed the road, and ran down Brixton Hill.

I walked slowly after him, watching the yellow of his T-shirt disappear from sight, then turned down Coldharbour Lane and went to find a table in the Phoenix.

I thought again about Anthony's arrest while I drank my coffee.

Police officers want to catch criminals. But who are these criminals and what are their crimes? After almost a year of night shifts, I found those labels increasingly arbitrary. Seventy-seven arrests down, Anthony could justifiably be labelled a seasoned criminal. But the term seemed a poor fit for someone locked in cycles of damaging behaviour, struggling with addiction and mental ill health.

We could say that Anthony had chosen to break the law by choosing to smoke crack in a phone box and that now he must face the consequences. But as John Berger wrote, 'to understand a given choice another makes, one must face in imagination the lack of choices which may confront or deny him.'

Given how much support Anthony needed, and the limits to the state's ability to provide it, was it useful or meaningful to call his actions crimes? In doing so, we simply made his situation look more straightforward than it was. It is neater to call something a crime than a shared, unresolved social dilemma.

'I don't like the term crime,' said the great Norwegian criminologist Nils Christie, 'it's such a big, fat, imprecise word.'

But perhaps the value of the word 'crime' is its very elasticity. It says nothing about an action's root causes or effect on others, it simply denotes that a behaviour is forbidden by law and punishable by the state. Crime is a term that contains rather than explains. Complexity disappears behind its facade.

After arresting and strip-searching Anthony, then leaving him angry and alone in a cell, I felt more uncomfortable than ever treating people suffering from addiction, trauma or mental ill health as criminals. Simplistic thought leads to simplistic action. Until we saw situations like Anthony's differently, we were unlikely to deal with them more effectively.

When the police response to a situation is inadequate, it is frequently a sign that society as a whole has not developed an adequate response. The shortcomings of the police are also the shortcomings of a society, our confusion the reflection of something wider. Societies ask their police to deal with the things they have not worked out how to deal with, to solve problems they would rather not think about. We are aimed at intractable issues by a hopeful population, only to arrive and find that our capacities are ill-matched to the challenges that confront us. We try to enact a society's hopes, but often dramatize its frustrations.

I thought of Egon Bittner's remark that police are there to deal with 'something-that-ought-not-to-be-happening-and-about-which-someone-had-better-do-something-now'. Homelessness, loneliness, teenage gangs, domestic abuse, addiction. There is no consensus on how to resolve such complex social issues – the question of who should do what circles endlessly. Bittner's point was that, while the debates rage, the police are the stop-gap institution, doing what they can in the absence of someone-more-suitable-doing-something-more-appropriate.

Anthony was trapped in a vicious cycle – but it was also our cycle. Until something changed, we would keep arresting him.

I got up to pay. The manager of the Phoenix was mouthing street names without looking at the *A–Z*, crossing London in his mind.

I was off duty in Waterloo station early on a Friday afternoon when I spotted a pair of children, twelve- or thirteen-year-olds, an IC1 boy and an IC3 girl who ought to have been at school. I had my warrant card in my pocket. I always carried it with me, ready to put myself on duty if required.

It is a strange sensation, walking around a train station in casual clothes, knowing you have a trump card in your pocket, something you can pull out to become more than just a passer-by. Shortly after I was sworn in as a police officer, I was having my hair cut on Coldharbour Lane. The customer in the chair next to me, IC1 male, forties, started talking about his drug habit to the barber, and about the places nearby where he went to buy sex. 'There are three places I could go for sex right now,' he said. Then he turned, looked me in the eye, and said: 'You're not a copper, are you? I'll bet as soon as I'm finished in here, you're going to follow me down the road.'

I watched the children dart around the concourse, over-excited, the girl chasing the boy, both laughing uncontrollably. I followed them to the bottom of a down escalator, watching them throw an empty plastic bottle up it, beneath the feet of descending travellers, wait for it to descend, and then throw it up again. I followed them to WH Smith and watched from the doorway while the boy filled his satchel with Robinsons Fruit Shoots, unnoticed by the cashier.

As the pair made to leave, walking slowly but with smirks on their faces, I confronted them. 'I've been watching what you've been doing. Show me what you've got in your bag.' They did not respond. 'Open your bag.' The boy unzipped the satchel and showed me the stolen juices. He looked up at me. 'Shall I put them back?'

Standing in the train station, looking down at two children not long out of primary school, I felt a stab of cognitive dissonance. I felt the instinct to be both teacher and police officer. I wanted to squat down and tell them off, then call their families and make sure they were OK. But I also wanted to march them to the manager and summon officers to arrest them.

They needed boundaries, but I was unsure what kind. According to Donald Winnicott, the anti-social act is 'an expression of hope', 'an S.O.S. for control by strong, loving, confident people'. The strong, confident part felt easy as a police officer – the loving part less so. Love seemed a lot to ask of a police officer. And yet, great schools were not afraid to say that they loved their pupils and loved their community. I thought how different policing would be, if every officer could sincerely say: *I love these people, I love this place.* Perhaps this is close to what Robert Peel was getting at when he said that constables should offer the public not just service, but friendship.

Only through becoming a teacher, did I realize that children crave things they do not often ask for – boundaries, authority, someone to say stop. They seem to desire a kind of weightless independence, their actions free from both consequence and control. Yet without boundaries, they cannot be happy. As children shapeshift into young adults, this paradox becomes increasingly stark. Teenagers often defy the people they care about most. Adults can feel they are being pushed away – when in fact they are being invited to come closer in.

Adolescents are characterized by a 'mixture of defiance and dependence', wrote Winnicott. They need to express both, and they need the adults closest to them to accommodate both. They need space. They need limits. They need to feel contained. They need to feel unconstrained. Truanting and playing pranks in the middle of one of London's busiest train stations, these two children were asking to be noticed, to be pulled back to the place where things are expected of them.

I was not sure what to do. I clamped a hand around the boy's upper arm and led him back into the store.

'Why aren't you at school?'

'I don't have one at the moment,' he replied. 'I left one place and we haven't found a new one yet.'

The boy was trembling, more frightened than I had expected. I walked him to the till and asked to see the manager. The checkout assistant directed me to a room not much bigger than a cupboard and I marched the boy towards it.

I looked over my shoulder for the girl, but she had slipped away.

A busy night shift feels disjointed and dream-like. Figures loom up and drift away. Voices come out of the dark. Everywhere you walk, people and problems pop up.

> 'We're going to a boom night.'
> 'What's a boom night?'
> 'I don't even know, you know.'

People prop themselves up on lamp posts, vomit in doorways, fall over their feet. They slump in bus stops, sleep upright against walls. People stagger towards transport, hanging off the necks of stabler friends.

> 'Do you want to touch the World Cup? Here, hold it,
>     hold it.'
> 'Hold on. What is this? The Quantity Surveyors' World
>     Cup?'
> 'Yeah, we won the league!'

Three men are fighting. We run across the road, stopping the traffic with our raised hands, but by the time we reach the men they have their arms around one another, dancing the can-can and singing, 'I love you baby and if it's quite all right I need you baby to warm the lonesome night.'

'What are you doing tonight?'

'Bashment. We're going to a bashment night. It's a
    Caribbean thing.'

An intoxicated IC1 male picks something up and launches it
with all his strength at a betting shop window. It is a recycling
bag full of waste paper, so light that it bounces off the glass
without a sound and wafts gently to the pavement.

'I pay for you! You're racist, the lot of you!'

Two IC1 females, early twenties, are flat on their backs in the
middle of the road, their strappy shoes next to them on the
tarmac. We run over and they begin to stir, pushing themselves
up on their elbows and flapping their hands to shoo us away.

'Can I borrow your hat for a minute? Just one minute
    I promise.'

An intoxicated IC1 male, early twenties, is asleep at a bus stop
with his phone, wallet and penis sticking out of his tracksuit
bottoms. His crotch and the pavement are covered in piss. He
is hard to wake and only stirs when we pinch his ear lobes as
hard as we can. We set the man on his feet and get back in the
van. He takes a few directionless steps before colliding with the
side of a burger truck. He leans his forehead against it and
closes his eyes.

'But which is the best?'

'It's got to be *The Prisoner of Azkaban.*'

'Azkaban? Are you talking about Azkaban?'

'Yes, we *are* talking about Harry Potter.'

'Are you the prisoner of Azkaban? Are you Sirius
    Black?'

'No, but you would, wouldn't you? Which woman
    wouldn't?'
'Gary Oldman? I bet he gets a lot of pussy.'
'He does.'
'Anyone know the way to North Clapham, Clapham
    North?'
'North Camden? You're going the wrong way, mate.'

It took a long time to get to the magistrates' court. I arrived in heavy rain an hour earlier than I needed, my uniform in a kit bag. The court was a squat concrete building with small windows, turned in on itself like a fortress. I walked up a ramp that felt like a drawbridge.

Inside, the pale blue walls were covered in drill holes, empty leaflet dispensers, dark rectangles where posters had been and stray strips of Sellotape that had once held them there. I went into the gents' toilet to change, its ceiling covered in black smudges, initials burned onto it with lighters, and then sat down on a bench outside Court 5. I was surprised by the design of the bench: it was made of moulded metal, covered with small round holes like a colander, as though it had been designed to let fluids drain through it. It was bolted in place and, although it was indoors, it was not a piece of indoor furniture.

The magistrates' court is the ground floor of the legal system, the place where the most minor cases are heard without a jury. I was giving evidence in a case of Driving Without Due Care and Attention, having given a Fixed Penalty Notice to a man in a rental van who had obstructed the path of an ambulance and failed to stop when we tried to pull him over. He had subsequently failed to pay the ticket, so the matter had come to court.

On the benches around me were defendants, lawyers, witnesses and a few other police officers. An IC3 teen in a black puffer jacket was talking on his mobile: 'If I get tagged, bruv, does that mean I can only stay out till seven?' There was a bizarre atmosphere outside the court-rooms, everybody tense and bored in equal measure, tight jaws and creased brows collapsing into sighs. My uniform felt clunky in the courthouse and my boots, made for scaling walls and walking miles, looked crude alongside the neat leather shoes of the lawyers and defendants. After I had been waiting on the metal bench for an hour, a young suited lawyer sat down next to me. 'Don't do what the last two officers did and just stand and read out your notes,' he said. 'They were fucking useless. I wouldn't be surprised if we lose the conviction because of it.'

I was grateful for my notes. I barely remembered the incident, never mind the specifics. Were it not for the driver's trilby, and the comment he had made when I gave him the ticket, that he had just inherited millions of pounds, I would have forgotten him. I read and reread the statement I had made at the roadside, then looked for the incident in my red pocket notebook.

While I waited for the hearing, I kept leafing through the notebook, intrigued to see which details had found their way onto its pages over the preceding months, trying to imagine myself back into the situations they described, wondering whether any of those rough remarks might one day prove consequential for reasons I could not have foreseen. 'Write everything down,' said the anthropologist Bronislaw Malinowski, whose ethnographic studies taught him that, in the midst of a situation, you are not in a position to decide which details matter.

The notes in my pocketbook were rushed and frequently incomplete, passages of narrative interrupted midstream, then ruled off and never continued. Certain scenes were still vivid. Others felt impossibly remote. Some were not at all as I remembered them. It was as though every memory had a half-life and I could not predict when it would decay. Some corrupted within minutes, others were remarkably persistent, although their persistence was no guarantee of accuracy. The only solution for the caprices of memory is to film things or to write things down straight away. Making a record at any distance from an event, James Boswell wrote, is as meaningful as 'pickling long-kept and faded fruits'. You cannot reverse the ageing process, so memories must be bottled fresh.

As a diarist, I find few things as frustrating as realizing a memory has eroded before I have fixed it on paper, knowing that whatever I now record will be fuzzy and approximate. As with a dream, the harder I grip it, the faster it fades. The only way I have found to recover it is to let my mind wander, to leave the door open for the memory to walk back in.

I closed my notebook and looked again at the statement I had written on the ticket, trying to imagine the questions the Magistrate might ask. My anxiety mounted, imagining the moment when I would come face to face with a man I had met once in the middle of the night, and had to justify why we were all in the court-room together. I had longer to prepare than I expected. The defendant did not arrive when he was supposed to. Every time somebody approached, I looked up expectantly. Two hours after our hearing was due to begin, I felt confident that the man was not going to appear and felt suddenly disappointed and stood-up.

From my bench, I watched the court-rooms fill up, and

observed the faces, frustrated or relieved, of the people leaving them. After months of policing, this was the closest I had come to the later stages of the legal system, to the onward journey for the incidents we passed along the line.

State punishment, minor or major, is a serious matter. I had read a book by the criminologist Nils Christie, who believed that our language makes us forget how serious punishment is and allows us to discuss unpleasant realities without confronting them. To shock people into recognition, Christie substituted the conventional terms with prickly alternatives which explicitly communicate what is intended by each. In Christie's writing, crimes become 'deplorable acts', criminals are 'suitable enemies', and punishment is 'pain delivery'. The chill of his wording makes the reader wince, removing the cushion between mind and meaning.

Our case was the last to be heard that morning and it took place without the defendant. Walking into Court 5, I found myself in a smart polished room, so different from the scuffed corridor that I struggled to believe we were in the same building. It felt like emerging from backstage onto a lavish theatrical set. The dissonance was profound. After several hours in a space that communicated a profound lack of concern for people's comfort and well-being, this space felt as plush as an old hotel.

The Magistrate was sitting behind a dark wooden desk and I took my place behind the chair he indicated. I looked around at the lawyer and two clerks. The court-room felt absurdly large for five people. I recited the oath printed on a laminated sheet of paper and answered the questions from the lawyer and the Magistrate. 'How did the vehicle in question come to your attention? . . . How many lanes were there on the road? . . . For how long did the vehicle obstruct the ambulance?' I gave full, diligent answers – too full. Try as I might, I seemed incapable of answering only the question at hand, unable to resist racing ahead or adding details. Each time, the lawyer cut me off.

'Case proved,' the Magistrate announced, far sooner than I expected. I wanted to object. I had more to say. We had barely been in there for ten minutes. He added six points to the defendant's licence and issued a £110 fine, £110 costs and £20 of other fees.

'Thank you for coming, officer, you may go,' the Magistrate said.

'Thank you for having me,' I replied, without thinking, and walked out feeling tired and flat, like a student who has over-prepared for an exam. There was nobody left in the waiting area. In the men's toilets, I changed into normal clothes for the bus ride home.

I had to hand back my warrant card and my kit later in the week. This would be my final outing in uniform. Our New Park Road flat was empty. A moving company had boxed up our belongings and sent them overseas. We would be living out of suitcases until we flew to South America, escaping the London winter for the height of a southern summer. I stood at the bus stop with a pair of IC3 teens and we travelled down Brixton Hill together.

There was a buzz at the station. The rosy-cheeked Sergeant was in a huddle with several regulars, and I walked over to find out what had happened. 'We lifted the twenty most senior members of GAS,' someone said. There had been a huge raid on the GAS gang leadership. Hundreds of officers had been deployed to dismantle their operations, which extended far beyond London, battering down doors in Angell Town, the Home Counties and Edinburgh. They had caught twenty-nine suspected senior members, having arrested eighty-eight suspected junior members on a previous raid. 'There's a power vacuum now,' someone said, 'there'll be splinter groups jostling for control of the estates.' There was a celebratory atmosphere. It was a big win. A dynasty had fallen and we had sent a message to the gangs: we were coming for them; their money and their power would go as quickly as it had come.

I struggled to share in the jubilation. The wheel had turned. New leaders would emerge. How much had actually changed?

For my final shift, I had signed up to patrol Brixton with the Neighbourhood Policing Team. I wanted to stay close to the ground, to walk a farewell lap of the streets where I had lived and taught and policed for almost six years. I was paired with a regular who had been policing Lambeth for three decades.

The Neighbourhood Policing Team was the least prestigious and desirable assignment for regular officers. It lacked the speed of the response teams or the rough glamour of the Gangs Taskforce.

'What do you do?' I asked when I got to their office.

'Deal with shit,' a regular replied.

I was surprised to learn that my partner had actively chosen the Neighbourhood Policing Team. Unlike many of his colleagues, he preferred this slow, fine-grained work, encountering the same vulnerable families and individuals again and again, helping them to improve things bit by bit. 'It suits me down to the ground,' he told me as we walked to the Tulse Hill Estate to make house calls, beginning with a family with learning difficulties, whose grown-up son had been repeatedly bullied, burned with a lighter and robbed.

The young man welcomed us in and the family told us how they were doing, that things had been slightly better recently. While the parents spoke, their son bustled around the kitchen, emptying and filling the pockets of his fleece jacket, taking little plastic bags out and then putting them back in again. 'He likes to keep his pockets full of little bags stuffed with paper tissues,' the regular told me as we left. 'Such a sad situation, that one. They're good as gold, but some people just won't leave them alone.'

We wove between the high brown-brick blocks, nodding to people as we passed. The regular gestured at a pair of flats next door to each other. 'We've been dealing with a neighbour dispute there for nine years now,' he said. 'It's the never-ending story.'

When I began policing, I hoped that the experience would help me to make sense of the complex social issues in my local area. I soon realized that this would not be the case. Proximity might illuminate complexity, but it does not reduce it. The intricacies simply become more visible, the patterns more pronounced. Police officers see vulnerability in all its forms, the interconnectedness of different issues, the cycles in which people become ensnared. We see them over and over again. We look at a city through a kaleidoscope, seeing its endless variety and its endless repetitions. But that does not mean we know what to do about them.

My partner and I walked slowly through the corridors and courtyards of the Tulse Hill Estate. I knew my way around now. I would forget it again soon; I would probably never come in here again. I thought about everything I had seen with the police. The domestics, the stabbings, the homelessness, the loneliness. They seemed to resist attempts to understand them. They were like wet knots. We tug at them, but nothing gives. They tighten.

I had sensed these frustrations as a carer, a teacher, a volunteer in a homeless shelter, but I felt them most keenly as a police officer. These issues are bigger than any single institution. They reflect the kind of society we are: who and what we value; how equal and inclusive we are; how and how much we support the most vulnerable. Inequality, intergenerational poverty and trauma are all bigger than the police. Sometimes I thought there was too much talk about the police – and not enough about the issues we ask police to deal with and what we actually want to do about them.

Most of my colleagues were frustrated at their inability to make a difference to the challenges we confronted. Some of this was weary cynicism, but some of it was enlightened bewilderment, as officers wondered why these tasks had fallen to them and what the bigger plan was.

With local services and safety nets cut away, we often ended up controlling people who were not being cared for, and in the process we enabled that lack of care.

There was something purgatorial about that, and we could sense it.

We continued our tour of the Tulse Hill Estate, skirting the perimeter of a large communal lawn, and cut across a car park. As we did, a low white sports car pulled up next to us and the driver, IC3 male, early twenties, lowered his window:

'All right? How you doing, yeah?' he said to the regular.

'I'm all right,' the regular said. 'Look at this! Is this a new car?'

'Yeah, man, what do you think?'

'Very nice. You know, I'm looking to get a new car myself. I'm thinking of the new Ford Focus.'

'No, man, look, forget that shit. Get yourself a Porsche.

All right it's sixty, seventy grand more, but you'll never regret it.'

The two of them spoke for a few minutes, then the young man wound up his window and drove away. 'We've known each other for years,' the regular said. 'Let's pop into Nan's house.'

The regular knocked on a nearby door. While we waited, we could hear a woman shouting, although we could not make out what she was saying. It took two or three minutes for Nan to come to the door, an ICı female in her eighties, but when she saw who it was she greeted us with a broad smile and ushered us into her living room.

'It's the Old Curiosity Shop in here,' the regular whispered as we entered. The narrow entrance hall was lined with display tables, laden with dozens of tiny ceramic gnomes and knick-knacks – rabbits sitting on toadstools, squirrels holding acorns – and the walls were covered with scenes of country life, paintings of hayricks and harvesters. We squeezed along the corridor to the living room, which was even more packed, every surface obscured by ornaments, the upholstery strewn with stuffed toys and elaborately embroidered cushions. The regular asked Nan how she was. 'I don't see many people these days,' she said. 'Sit down and have a cup of tea.' We said we would have loved to but we could not stop for long.


Egon Bittner said that the property that makes police distinctive is their ability to use force. My experiences made me think that the heart of policing, the quality most needed, is care: caring for fragile people at moments of extreme stress, and caring about intractable-seeming issues, even as they thwart your attempts to solve them. The police, the vehicle for force in society, are handed not just society's most physically risky situations but also its most complicated caring duties.

Most officers liked chasing, catching, rescuing – not the messy, ongoing work of care. But whether we liked it or not, that was the work. Most of our urgent calls were not aberrant one-offs. The emergencies of community policing are slow-motion emergencies, playing out over months or years. They need sustained care, not sporadic bouts of control.

I was interested to have met an officer who sought out the very challenges we struggled to address, who was comfortable dwelling in that complexity without becoming enraged or trying to explain it away.

Watching my partner on his rounds of the Tulse Hill Estate, he demonstrated an enduring concern for problems that lacked ready solutions. He seemed happy to spend his days and nights mired in the minutiae of communal life: mediating social relations when they broke down or, as in Nan's case, compensating for their absence. He listened to people, he built relationships; he had become an unwitting expert in care. His colleagues in the Neighbourhood Policing Team did not get it and thought he was an oddball.

Care sounds like the antithesis of crime fighting. But it is the only true way to fight crime. Anything else is crime control: putting problems on ice, putting problem people out of sight. Only when the police see care as the core of their work will they help to solve the problems that frustrate them; only then will they truly help the people they are continually sent to arrest, move on or subdue. Instead of being experts in coercion who grudgingly offer care, they need to become experts in care who grudgingly use coercion.

After a year with the police, I felt certain that Bittner was right about us missing our true vocation. Within our grasp was the opportunity to do satisfying, life-changing work – to help create safe, resilient communities. Yet we could not see it, and we remained on the outside, risking our safety every shift, only to see the same issues on the next.

I wondered whether we could change. And, if we did, would we still be 'the police', or something else entirely?

'Wonderful lady,' the regular said as we left Nan. We walked to the edge of the estate and turned back down Tulse Hill. As we approached Hootananny, an IC3 female ran towards us. 'There's a dog in the road!' she shouted.

We passed a white van with the word ABSURD spray-painted on one side. Looking along Effra Road, we could make out a Jack Russell disrupting the traffic, weaving between the vehicles in breathless spurts. Four lanes of buses, vans, bikes and cars stopped, started, honked and swerved. The regular and I ran into the road, waving our arms to stop the traffic, trying to grab the dog. Drivers leaned out of their windows, eyes lifted from phones at a bus stop. The Jack Russell saw us approaching and bolted away, invigorated by the chase. We kept running, struggling to get anywhere near it, feeling ridiculous, aware that people were filming. After several aborted attempts, we managed to trap the dog along the side of a Number 2 bus, catching it with a pincer movement, and carried it to the pavement, smiling at a ripple of applause. 'He lives just over there,' a passer-by said to us, pointing at a brown-brick terrace.

When we knocked on the owner's door, she was surprised. She had not realized the dog had got out and looked at us accusingly, as though we had abducted it. She took the Jack

Russell, held it tightly to her chest and closed the door without a word.

A van picked us up and we circled South Lambeth. It was gone eleven, dark with no moon. It was midwinter and it had been dark for almost eight hours. Patrolling on cold, moonless nights the city feels aquatic. Visibility is blurred, shapes swim up then away. The streets behave like the sea floor, moving and changing, currents moving over them, the surface shifting, lifting and settling, before shifting and lifting again. There are layers of movement. People and things fold endlessly into and over one another. Someone passed round a bag of Percy Pigs. I leant my forehead against the thrumming window and watched as one neighbourhood bled into the next, keeping half an ear on the radio.

'We've had a call about a male swinging a cat basket on Streatham High Road,' the operator said.

'Yes, well, there is enough room to swing a cat on that road,' an officer replied.

A DV call came out, a stabbing at the other end of the borough, a report of a man being aggressive to a woman outside a pub. We drove there on blue lights, but there was no sign of any trouble when we arrived. We asked the people at the bar whether they had seen or heard anything. 'No,' they said, and asked if we wanted a pint.

A pair of intruders had been spotted in a back garden on Brixton Road. We rushed to the property, a tall terraced house, and the couple who lived there ushered us along a narrow side passage. The garden was long with no outdoor lights. Even when we turned on our torches, the objects around us were fuzzy and indistinct, as though we were walking through CCTV footage of the incident we were investigating.

We searched both sides of the garden, checking under the bushes and in the recesses behind the sheds. Something surged forward as we opened a cupboard. We leapt backwards, reaching for our batons, as a pile of bin bags fell at our feet.

After five minutes, we were confident that there was nobody in the garden, but we thought that there might have been people there before our arrival. At the far end we had found an upturned dustbin against the garden fence, a possible escape route. On the ground next to it, we found the wrapper and hollow core of a Kinder Egg. We did not know what had happened and we did not discuss it in the van.

We were hungry and drove to Clapham High Street. The hot-dog vendor was working outside Londis but we ignored him and parked outside the Kebab Company. We got our pittas and drove to Brixton Police Station for refs. An officer walked up to us groaning. 'Someone threw my hat out of the window. Oh man, I lost my hat!' Outside we could hear somebody screaming. 'Racheeeeeeeeeeel! Racheeeeeeeeeeel! I looooove yoooooooooooou!'

Later, the Sergeant sent us out on foot patrol. I set off with the same regular as before, away from Brixton town centre, along Effra Road, and back to Tulse Hill.

An IC3 teen cycled past us.

'Don't fall off!' the regular shouted.

'Oink oink!' the boy called back.

8

A few days after my final shift, I went to the station and handed back my kit, itemizing it like a suspect checking in property at custody. I gave back my warrant card and walked out onto the street. I still felt like a police officer; it would take a while for that to wear off. I got on a bus and paid for my journey to New Park Road.

A few days later, my wife and I flew to South America. In the four years we lived there, I occasionally bumped into former Met officers who had landed government jobs, far from their old beat. On a trip to the Yucatán Peninsula, I bonded with a Mexican police officer, telling him about policing London while his colleague searched our car and emptied my wallet. I smiled, shook the officers' hands, and only realized what had happened the next time I tried to pay for something.

We had a daughter while we were living abroad and then, soon after our return to London, we had a son. We moved back to our flat and our view of the prison's chimney stacks. Brixton had continued to change. The Phoenix was gone, replaced by a restaurant called Fancy Funkin Chicken.

It was late winter. We had just flown in from the southern summer, from dust, mosquitoes and the sound of Reggaeton. I took a job in Islington and began a new routine of London commutes. Returning home late one evening, I climbed the steps from Brixton tube and smelled onions, frying meat. I stopped at the top of the staircase, beside the shuttered Starbucks. The chain had rushed into Brixton with the new restaurants and estate agents. Now it was gone again, the rent too high, the clients too erratic. I looked around for the source of the smell and there, next to the pedestrian crossing, was the hot-dog vendor.

I was stunned: how had he managed to keep this up, after all the pressure, the confiscations, the fines? I felt amusement, even affection. Here he was, unperturbable, still serving un-licensed meat to the masses. He had even upgraded his cart – it now had electric lighting and proper signage, the words JUMBO HOT DOG printed above a perfectly proportioned sausage and bun. Did the upgrade mean that his carts were no longer being taken off him? Were his old carts still rusting in the backyard of Brixton Police Station? I paused and looked him in the eye. He looked back but there was no recognition. He looked away and tossed the onions with his spatula.

It felt strange to encounter the hot-dog vendor without my warrant card. I felt myself melting back into the unofficial life of Lambeth, felt any sense of distinction between myself and the people around me dissolve. I had nothing up my sleeve. I was just a former teacher, a former police officer, and now I was a local dad, reading *Cops and Robbers* to my children and attending Wriggle and Rhyme at Brixton Library.

The children I had taught were nearly adults. I wondered what they were doing. Some of the teenagers I had policed would be in their early twenties. Some of the younger ones would be running their gangs. Four years is a long time in the lives of children, in the life cycle of a gang. Things had got worse since we left. Knife crime was rife, young people were killing one another at an unprecedented rate, and no one seemed to know what to do. The issues were the same, but the stakes were higher.

I left the hot-dog vendor and took a bus up Brixton Hill, looking into the empty shell of Olive Morris House. It was slated for demolition as part of the redevelopment of Lambeth Town Hall. Soon her name would no longer blaze over Brixton in foot-high letters. No new building would take her name. Yet Olive's legacy seemed secure. The 'Do You Remember Olive Morris?' project had succeeded. Everything they collected is now in the Lambeth Archives. Her life is being written about and discussed. In 2019, the *New York Times* ran a belated obituary. In 2020, on what would have been her sixty-eighth birthday, she was the subject of a Google Doodle. Olive Morris has been elevated into the official narrative, into our collective memory – at least for now.

I got off the bus at New Park Road and walked home. Our small flat felt claustrophobic with four of us in it. The owners of the flat upstairs had removed their carpets and were renting it out on Airbnb. We could hear every step, every word of every TV programme. In the middle of the night, we were woken by the wheels of suitcases and the voices of guests from around the world. Our revenge was the howling of our new-born son at night, waking at one, two, three, four. My wife would sit up and feed him, but often he still would not sleep, so I would carry him into the lounge.

Each night, I walked circles around our small lounge with my son in my arms, walking its perimeter hundreds of times, keeping a steady pace, a light bounce in my step to send him back off. I listened to the traffic on Brixton Hill, to the screech of foxes, to distant sirens. Every now and then a response car passed the lounge window, bathing the room in blue light. I was always surprised that the siren and the alien light did not bother my son. I walked around and around the coffee table, singing the same songs hundreds of times, trying to wear him down with repetition. When his eyes were closed, his body loose and heavy, when I was sure he was asleep, I would tiptoe to his cot and lay him down, praying that the stillness would not shock him awake.

Sometimes nothing made a difference, so I just kept walking, my head nodding, my eyes half-shut, waiting for the night to end.

# SELECT BIBLIOGRAPHY

Although I do not quote from all of these texts, the following had a particular influence on me while writing *Into the Night*:

## WRITING ABOUT THE POLICE AND CRIMINAL JUSTICE

Benyon, John, *A Tale of Failure: Race and Policing* (University of Warwick, 1986).

Bittner, Egon, *The Functions of the Police in Modern Society* (National Institute of Mental Health, 1970).

Cain, Maureen, *Society and the Policeman's Role* (Taylor & Francis, 1973).

Christie, Nils, *Crime Control as Industry* (Routledge, 1993).

Davis, Angela Y., Gina Dent, Erica Meiners and Beth Richie, *Abolition. Feminism. Now.* (Hamish Hamilton, 2022).

Dickens, Charles, 'On Duty with Inspector Field', *Household Words*, 14 June 1851.

Emsley, Clive, *The Great British Bobby: A History of British Policing from the 18th Century to the Present* (Quercus, 2009).

Fassin, Didier, *Enforcing Order: An Ethnography of Urban Policing* (Polity Press, 2013)

Fielding, Henry, *An Enquiry into the Causes of the Late Increase of Robbers* (A. Miller, 1751).

Foucault, Michel, *Discipline and Punish* (Allen Lane, 1977).

Gash, Tom, *Criminal: The Truth about Why People Do Bad Things* (Allen Lane, 2016).

Graef, Roger, *Talking Blues: The Police in Their Own Words* (Collins Harvill, 1989).

Greif, Mark, 'Seeing Through Police', *N+1* (2015); reprinted in Mark Greif, *Against Everything* (Verso, 2016).

Hall, Stuart, Charles Critcher, Tony Jefferson, John Clarke and Brian Roberts, *Policing the Crisis: Mugging, the State, and Law and Order* (Macmillan, 1978).

van Maanen, John, 'Observations on the Making of Policemen', *Human Organization* (1973).

Maher, Geo, *A World Without Police* (Verso, 2021).

Nutt, David, *Drugs Without the Hot Air* (UIT Cambridge, 2012).

Reiner, Robert, *The Politics of the Police* (Prentice Hall, 1985).

Rowe, Michael, *Introduction to Policing* (SAGE, 2008).

Shiner, Michael, Zoe Carre, Rebekah Delsol and Niamh Eastwood, 'The Colour of Injustice: "Race", Drugs and Law Enforcement in England and Wales', *StopWatch* (2018).

Vitale, Alex S., *The End of Policing* (Verso, 2017).

## WRITING ABOUT CITIES AND SOCIAL INCLUSION

Bernard, Jay, *Surge* (Vintage, 2019).

Boakye, Jeffrey, *Hold Tight* (Influx, 2017).

Corrigan, Paul, *Schooling the Smash Street Kids* (Macmillan, 1979).

Desmond, Matthew, *Evicted: Poverty and Profit in the American City* (Allen Lane, 2016).

Elkin, Lauren, *Flaneuse: Women Walk the City in Paris, New York, Tokyo, Venice and London* (Chatto & Windus, 2016).

Femi, Caleb, *Poor* (Penguin, 2020).

Irwin-Rogers, Keir and Craig Pinkney, 'Social Media as a Catalyst and Trigger for Youth Violence', *Catch-22* (2017).

Jacobs, Jane, *The Death and Life of Great American Cities* (Random House, 1961).

Johnson, Linton Kwesi, *Selected Poems* (Penguin, 2006).

Laing, Olivia, *The Lonely City: Adventures in the Art of Being Alone* (Canongate, 2016).

Mayhew, Henry, *London Labour and the London Poor*, 3 vols (London, 1851).

Owusu, Derek (ed.), *Safe: On Black British Men Reclaiming Space* (Trapeze, 2019).

Parker, Tony, *The Unknown Citizen* (Hutchinson, 1963).

Rankine, Claudia, *Citizen: An American Lyric* (Graywolf Press, 2014).

Robinson, Roger, *A Portable Paradise* (Peepal Tree Press, 2019).

Sandhu, Sukhdev, *London Calling: How Black and Asian Writers Imagined a City* (HarperCollins, 2003).

Schivelbusch, Wolfgang, *Disenchanted Night: The Industrialisation of Light in the Nineteenth Century* (Berg, 1988).

Thapar, Ciaran, *Cut Short: Youth Violence, Loss and Hope in the City* (Viking, 2021).

Wacquant, Loïc, *Urban Outcasts: A Comparative Sociology of Advanced Marginality* (Polity Press, 2008).

Weegee, *Naked City* (Essential Books, 1945).

Winnicott, Donald, *Deprivation and Delinquency* (Tavistock, 1984).

## MEMOIR AND BIOGRAPHY

Baldwin, James, *The Fire Next Time* (Penguin, 1963).

Cadogan, Garnette, 'Walking While Black', *Literary Hub* (2016).

Coates, Ta-Nehisi, *Between the World and Me* (One World, 2015).

Fuller, Michael, *A Search for Belonging* (Bonnier, 2020).

Louis, Edouard, *The End of Eddy* (Vintage, 2018).

Machado, Carmen Maria, *In the Dream House* (Serpent's Tail, 2019).

Masters, Alexander, *Stuart: A Life Backwards* (Fourth Estate, 2005).

Miller, Kei, *Things I Have Withheld: Essays* (Canongate, 2021).

Park Hong, Cathy, *Minor Feelings: A Reckoning on Race and the Asian Condition* (Profile, 2020).

Remembering Olive Collective, *Do You Remember Olive Morris?* (Remembering Olive Collective, 2009).

Woolf, Virginia, 'Street Haunting' (Westgate Press, 1930).

## IDEAS

Ahmed, Sara, *Complaint!* (Duke University Press, 2021).

Akala, *Natives: Race and Class in the Ruins of Empire* (Two Roads, 2018).

Arendt, Hannah, *The Portable Hannah Arendt*, ed. Peter Baehr (Penguin, 2003).

Barthes, Roland, *Camera Lucida: Reflections on Photography* (Vintage, 1981).

Benjamin, Walter, *Illuminations* (Jonathan Cape, 1968).

Berger, John, *A Seventh Man* (Viking, 1975).

Cohen, Stanley, *Folk Devils and Moral Panics: The Creation of the Mods and Rockers* (MacGibbon and Kee, 1972).

Cole, Teju, *Known and Strange Things* (Faber & Faber, 2017).

Eddo-Lodge, Reni, *Why I'm No Longer Talking to White People about Race* (Bloomsbury Circus, 2017).

Goffman, Erving, *Asylums: Essays on the Social Situation of Mental Patients and Other Inmates* (Penguin, 1961).

Hartman, Saidiya, *Wayward Lives, Beautiful Experiments* (Serpent's Tail, 2019).

hooks, bell, *Outlaw Culture: Resisting Representations* (Routledge, 2006).

Nelson, Maggie, *On Freedom: Four Songs of Care and Constraint* (Jonathan Cape, 2021).

Sontag, Susan, *Regarding the Pain of Others* (Hamish Hamilton, 2003).

# ACKNOWLEDGEMENTS

I am grateful first of all to the wonderful, welcoming community of South Lambeth, which provides the backdrop to much of this book. I moved to Brixton as a twenty-three-year-old. A decade and a half later, my family and I have made our London home in the area. I feel fortunate to have chanced on such a special place.

*Into the Night* was written over seven years and evolved enormously during that time. Enormous thanks to four friends who were with me every step of the way: Henry Eliot, Edward Posnett, Belinda Sherlock and Andy Wimbush. Their ideas and feedback have been pivotal in the book's development and their creative companionship is one of the great delights of my life.

Several other dear friends read work in progress and had a particularly significant impact on this book. Huge thanks to Hugo Azérad, Una Dimitrijevic, Bill Higgins and John-Luke Roberts for their wisdom, candour and encouragement.

I am extremely grateful to my remarkable agent Patrick Walsh, who believed in this book from its earliest incarnations, read multiple drafts and provided invaluable support and challenge throughout. Thanks also to John Ash and the whole team at PEW Literary.

It has been a pleasure to work with the team at Picador.

Many thanks to my fabulous editor George Morley, and to Marissa Constantinou and Marta Catalano, for their sharp eyes and expert guidance. Thanks to Stuart Wilson for a brilliant cover, to Connor Hutchinson for being such a dynamic publicist, and to Laura Carr, Jessica Cuthbert-Smith, Daisy Dickeson, Kate Green, Ross Jamieson, Mairead Loftus, Rabeeah Moeen and Lindsay Nash. Many thanks to Sarah Shaffi for an insightful sensitivity read.

Many other people provided illuminating advice, conversation or support along the way. Thanks to Steven Appleby, Charles Arrowsmith, Will Atkins, Caroline Austin, Alex Beard, Ben Benjamin, Ellen Blythe, Juan Pablo Canala, Irene Chikiar Bauer, Alex Christofi, Jamie Coleman, Tomás Downey, Kim Esnard, Davy Evans, Jennifer Feroze, Gabriella Ferrari, Georgie Gould, Alex Gruzenberg, Alice Hamlett, Martín Hadis, Will Hammond, Jessica Heal, Jude Heaton, Laura Henry-Allain, Laura House, Katy Ivko, Patrick Kingsley, Tom Kingsley, Sophie Lambert, André & Ros Mangeot, Hanna Naima McCloskey, Louis Mikolay, Julia Minnear, Jane Monson, Polly Morland, Denise Neuman, Fran O'Hanlon, Euan Paterson, Nicholas Pearson, Harriet Poland, Justine Raja, Oli Rose, Brett Scott, Dave Spencer, Vikki Spencer, Cecilia Stein, Barbara Trevitt, Tarun Varma, Christie Watson and Kevin Williams.

Several experiences were particularly formative in the writing of this book. Thanks to all involved with the Lambeth Special Constabulary and to the regular officers who took us out and taught us about policing. Thanks to the staff, children and families of the school in Brixton, where I had the privilege of working as a teacher. Thanks to everyone at Teach First, where I ran an educational research team and visited schools across the country. Thanks to the staff, volunteers and residents at Jimmy's night shelter; it was a delight to play a small part in that amazing work. Thanks to the whole community of L'Arche à Paris, where I spent a hugely uplifting, instructive year as a live-in carer. My outlook has also been shaped by working with Fearless Futures, Frontline, Minds Ahead, MIT Solve, National Institute of Teaching, Police Now, Reach Academy Feltham, Teach for All and tiney; thanks to everyone at those organisations for the life-changing work they do to address the knotty issues this book explores and for expanding my ideas of what is possible.

*Into the Night* started life as a book about policing but became a book about care. My own ideas about care originate in the incomparable generosity and selflessness of my parents Julie and Stephen Lloyd. Thanks to them, as always, for their incredible love and support as parents and grandparents. Thanks also to my wonderfully fun, thoughtful and caring sister and brother-in-law, Jennifer and Simon Lloyd-Bowen.

I am endlessly grateful to my children, Florence and Sebastian, for making each day so happy and hilarious. I began work on this book before they were born; caring for them and getting to know them is the most joyful and satisfying experience I have ever had. Finally, bottomless thanks to my bold, brilliant wife Lydia, my great love and closest friend, for being the best of companions and making our family life such a fine adventure.